D1551382

The Great Skills Gap

THE GREAT SKILLS GAP

Optimizing Talent for the Future of Work

Edited by Jason Wingard and Christine Farrugia

STANFORD BUSINESS BOOKS
An Imprint of Stanford University Press
Stanford, California

STANFORD UNIVERSITY PRESS
Stanford, California

Special discounts for bulk quantities of Stanford Business Books are available to corporations, professional associations, and other organizations. For details and discount information, contact the special sales department of Stanford University Press. Tel: (650) 725-0820, Fax: (650) 725-3457

Printed in the United States of America on acid-free, archival-quality paper

Library of Congress Cataloging-in-Publication Data
Names: Wingard, Jason, editor. | Farrugia, Christine A., editor.
Title: The great skills gap : optimizing talent for the future of work / edited by Jason Wingard and Christine Farrugia.
Description: Stanford, California : Stanford Business Books, an imprint of Stanford University Press, 2021. | Includes bibliographical references and index.
Identifiers: LCCN 2021001586 (print) | LCCN 2021001587 (ebook) | ISBN 9781503613539 (cloth) | ISBN 9781503628076 (epub)
Subjects: LCSH: Vocational qualifications—United States. | Labor supply—Effect of education on—United States. | Labor supply—Effect of technological innovations on—United States. | College graduates—Employment—United States. | Continuing education—United States. | Education, Higher—Economic aspects—United States.
Classification: LCC HF5381.6 G74 2021 (print) | LCC HF5381.6 (ebook) | DDC 331.11/420973—dc23
LC record available at https://lccn.loc.gov/2021001586
LC ebook record available at https://lccn.loc.gov/2021001587

Cover design: Rob Ehle

Text design: Kevin Barrett Kane

Typeset at Stanford University Press in 10.5/14 Minion Pro

CONTENTS

ACKNOWLEDGMENTS

We, the editors, would like to thank the following individuals for their support in bringing this ambitious book to fruition:

First, thank you to the University Professional and Continuing Education Association (UPCEA) for their partnership on the Forum on the Future of Work, the book's primary content source, held at Columbia University in 2019. Specifically, we appreciate the efforts of Robert Hansen, Molly Nelson, Jordan DiMaggio, and Joseph Fedak for their expert advisory and project management contributions.

Second, we would like to thank Pam Wong at Columbia University for her contributions throughout the developmental stages of the project.

Third, we offer special thanks to Steve Pelletier and Susan Shain for their editorial assistance, and Natalie Nixon for her consulting support.

Finally, we thank the contributors to this volume, whose thought leadership and eagerness to engage in this topic made the book possible.

FOREWORD

If there ever was any doubt, the fallout from COVID-19 has made it clear that technology will drastically change the jobs of the future. The only question remaining is, how will workers adapt? How will seasoned professionals who have spent their lives in one career successfully make the leap to something new? How will young people lay the foundation for a lifetime of meaningful, engaging work? No one has all the answers right now. But one thing we know for sure is that new skill sets will be critical.

A remake of skill sets is already underway. Done successfully, transitioning workers to new skills and new jobs can close the gap between those reaping the rewards of the digital age and those yet to realize its gains—in other words, between the haves and the have-nots. But if the transition fails, the gap between these groups will widen. This transition is being steered by a variety of agents, including educators, policymakers, entrepreneurs, and, of course, corporations.

As the CEO of a multinational Fortune 50 company, I believe that corporations have a responsibility to help their employees navigate the challenges of reskilling for the digital age, so that both employees and companies emerge stronger than before. Not only do employees need transparency about whether their skills are in demand today and if they will still be needed tomorrow, but also companies need to ensure that employees are comfortable enough with digital technology to make it work for them.

Education is a solution. But not just the traditional kind. Employers have for too long focused on bachelor's degrees as the ticket to good jobs, but the truth is that many of today's jobs require skills, not degrees. At PepsiCo, we take a multistep approach to upskilling and reskilling our workforce. A range of on-demand learning resources is available anytime, anywhere, on any device. These resources are tagged by skill set, so people can create learning paths based on their development goals. For deeper capability building, we offer tuition support for certificate and degree programs. We also encourage our leaders to teach, bringing together external perspectives with PepsiCo-specific application to bring the learning to life. The problem of reskilling is ultimately solvable, but it takes the public and private sectors working together to change the face of education. Neither companies, nor government, nor education can do it alone. The need for reskilling is larger than any individual or organization.

Successfully navigating complex change requires the ability to lead people through uncertainty. Continually scanning the external environment, envisioning future scenarios, and building capabilities to thrive under any circumstance is a top priority for PepsiCo. Our mission to create more smiles with every sip and every bite means we must stay in lockstep with our consumers, adjusting our portfolio and finding new ways to delight in more sustainable ways. This versatility is due in no small part to the agility of our leaders—an agility we consciously nurture through challenging assignments, frequent job transitions, and a robust learning culture.

The Great Skills Gap: Optimizing Talent for the Future of Work offers an abundance of provocative ideas for how higher education can collaborate with the business community and system facilitators to align educational programs with the long-term needs of employers and workers. The editors, Jason Wingard and Christine Farrugia, are leading experts on the future of work and its implications for higher education and training. Their research on the human impact of automation highlights the importance of prioritizing strategies for inclusive talent development, reaching across industries and demographics—strategies that will be more important than ever as companies look to rebound from the devastating social and economic consequences of COVID-19.

In this book, Wingard and Farrugia have curated an insightful exploration of how transformative forces are—or should be—driving changes in the ways colleges and universities prepare students for careers. Combining their own work with the perspectives of leading educators, prominent employers, and other thought leaders, they deliver a wealth of insight into the skills challenges facing our economy. They explore innovative ideas for how to solve these challenges through higher education and alternative learning models, as well as how to scale solutions through cross-sector partnerships. From the first page to the last, the book's insights and analysis are invaluable to all of us, both in business and higher education, who hold a stake in the success of the twenty-first century workforce.

Ramon Laguarta
Chairman and CEO, PepsiCo

The Great Skills Gap

INTRODUCTION

AN EXTRAORDINARY CONFLUENCE of powerful forces is transforming both the world of work and the ways we educate current and future employees to contribute productively to the workplace. Automation and digital technologies are already profoundly transforming how business is done at every level, and alarming predictions of our jobs being replaced by robots abound. While the most catastrophic of these scenarios is overblown, there are seismic shifts afoot across industries and roles that reach beyond manufacturing—where industry disruption has been a mainstay for decades—to professional occupations where the prospect of job displacement due to automation seems to many like a far-off possibility rather than a looming threat. With these changes comes immense uncertainty for what the future holds in terms of what our jobs will look like and whether they will exist at all.

As with all things, the truth lies somewhere in the middle of two extremes. The realistic scenario is that jobs will not evaporate entirely, but they will change, perhaps substantially. Robots will not replace us. Instead, humans will work with machines and artificial intelligence in new ways. As technologies develop, they will open new lines of business and create roles that will demand skilled workers. The jobs we know today will be reinvented into something new—and perhaps unrecognizable—in the future.

A transformation is underway at the nexus where the world of work meets the world of higher education. The exploding scope and pace of technological innovation in the digital age is fast transforming the fundamental nature of work, and many of the shifts have already begun. The gig economy is prevalent. Companies like Lyft and Airbnb offer technologies that capitalize on this trend, and Google now has more contract employees than regular full-time workers.[1] Automation is also influencing the way people work. For example, to better respond to customer demand for personalized cars, Mercedes-Benz moved from a "dumb" robot system on the S-class sedan assembly line to a "cobot" system. Cobots—robotic arms operated by human workers—combine the power of robotic methods with the agility of humans who are able to execute judgment and adapt quickly.[2] These developments, and their rapid pace, are shifting the skills and preparation that employers need from their talent pool.

At its core, the ability to successfully navigate toward the future of work relies on workers receiving training that is relevant for the jobs of today *and* the jobs of tomorrow. Employers are grappling with these dilemmas of how to transform their current workforce to meet future business needs in a rapidly changing environment. Employers face the challenge of anticipating how their industries and companies will change, and then crafting training and hiring strategies to meet their needs now and into the future. The difficulty of this task rests in the element of the unknown. What will the jobs of tomorrow look like? Which of the skills that workers possess today will still be relevant in five, ten, or twenty years?

Employers are already developing strategies to expand their pipelines of skilled talent and to train and retain their workers. Google and Ernst & Young are turning away from a college degree as a predictor of on-the-job success and have opened numerous professional positions to workers with the requisite skills, regardless of whether they have a college degree.[3] Corporate-backed training options are growing in prevalence and type. TSYS has implemented a program to retrain their older workers with the future skills that their company needs so they are able to adapt within the company.[4] IBM now offers a menu of training options for "new-collar" jobs that require some training but fall short of needing a college degree. The company offers programs such as digital badge portfolios, apprenticeships, and bootcamps to groom the talent it needs.[5] In an effort to attract and retain young talent, Walmart offers college tuition benefits and a platform to access online degree programs.[6]

While employers are grappling with how to ensure a pipeline of skilled talent for the future, higher education also has a role to play. Colleges and universities have traditionally fed their graduates into skilled occupations, largely relying on the liberal arts model of education that has defined US higher education since its inception. However, within the changing employment landscape, there are questions about how well the current higher education model is positioned to continue launching its graduates into productive careers. Indeed, the future of work creates an imperative for radically rethinking the purpose and current approach to employment readiness by higher education institutions.

The Future of Work and Its Implications for Higher Education

Workforce disruption is a dominant theme in the future of work. Increasing levels of automation and artificial intelligence (AI) are replacing workers and reshaping the world of work. McKinsey estimates that by 2030 about half of work activities could be automated.[7] For example, in the medical field, AI approaches are being developed to harness massive amounts of health data so that machines can diagnose illnesses, and these tools are showing the potential to be more accurate than doctors.[8] Media companies are already using AI to mine data sets to generate newsworthy insights, to create article content, and to automate and optimize content distribution across channels, placing pressure on traditional jobs in journalism.[9] Industries, employees, companies, and technologies are already being developed, disrupted, or reconfigured in unforeseen ways, illustrating how the jobs we know today may not exist in the future.

The accelerated pace of evolution and disruption in the competitive business landscape demands that workers not only be technically proficient but also exceptionally agile in their capacity to think and act creatively and quickly learn new skills. Employee capabilities in leadership, teamwork, and communications are also paramount. In turn, those changes are motivating significant, even revolutionary change in the way educational institutions prepare learners for careers. Forward-thinking colleges and universities are reshaping instruction and the curriculum to ensure that they invest learners with skills appropriate to the twenty-first-century economy.

In addition to technological disruption, demographic forces are also affecting the workplace, compelling higher education to respond in turn. The increased longevity of human beings means that many careers will span sixty years or more, creating a sustained need for continual "reskilling" so that workers remain productive with relevant skills.[10] Meanwhile, evolving demographic trends are shattering the relative homogeneity that once defined the workforce by opening the pipeline to employment for a more diverse employee population. The ability to achieve workforce parity and diversity relies on higher education graduating a diverse pool of talent with the skills and knowledge needed to move into professional occupations.

To meet the challenges of a dynamic, fast-evolving workplace, employers seek workers who can think creatively and act nimbly. Employees need both the preparation to contribute substantively to their workplaces from day one, as well as an educational framework that will enable them to retool their skills continually over the course of a career that might endure for sixty years or more.

Within this context, higher education faces new demands in supporting the development of a workforce invested with twenty-first-century skills. Higher education has a paramount role to play in ably preparing learners to meet the immediate requirements of the workplace, as well as the uncertain demands of the future. Many higher education leaders believe they do this well. However, the Strada-Gallup 2017 College Student Survey found that while nearly all (96 percent) of chief academic officers in colleges and universities believe their institution is effective in preparing future workers, just 11 percent of business leaders strongly agree with them.[11]

As the workplace undergoes transformation wrought by automation, technological innovation, globalization, and demographic shifts, the skills and training that employers require are evolving. At the same time, higher education is facing pressures to prepare students so that they are employable, ready to contribute to innovation, and able to craft meaningful careers over their lifetimes. In the future of work, the ability of higher education and industry to work collaboratively and productively is paramount to achieving these ends.

About This Book

This book examines the gap between employers and higher education and considers their ability to collaboratively address the coming challenges in the future of work. The book's content is guided by the overarching question of what higher education's special role is in addressing employment needs of the future. Employers and higher education do not always talk well with each other, so in this book we bring these two groups together, along with intermediary organizations—such as nonprofits, foundations, and think tanks—that work between higher education and employers to help facilitate system solutions. The book's contributions from leading educators, prominent employers, and other thought leaders frame relevant considerations for both business and higher education and suggest specific strategies for improving workforce preparation.

This book is structured in three parts that present the views of each stakeholder group. Part I ("Talent of the Future: Are We Missing the Mark?") examines issues around automation, demographics, economic disruption, and related trends that are transforming the fundamental nature of work and the workplace, exploring the ways technology will transform the world of work and how the workplace should respond. With such change as context, how can we ensure that employees have the right skill sets for work in the future?

The chapters in Part I explore how automation and other technological advancements will affect workplace practices and employers' demands for workplace skills. The authors consider how best to tackle the challenges of training emerging professionals and reskilling seasoned talent through higher education, workplace training programs, or alternative credentialing models. Several contributors argue for the primacy of the human experience through humanistic workplace practices, retraining efforts that advance individuals' development and employment prospects, and a global understanding of the world and the people in it.

Part II ("Higher Education: Still the Solution for a Workforce in Flux?") raises the question of how higher education can or should adapt to better meet the needs of tomorrow's workplace. Fundamental changes in the workplace are driving significant changes in the ways that colleges and universities help prepare learners for careers and for their lives as citizens. Responding in part to concerns from employers that many new employees lack the requisite skills that businesses need, colleges and universities are engaging in change on several fronts.

Institutions are developing academic programs and cocurricular tools like makerspaces and apprenticeships to help students across a spectrum of majors to develop practical skills in emerging technologies. Across the curriculum, institutions are focusing on ways to help students develop crucial workforce skills like teamwork, goal setting, effective interpersonal communication, and conflict resolution. There is increasing recognition that the liberal arts—recently in disfavor in some more career-centric circles—invests students with a rich panoply of skills that employers value, including creative thinking and idea synthesis and the capacity to solve problems and drive innovation. Higher education is embracing an evolving palette of tools—including online learning, microlearning, credentials beyond degrees, experiential learning, bootcamps, competency-based education, and more—that help better prepare their students for the jobs of tomorrow. Professional and continuing education are booming, serving expanding needs of adult workers for lifelong retooling and "upskilling" across the course of increasingly longer careers.

In light of these contexts, Part II explores key questions, such as how continuing education can help adult learners "unlearn" deeply held identities and reinvent themselves in the process of upskilling to new occupational roles. Chapter authors reflect on the new relevance of the liberal arts in the era of rapid technological advancement and explore how students and professionals in today's workplace can marry expertise drawn from the liberal arts with more purely technical skills. The ways in which alumni learning and university strategies to better serve their graduates are evolving in the digital era are explored in depth.

Part III ("Bridging the Gap between Learning and Labor") delves into the perspectives of system facilitators to explore solutions and innovations to help business and higher education to find more effective ways to join forces in support of their respective needs, in order to help traditional and posttraditional students gain the skills they need for tomorrow's workplace. How can the worlds of commerce and academe collaborate effectively to better understand their respective motivations and work together to capitalize on emerging opportunities?

Insights about the changing nature of work and preparation for the workplace of tomorrow underscore the need for better communication and richer collaborations between employers and institutions of higher learning. Chapter authors reflect on how business and higher education can develop agile partnerships to meet the challenges of changing labor markets and evolving economies.

Among other critical questions, Part III examines the systemic problems in higher education that prevent students from graduating with the capacity to fully serve the demands of the contemporary workplace. It further considers how universities can sustain their mandate to prepare future citizens while also delivering highly relevant vocational training, including apprenticeships, and what role business can play in supporting lifelong learning for employees. Also explored are the challenges of fostering a culture of learning and growth to motivate workers to embrace and capitalize on technological change, as well as persistent questions about how to ensure that tomorrow's workplace is broadly accessible to a diverse cadre of workers.

TALENT OF THE FUTURE

Are We Missing the Mark?

PART I PRESENTS THE PERSPECTIVES of leading employers who describe how the future of work will impact their industries and organizations. They share their visions of how the skills needed from their employees will evolve in response to these larger environmental shifts. Lund and Hancock present McKinsey's research on the impact of automation on the future workforce and discuss how the demand for skills will change across industries. Braunstein from BlackRock extends this conversation through his reflections on how technology now pervades all aspects of life and work, creating a demand for "citizen developers"— technological laypeople who, notwithstanding their nontechnical roles, have the skills and knowledge to develop technological solutions to solve work problems. Pittinsky, cofounder of Blackboard and now CEO of Parchment, discusses the value of credentials in the workplace and explores opportunities and challenges for creating systems to communicate workers' skills to employers in the absence of formal credentials. Ulica, president and chief operating officer of the National Geographic Society, makes the case that the field of geography is vital for success in an interconnected world. Pfizer's Ray, Hong, and White discuss the importance of integrating a commitment to humanity and mission with a technological and scientific focus. NASA's Robinson reflects on how technological development in prior decades altered the ways we worked and then situates past changes on a continuum of the shifts we are likely to see in the future. Heitzlhofer of Lyft explores the need for continuous corporate learning in the face of rapid technological developments and proposes that learning and development programs be expanded beyond single companies to span multiple employers.

The array of employer perspectives in this section provides a multifaceted vision of what the future landscape of work will look like and how it will impact both employers and workers. This section sets the stage for discussions in later sections of how higher education and multisector partnerships can evolve to meet changing training needs.

INTRODUCTION

Neil Irwin

IF YOU ARE SOMEONE WHO SPENDS a lot of time thinking about the future of work, it sometimes feels like the real future of work is millions of people organizing panel discussions about the future of work. That is to say, this is an endlessly important question—how we, and future generations, will make a living—but one that lends itself more to endless gabfests than definitive conclusions.

This is partly because foreseeing the future is inherently hard. But I think that's only part of it.

Part of the challenge of reaching confident predictions about the nature of work is that the forces we see around us in the present are themselves subject to interpretation. There are lots of unresolved contradictions as to what is happening in the here-and-now, which in turn makes any kind of prediction about the future difficult.

Here's one of those contradictions: everyone worries a lot about automation rendering millions of once-secure jobs needless. And you can come up with anecdotes about advances in artificial intelligence and robotics resulting in a company shrinking its workforce. But at the economy-wide level, none of the things you would expect to happen in a world of mass displacement of humans by machines seems to be happening. The unemployment rate, as of late 2019, is near its lowest level in five decades. Employers complain of labor shortages. Capital spending is relatively low as a share of the economy, by historical standards. And productivity growth has been weak roughly since the beginning of the twenty-first century, not uncommonly strong.

In more anecdotal terms, in the same publication you might read an article in which a technologist bemoans the future loss of millions of good blue-collar trucking jobs as driverless freight trucks become a reality—and also an article about how the trucking industry is struggling to find enough drivers.

But that's not the only contradiction. Consider one tied to what it means to "have a job." As everyone knows, the implicit contract between a worker and an employer has changed a great deal over the past few decades. Even for traditional payroll employees, there is no implicit promise of a job for life of the sort that large, successful companies offered in the decades immediately following World War II. To the contrary, workers understand that as an employer's business needs change, so will the workforce. Layoffs are common even at profitable companies and even when there is no recession.

And that sense of uncertainty is even more extreme for the armies of contract and freelance workers modern organizations rely upon to do their work. Indeed, part of the appeal of using contracting firms for companies is that they can offer less lavish benefits and less job security than they would for payroll employees.

Consider an example that formed the basis of a 2018 article I wrote for the *New York Times*. In the 1980s, a janitor for Eastman Kodak—one of the most innovative and profitable companies of that time—may not have been paid much money, but she did receive paid vacation time, excellent health care, and an annual bonus based on the company's profits. Her equivalent today, a janitor at Apple Inc., does not work for the company at all, but for a janitorial services company. Her pay might be similar in inflation-adjusted terms to her Eastman Kodak equivalent from a generation ago, but with few benefits, less job security, and little opportunity to advance.

One might reasonably predict that this bifurcation of the labor force is a one-way train, that the gap will keep widening between a small number of highly educated professionals and masses of less skilled, financially insecure contract workers.

But the contradiction at play is that we can also see before us evidence of the limits of this approach—reasons to think that the shift toward less secure employment arrangements with less extensive benefits was a political choice that society made, not some technological inevitability.

For one thing, predictions that the "gig economy" model would rapidly overtake all sorts of work simply aren't coming true. Digital platforms like Uber and TaskRabbit remain niche forms of employment and are more commonly used as a "side hustle" by people who earn their primary income from more conventional jobs than as full-time work. Some of the early evidence that these forms of work were becoming more widespread has turned out to be faulty, a fact notably acknowledged by Larry Katz of Harvard and the late Alan Krueger of Princeton, who revised their own earlier work based on the latest data.

It turns out, in most jobs, the ability to collaborate and develop specialized skills and training is really important, and those are only really plausible in more traditional work arrangements.

And some major employers are finding that the "low road" of minimizing labor costs isn't in their long-term interests. Walmart, for example, the largest private employer in the United States, found itself wrong-footed in 2014 after it found that years of trimming labor costs to the bone had undermined its ability to compete amid the digitization of the retail industry. It invested $3 billion in higher pay and more expansive training programs to reclaim that competitive advantage.

Walmart is not the only company that has found business success by moving toward a more old-school way of relating to its employees—keeping them as payroll employees and offering higher pay and more extensive training than is strictly necessary. You can also see it in industries with powerful unions, which tend to have persistently higher wages and better benefits relative to those with otherwise similar workforces but without organized labor. Hotel staff are unionized in many major cities, for example, and the industry tends to have persistently higher pay than the rarely unionized restaurant industry.

In other words, much of the shift in the definition of a job and bifurcation of the workforce appears to be less of an inevitable function of technology and globalization, and more like the result of political choices, such as making it harder for unions to organize, to allow the concentration of major industries.

When something results from a political choice, it could be reversed if the political winds change. From the 1980s through the 2010s, power shifted from workers to employers. There's no reason it couldn't shift back in the right circumstances.

Those contradictions help explain why the debate over the future of work is such a debate. The chapters in this part meet that uncertainty and ambiguity with facts and insight.

This aligns well with the ideas offered by Susan Lund and Bryan Hancock of the McKinsey Global Institute, who show the ways that educating a workforce with the correct mix of skills will be key to the future. In particular, they show how it is a false dichotomy to think of the need for STEM (science, technology, engineering, and math) skills as being in tension with a broader, liberal arts education. Indeed, they make a compelling case that we should use a different acronym, STEAM, to incorporate "arts" as a fifth type of skill. The future of competition involves not just developing clever algorithms and new artificial intelligence techniques but also deciding how to put those new technologies to work. And a tunnel vision on the technical dimensions can leave a worker of the future unprepared to use good judgment and interact with other people effectively.

This aligns with what I've heard over and over in my reporting with executives and recruiters from major companies. A great software engineer is valuable, of course, but even more valuable is a software engineer who can also communicate effectively with less technically minded colleagues, who can interact well with clients, and who can help make good strategic decisions about how to put lines of code to use.

Relatedly, Lance Braunstein, head of the Aladdin product group at asset management giant BlackRock, describes the need for "citizen developers," people with deep subject matter expertise who are not software developers per se but who have enough experience coding to put software tools to work to solve business problems. I would draw a comparison with spreadsheet software. A generation ago, spreadsheets were most commonly used by financial professionals, and it took in-depth training to put them to use. Now, it's expected that almost everyone in a corporate environment would know how to do simple quantitative analysis using spreadsheets, which are far more intuitive and easier to use than in earlier decades. Programming tasks of moderate complexity are the equivalent, which implies that universities should educate even those who have no inclination to become computer science majors in one or two of the simpler coding languages.

How can educational institutions ensure that they are producing graduates with the skills they will need to thrive regardless of how the future of work plays out—whether that is a more dystopian or a rosier scenario? Matthew Pittinsky, a veteran entrepreneur at the intersection of technology and education, offers answers. He describes how universities might combine education in fundamental lifelong learning skills layered with specific credentials that are optimized to the needs of employers. His observations align with what I have found in my own reporting on the needs of modern companies. They seek workers with strong abilities in skills like quantitative analysis and communication, but also with the adaptability to learn the latest programming language or data science technique.

Mike Ulica of the National Geographic Society explores how geographic and cultural diversity matters in the modern workplace. Building successful teams, it seems clear, is not just about achieving diversity among technical skills but also entails achieving diversity in where people come from and how they understand the unique challenges to deploying a product across different geographies.

What might an employer of the future do to make their workplace one that gets the best out of people and enables them to thrive? Amrit Ray, Lu Hong, and Trish White provide a narrative of how Pfizer's Upjohn division is attempting to do just that. They describe a workplace that em-phasizes flexibility among teams and clear, honest communication among colleagues. It is striking that younger workers do seem to embrace the idea that there is no such thing as a job-for-life anymore, but, in exchange, they want their employers to embrace values like offering opportunity, flexibility, and honesty.

For a case study of how all this works in one particular environment with immense technological complexity, we hear from Gregory L. Robinson, the director of NASA, who reflects on how aerospace research has changed in the last generation and what that means in his field. He notes, among other things, how some of this integration of people with different technical skills is not entirely new and that at NASA it is common for engineers to expand their skills across other types of engineering.

Uli Heitzlhofer, of the transportation platform Lyft, meanwhile, takes us deep into the role that L&D—learning and development—should play in maintaining a vibrant workforce as artificial intelligence and other tech-nologies mature. It seems inevitable that smarter computers will mean that humans interact with those computers differently than in the past. Think of the difference between driving a car made in 1969 compared with one in 2019, and imagine what another fifty years might change—or, more dramatically, the difference between using a 1960s typewriter versus a modern word processing program.

In particular, Heitzlhofer argues that there is room for collaboration among companies that might normally be cutthroat competitors in the area of training workers. The flip side of this more volatile environment for workers is that employers have been reluctant to spend money helping their staff develop new skills, in that loyalty cuts both ways. Why spend money training someone who might leave for a competitor? But if many companies in an industry contributed to joint training programs, perhaps that dilemma could be avoided.

Taken together, the chapters in this part may not resolve the question of what the future of work looks like. But they show how many sharp minds are at work trying to ensure that workers of the future can have rewarding, successful careers even in a world of rapid technological change.

1 EQUIPPING A NEW GENERATION WITH THE SKILLS NEEDED IN THE AUTOMATION AGE

Susan Lund and Bryan Hancock

ABSTRACT

Research by the McKinsey Global Institute into the effect of automation and artificial intelligence adoption highlights key workforce transitions over the next ten to fifteen years. One of the major changes will likely be shifting demand for skills: the jobs of tomorrow will require more technological skills, but they will also need more higher cognitive and social and emotional skills. These changes will affect workers across sectors and countries—and will require rethinking existing educational models. This chapter proposes five paths forward: more STE(A)M degrees and greater student diversity within them; a renewed focus on liberal arts for "robot-proof" jobs; expanding postsecondary credentials; greater collaboration between higher education and companies to prepare students for the labor market of the future; and creative new ways for colleges to make lifelong learning a reality.

IN THE PAST FIFTY YEARS, the skills used in many professions have fundamentally changed, even as the professions themselves have thrived. The changes can be seen by comparing official descriptions of roles as defined by the US Department of Labor.[1] For example, nurses in 1957 were required to administer medication, monitor patients' pulse and temperature, and help with therapeutic tasks such as bathing and feeding patients. Today, they still administer medication, but nurses also help perform diagnostic tests and can analyze the results, employing skills and filling roles that were common to doctors a half-century ago. As automation and artificial intelligence (AI) are increasingly deployed in the workplace, such shifts in skills and roles will become more pronounced. This will challenge educators globally. They will need to both anticipate the changes and equip young generations today and tomorrow with the tools needed to thrive in a rapidly evolving technological age.

Automation, Artificial Intelligence, and Workforce Transitions

A new wave of technological innovation is upon us. As with previous waves, the arrival of advanced automation and AI has the potential to bring immense benefits to our lives but also challenging disruption, especially in the workplace. Rapid advances in algorithmic capabilities combined with an explosion of computing capacity and data are enabling beyond-human machine competencies and a new generation of system-level innovation, from self-driving cars to promising advances in medicine. For businesses and the economy more broadly, the potential productivity gains across sectors are substantial, even if these technologies still have limitations and deployment can be complex. In the public debate, polls tend to show a nuanced view: although there is excitement over the potential for machines to improve lives as consumers, this is often tempered or overshadowed by fear of what adoption will mean for jobs.[2]

Our research provides some reassurance on the employment front. First, we find that companies at the forefront of adopting AI are likely to increase employment rather than reduce it, as innovation-focused adopters position themselves for growth, which tends to stimulate employment.[3] Second, scenarios we have developed for the impact of automation on the workforce, based on the pace and extent of adoption, suggest that although about 15 percent of the global workforce, or the equivalent of about 400 million workers, could be displaced by automation in the period 2016–2030, some 550 million to 890 million new jobs could be created in the same period from productivity gains, innovation, and the catalytic effect of new labor demands, including rising incomes in emerging economies and increased investment in infrastructure, real estate, energy, and technology.[4]

Barring extreme scenarios, the jobs lost and jobs gained through automation and AI adoption may thus more or less balance themselves out. Nonetheless, our research beyond these numbers also suggests that significant and often disruptive workforce transitions can be expected over the next ten to fifteen years. Almost all jobs will change as machines increasingly complement human labor in the workplace. Our research has found that about 30 percent of the activities in 60 percent of all occupations could be automated by adapting currently demonstrated technologies.[5]

The workforce implications are likely to include large-scale change of occupations for some workers. Occupations that are highly susceptible to automation—for example, those involving physical activities in highly structured environments and in data processing—will decline, whereas others that are difficult to automate will grow. This latter category includes activities such as managing others, providing expertise, and interfacing with stakeholders. Workplaces and workflows will also change as people interact ever more closely with machines; for example, whereas industrial robots used to be potentially hazardous to people and were kept in cages, today "cobots" work side-by-side with humans on assembly lines and at times are trained by their human coworkers. Workplace changes are not unique to industry: in many supermarkets, for example, the job of cashier has shifted from scanning barcodes to helping customers who do it themselves. Such workflow changes will be challenging both to individual workers, who will need to be retrained, and to companies, which must become more adaptable. Automation could also put pressure on average wages in advanced economies. In advanced economies, for example, many middle-wage jobs are dominated by highly automatable activities in fields such as manufacturing and accounting, which are likely to decline.

Shifting Demand for Skills

One of the biggest challenges and potential transitions involves the skills that will be needed in the workplace of the future. To examine those implications in detail for our research at the McKinsey Global Institute, we created a model of work activities that automation and AI can perform. We then defined a taxonomy of twenty-five workforce skills grouped into five categories: physical and manual, basic cognitive, higher cognitive, social and emotional, and technological skills. We quantified the amount of time that workers in the United States and Europe spend using each of these skills today and how that will shift as a result of technology adoption by 2030.[6]

Broadly, we see a significant increase in demand for technology, engineering, and math skills, including both basic digital skills and advanced skills such as computer engineering, machine learning, and AI development. Simultaneously, we envision an increase in the need for higher cognitive skills, such as creativity, critical thinking, and complex information processing, as well as increased need for social and emotional skills, including leadership, managing others, empathy, and initiative taking (Figure 1.1). These latter skills, often characterized as "soft," are difficult to measure or teach. Yet they are relatively "robot-proof," since machines for now do not come close to matching human performance levels.

Indeed, based on our research, we anticipate that demand for social and emotional skills will grow almost as fast as demand for many advanced technological skills. By contrast, demand for physical and manual skills will decline but will nonetheless remain the single largest category of workforce skills in 2030 in many countries including the United States.[7]

This shifting skills outlook is likely to have substantial implications for educators. Indeed, it challenges some core assumptions of today's educational model. By way of example, consider creativity. Our research shows that creativity will be increasingly in demand in the future; we estimate the number of hours in the United States for which it will be an essential element for work could rise by 40 percent. Creativity is an innate human skill that even the most advanced AI systems today struggle to emulate. True, algorithms can "write" fugues that sound like they may have been composed by Johann Sebastian Bach if they have been trained on existing Bach fugues, but the end product is entirely derivative.[8] For a machine to

United States, all sectors

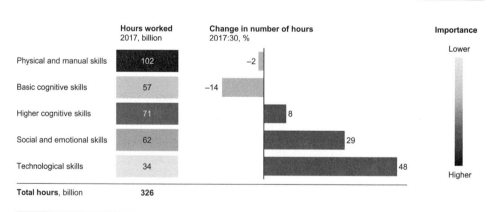

Figure 1.1 The skills required in all jobs will shift toward more technological and socioemotional skills

SOURCE: McKinsey Global Institute

devise a new style of music that is pleasing to the human ear, write a novel, or invent a new product that will excite consumers is still just a gleam in the eye of AI developers. Yet how does one teach creativity? For more than a century, various thinkers have wrestled with this question, and numerous attempts have been made to introduce some forms of creativity into the curriculum. Montessori, Steiner, and other methods (including the Reggio Emilia approach) are sometimes characterized as being adept at fostering creativity, although there is a lack of rigorous scientific evidence to back this up. Moreover, definitions of what constitutes creativity and how it can be imparted vary widely.

New thinking will also be needed to work through the implications of greater demand for other higher cognitive and social and emotional skills. How can the teaching of information synthesis and critical thinking, among other higher-level cognitive skills, be upgraded in schools and colleges? Social and emotional skills, such as empathy, leadership, and teamwork, are today developed mainly through participation in extracurricular activities such as athletic teams and clubs. But participation in these activities is voluntary, and they are likely to attract students already endowed with stronger social skills. As a part of a revamped core curriculum for the automation age, new approaches will be needed in the classroom to foster higher cognitive and social and emotional skills.[9]

The Challenge for Education: Five Paths Forward

Given the challenges around skills that our research has highlighted, how should educators and other stakeholders focus their efforts? Change is required, but where should the priorities lie? Without seeking to be prescriptive or exhaustive, we offer here five potential paths forward. Expanding on existing ideas, methods, and institutions, these paths are designed to equip a new generation with skills that will enable them to thrive in the automation age. Some are relatively short-term and tactical. Others are longer term and highly strategic. Some combination of both will be needed if individuals, educators, and society more broadly are to successfully navigate the coming technology-related transitions and reap the full benefits of adoption with a minimum of workforce disruption.

We welcome other ideas that can also advance skills training. Indeed, other authors in this book offer their own viable pathways. Earl Lewis and colleagues from the University of Michigan, for example, speak to the need for a channel that works directly with chronically under- and unemployed workers. Greg Robinson describes how one highly technical organization, NASA, has found a path forward through cultural change within the organization to support continuous learning.

More STE(A)M Degrees and Greater Diversity among Students in These Programs

In the new age of automation, everyone will need some basic digital skills. Already in the past decade, people in once low-tech occupations from nursing to truck driving have had to adjust to a rising need to work with machines ranging from sophisticated vital sign monitors to GPS systems.[10] In coming years, we expect the demand for basic digital skills to continue increasing.[11] At the same time, many more people will need to be fluent in advanced technology skills, such as programming, in order to create, implement, and maintain the plethora of new technologies in the workplace.

Yet the future workplace will not just be a technological one. The arts and humanities will also have a growing role. Although AI is good at answering questions, for example, humans are better at asking them. Given the growing importance of nontechnical skills, including critical thinking, creativity, and complex problem solving, the classic STEM skills—science, technology, engineering, and math—will need to add an *A* for arts, transforming STEM into STEAM.

The integration of technology and the arts is accelerating—and in some eye-catching ways. At the high school level, the convergence is taking place in different forms across the United States; for example, more than two dozen school districts and programs in Pennsylvania have been awarded $530,000 specifically for the development of STEAM programs and facilities. Such programs tend to use project-based teaching to foster student skills in creativity, design thinking, tech literacy, collaboration, and problem solving.[12]

At the college level, the Rhode Island School of Design (RISD) exemplifies how technology and science are cutting across the traditional curriculum. RISD offers an interdisciplinary undergraduate concentration in computation, technology, and culture; students hone their ability to write source code, author software, and program machines for making works of art and design. RISD, which has been receiving federal research funding from the National Science Foundation for its work to visualize environmental research, offers a dual degree with Brown University that enables students to pursue multidisciplinary work combining arts and design with life sciences as well as humanities and social sciences.

Elsewhere, Virginia Tech's Institute for Creativity, Arts, and Technology is one of ten university research groups in a Mellon Foundation–funded national consortium designed to explore best practices for integrating arts practice into the research university. The other institutions in the program are Carnegie Mellon University, Pennsylvania State University, Massachusetts Institute of Technology (MIT), Stanford University, the University of California, Berkeley, the University of Colorado, the University of Michigan, Vanderbilt University, and Washington University in St. Louis.

Engineering schools are also moving to break down traditional barriers between science and arts. MIT, notably, has long sought to encourage learners to work across disciplines; today, for example, students there can combine engineering subjects with electronic music, computer science with virtual storytelling or theater, or synthetic biology with visual art.[13]

Greater student diversity will also be needed within STEM degrees, where women and minorities tend to be heavily underrepresented for now. In the United States, for example, women comprise just 23 percent of high school Advanced Placement computer science exam takers, 19 percent of bachelor's computer and information science degree recipients, and 26 percent of the computing workforce.[14] Creating more diversity is not just an end in itself but will also help counteract some of the bias that has become baked into algorithms as a result of unrepresentative data that perpetuate human biases about race and gender. Julia Angwin and others at ProPublica have shown how COMPAS scores, used to predict recidivism in Broward County, Florida, were nearly twice as likely to incorrectly label African American defendants as higher risk compared to white defendants. Work by Joy Buolamwini and Timnit Gebru at MIT found error rates in facial analysis technologies differed by race and gender.[15]

Alternatives to Being a Technologist

Many of tomorrow's jobs will be in occupations where machines have yet to make significant inroads. Activities such as managing or coaching others; addressing stakeholder questions; and providing expertise, judgment, and discernment remain innately human actions. Social and emotional skills are not entirely robot-proof, but even if, say, a nurse's or a teacher's role could be replaced by a machine, consumer acceptance is not a given.[16] Our analysis of global demand for occupations thus continues to see a broad range of workforce roles that only humans will be able to fully do—that includes the work of teachers, managers, and doctors but also that of interior designers, therapists, musicians, nutritionists, and community service managers, to name just a few such occupations.

Many new jobs are emerging to meet needs created by new technologies. These include such roles as AI photo taggers and search engine–optimization specialists but also solar panel installers and wind turbine engineers, occupations that simply didn't exist a few years ago. At the same time, many classic engineering jobs could shrink rather than grow as the impact of technology expands, and many entry-level accounting and actuarial jobs will be replaced by AI. Meanwhile, some types of occupation that require little or no technology could grow, as people look for other types of work, including in areas such as personal enrichment. That could lead to more demand for teachers in areas such as yoga and pottery but also for makeup artists, video camera crews, and DJs—which the Bureau of Labor Statistics officially added to its roster of professions in 2018.

Expanding Postsecondary Credentials and Degrees

Classic credentials such as a college diploma have long been proxies for skills, but in the digital era that may no longer hold true. Skill-based courses that are linked to employer demand and that can be delivered in alternative ways such as online have the potential to help close existing skill gaps and prepare young people for jobs of the future.

A range of possibilities have emerged that increase the number of pathways to postsecondary certificates and degrees. They include creating clearer pathways from high school to technical/community college; guaranteeing funding for community college education; guaranteeing transfer admission to four-year colleges from community colleges; and moving from degree to certificate program, where appropriate.

Creating such pathways is critical, as they can enable everyone to move up the education ladder. People whose education has not extended beyond high school may be among the most susceptible to the employment effects of automation, and so their ability to receive certificates and associate degrees can open new doors. To make room for them, in turn, people with associate degrees will also need to move up a level, and so on.

Several new models link high schools with community or technical colleges to new pathways to employment. Early-college high schools, which now are found in almost thirty US states, allow students to earn college credits in four-year college programs while they are still in high school.[17] The P-Tech model, pioneered by IBM, is a public-private partnership that offers a six-year diploma plus an associate degree in a STEM field. High schools working with community colleges and at least one local employer design the program and provide coaching and mentoring as well as instruction in classes.[18]

Guaranteeing funding for community college education, along with intensive coaching, can be critical elements to ensure that low-income students, in particular, stick with and complete programs for which they have enrolled. To that end, for example, the state of Tennessee in 2014 pioneered the "Tennessee Promise" program, which offers free tuition and paid fees to community college students provided they finish high school and apply for federal financial aid. At least thirty other states have started or are considering such programs.[19] As well as providing coaching and mentoring, these schemes also create a digital record for each student that includes his or her high school transcript, test scores, work experience, and extracurricular activities. This record functions like a LinkedIn profile for high school students, enabling them to send key information about themselves to colleges with one click.

A third pathway is guaranteed transfer admission from community colleges to four-year colleges. This is already the case in California, where six University of California campuses offer a transfer admission guarantee program for California community college students who meet specific requirements. Northern Virginia Community College has a number of guaranteed admission agreements with four-year colleges, including the University of Virginia, George Mason University, and George Washington University.

The idea of moving from full degree programs to certificate programs, where appropriate, is currently being tested. Western Governors University, for example, recently announced its first less-than-full-degree program in medical coding; under the initiative, which is being implemented in partnership with the Service Employees International Union-United Healthcare Workers West, students will earn a Certified Professional Coder credential, the most recognized medical coding certification in the health-care industry. The program is expected to take about nine months to complete. As tech skills grow in importance in health care, Western Governors estimates that, in California alone, medical providers will need to fill 400,000 positions with skilled workers other than doctors, nurses, and dentists over the next five years.[20]

Greater Collaboration between Higher Education and Companies to Prepare Students for the Labor Market of the Future

Educators have opportunities to collaborate with companies to provide degrees and credentials to people in the workforce. Several higher education institutions and companies have taken the lead, including Arizona State University (ASU), which has partnered with Starbucks to enable baristas to earn college credit in more than eighty undergraduate degrees, and Georgia Tech, which has partnered with AT&T.[21] At a time when "reskilling" has become a key topic for many CEOs and boards, such forms of cooperation fill some important gaps and could lead to at-scale retraining efforts if widely adopted. ASU is looking to expand its partnerships in the private sector with a forthcoming for-profit venture that will be financed and majority owned by the $2 billion TPG Rise Fund.[22] Several authors in this book propose other specific ways through which business and higher education can collaborate to advance skills training. See, for example, the chapter by Jason A. Tyszko and Robert G. Sheets, which describes a job-data exchange where information on skills and competencies could be shared. Another chapter, by Brian Fitzgerald and colleagues from the Business–Higher Education Forum, outlines a different model for sharing relevant information across multiple corporations and multiple sectors. And Uli Heitzlhofer argues that businesses ought to collaborate in support of meeting their training needs.

As the pioneers have been finding, however, cooperation can work effectively only if companies make sure that people embarking on training are qualified to pursue higher education. When learners are not fully qualified, institutions may have to provide remedial education that brings employees up to standard. A key problem, early adopters suggest, can be the lack of basic literacy and numeracy.[23] Online programs can allow students to brush up on these basics to qualify for online college.

Some employers are going further to open doors to employees—and help them overcome limitations. Walmart offers all its employees the chance to attend college for just $1 a day in a partnership that includes Florida State University, Brandman University, and Bellevue University.[24] This is just one example of employers envisioning employee skills development more holistically than just "in-house training" and tuition reimbursement.

At a local level, too, business and educational institutions work closely together in some places. For example, the Technical College System of Georgia's QuickStart program provides customized workforce training for Georgia's businesses in a wide range of disciplines, including making donuts, forging cast iron, shaping plastic, and sorting peanuts.[25]

The Critical Role of Colleges in Fostering Lifelong Learning

Higher education has long been a limited-period experience, geographically limited, and a stepping-stone between high school and work. In the new era that is dawning, as occupations change and all workers need to adapt, the mantra of "lifelong learning" will need to pertain broadly to all employees. A typical student of the future may not be an eighteen-year-old, but a thirty-five-year-old or a forty-five-year-old looking to reboot her or his education. Moreover, as the pace of technological change accelerates, learning new skills may be essential at several different junctures of a career.

Although some learning happens on the job, there is also a need for short-term continuing education programs for midcareer workers. In this regard, colleges, not just employers, have a critical role to play. Some schools are already tapping into this opportunity. The Ross School of Business at the University of Michigan, for example, offers MBA students career counseling and online coaching resources any time after they have graduated.[26] At the University of North Carolina at Chapel Hill's Kenan-Flagler Business School, graduates of the online MBA program have permanent access to coursework, allowing them to return at any time to refresh their education and explore new skills. Harvard University makes many of its most popular courses available online to alumni, while Columbia University offers alumni online library access.[27]

If undergraduate study is just the start of a lifelong learning partnership between institution and students, the distinction between student and alumnus will become increasingly blurred—and indeed could become akin to an "open loop." Former students who graduate may return to their alma mater years later for further education aimed at upgrading their skills or learning new ones—and keep returning over the course of their working lives.

The advantage for colleges in taking such an approach is not just altruistic. Helping alumni cope with adjustments in their professional lives can make financial sense, too, by strengthening an institution's bonds with alumni and giving greater direct purpose to fundraising appeals.

*   *   *

In this era of technological ferment, higher education providers have a critical role to play in preparing new generations for the world of tomorrow. The starting point for change is a clearer understanding of how technology will change occupations and the skill requirements of the workforce. Just as creativity and critical thinking will grow in importance in the workforce, so, too, do college leaders need to be creative and critical in their approach to an uncertain—but exciting—new world that will require them and their institutions to change with the times.

2   THE ROLE OF CITIZEN DEVELOPERS IN DEVELOPING TECHNOLOGICAL LITERACY

Lance Braunstein

ABSTRACT

Technological shifts are not isolated to any particular industry but are pervasive in a way that is causing everyone to rethink business models, social interactions, and education structures. Specifically, the way children and employees are trained and educated means we can no longer just watch this digital transformation. We must now begin to actively take part in automation, data analytics, and software development across industries and professions. There are many dimensions to this evolution in education, with significant implications to the notion of the "digital native," the child who has grown up with the ubiquity of smartphones, touch screens, and voice-enabled digital assistants. This chapter discusses the importance of software and digital literacy, the concept of vocational education, the expansion of technical skills, and current skills gaps.

MARC ANDREESSEN'S FAMOUS QUIP "software eats the world" is one of my favorite expressions.[1] It's at once playful, evoking images of a Monty Pythonesque cartoon monster quietly munching parts of the Pacific Rim, and prophetic in that our lives are becoming more digital, served via online software. This shift, which feels tectonic, isn't isolated to any particular industry but is pervasive in a way that is causing us to rethink our business models, social interactions, and education structures. The way that we train and educate our children, employees, and ourselves today means that we can no longer stand by and merely watch this digital transformation; rather, we must now begin to actively take part in automation, data analytics, and software development across industries and professions.[2]

There are many dimensions to this evolution in education, with significant implications for the notion of the "digital native," the child who has grown up with the ubiquity of smartphones, touch screens, and voice-enabled digital assistants. A specific and interesting question has emerged in higher education: Are we providing our students with an education that prepares them for the digital landscape they'll navigate once they join the workforce as engineers, graphic designers, journalists, and, yes, software developers?[3] For now, I believe, the answer is no.

Let's start with the idea of a vocation. According to *Merriam-Webster*, *vocational* is defined as "of, relating to, or undergoing training in a skill or trade to be pursued as a career."[4] The fundamental element of a vocation, then, is the skill needed to do work—not just the theory and knowledge of a subject, but the skill specifically. In fact, most vocational program assessments are based on competencies rather than grades, the most common metric in higher education.[5] A plumber, for example, needs to be able to solder pipe. A software developer needs to be able to write a data-sorting algorithm. Graduates from a vocational school will pass a set of competencies based on a skills matrix rather than a graded measure of their theoretical knowledge. In respect to this practical focus on skills, I am suggesting that, in a digital world, all of us will need technical skills as a core competency of any career. Like literacy or numeracy, technology literacy is increasingly becoming a necessary skill for work.[6] And not just technology work, but any work. For example, if you are training to become a graphic designer, it's no longer sufficient to understand typography, color theory, user experience design, and information architecture. You also require vocational training that will impart an understanding of digital channels like web or mobile and will likely include the underlying tools needed to create designs for those channels, including coding pages, data methods for tracking usage, and visualization tools for ensuring that outcomes meet success measures.

In this chapter, I argue that technological literacy is foundational for all work. I discuss retraining existing workforces to increase technology literacy as well as the evolving role of higher education in training our next generation of doctors, engineers, lawyers, and graphic designers with a greater ability to navigate the digital landscape in which they work.

Citizen Developers

There have been two important developments in humanity's interaction with its work: the invention of machines that help humans move and machines that help humans think.[7] The Industrial Revolution was marked by foundational inventions like dynamite, the steam engine, and telegraphy, all of which helped people perform mechanical tasks significantly more efficiently and changed the relationship of humans to their work. For example, when James Watt invented the steam engine in the late 1700s, the way people and goods moved from place to place became dramatically more efficient and faster. The focus of the people who worked in transport shifted from managing people and animals to engineering solutions for railways, engines, and fuel.

In the Information Age, we have seen an analogous shift to enhanced cognition in which humans rely on machines to drive efficiency in the access, organization, and manipulation of data. The rise of computers and the internet has had profound effects on every part of our lives, including how we work. We have automated away many tasks—think about how you book travel or research a topic—in a way that has evolved our workforce to higher level jobs that no longer focus on data entry, retrieval, and management versus the analysis and visualization of information. Like the shift from people managing pack mules to people running steam engines, the very nature of our work lives shifted from paper and abacuses to personal computers, mobile devices, and the cloud. Our jobs have now become an exercise in making insights from a vast array of data that are available to us across many channels and devices and demand an understanding of the underlying technology more than ever before. Let's narrow this focus to the enterprise and discuss a phenomenon that I've observed called the "citizen developer."

The Rise of the Citizen Developer

What is a citizen developer? I first came across this term at BlackRock, but it captures a phenomenon that has been growing for some time. Citizen developers are users who create business applications for consumption by others. In a general sense, these developers are not technology professionals who are paid to code applications; instead, they use available tools for building applications that their teams can use during the course of their work. We saw many applications of this kind develop with the rise of personal computers, including shared spreadsheets and macros and, in more sophisticated examples, people creating local databases and applications to perform specialized tasks. These part-time coders rose out of necessity and, perhaps, the scarcity of technology resources. Often, these citizen developers are highly fragmented and not managed or controlled outside the local developers.

As the need for this form of development became clearer, a number of tools emerged to make data more readily available and to make analysis and visualization easier for the non–technology professional.[8] This enablement provided greater control and consistency while also improving productivity for the teams that embraced the model. The next stage of the evolution was the ability for people who did not have coding experience to start to write basic software to enable manipulation of and transactions involving the data. Like data, the ability to code started in a highly distributed way. We are now seeing greater centralization, enabled in large part by the cloud and the rise of standards-based application programming interfaces (APIs) that allow developers, professional or otherwise, to access services through standard, published means in a controlled way.

The result is that we are now seeing an entirely new demographic in the workforce of citizen developers who are adept at manipulating data and executing transactions in a consistent, controlled, and highly efficient manner. This new paradigm pushes the technology solution closer to the technology demand, so that people with deeper insight about the needs for given solutions are driving development of those solutions. The efficiency in narrowing the distance between supply and demand should be clear; but, perhaps more important, the innovation that results from this model is significant.

So how does this citizen developer phenomenon occur? There are several enablers, including the recognition that technical solutions are not the sole domain of the technology professional; the availability of controlled tools, environments, and processes for developing solutions; and the training of the citizen developers.

The Need for Citizen Developers

The need for increased technology literacy in the workforce has emerged in different industries at different paces. One of the earliest examples is from finance. In the late 1960s and early 1970s, electronic trading companies like Instinet and Nasdaq emerged that allowed clients to exchange data and transactions about stocks without human intervention.[9] This began a revolution in trading that ultimately led to a dramatic change in the industry in terms of volumes, pricing, and the business models of many firms. However, one of the more interesting footnotes to this history is the way in which the skills evolved in large trading firms.

Traditionally, large institutional trading firms like Goldman Sachs and Morgan Stanley hired many salespeople and traders to handle the trade flow for their businesses. Staff in these roles often sat together in large, often boisterous "trading floors." As the electronic trading revolution increasingly took hold, these trading floors began a transformation. They became quieter and the number of people who sat on them shrank. What caused this? The people who were driving this industry were no longer salespeople and traders. Rather, they were now software developers who understood trading and were writing algorithms and workflow systems to drive the business.[10] The days of calls coming in for a stock quote or to place a trade had given way to digital access to data with electronic order-taking and execution.

This is a clear example of an industry undergoing seismic changes that required a recognition of a new skill set and the enablement of the business to develop new technical solutions. In this case, the industry had already seen a digital revolution and evolved its workforce as a matter of survival. Other industries may not yet have seen that kind of radical shift. But is any industry immune from this digital revolution? That seems unlikely.

Tools for Citizen Developers
The basic tools for citizen developers are not unlike those used by other developers. They include tools and environments to write and test software; tools and processes to release it to production; tools to access data; and the ability to ensure that development is completed with the proper documentation, reviews, and process controls. This is often collectively called the software development life cycle, or SDLC, and is typically the domain of the technology professional.[11] A primary enabler of citizen developers is access to the SDLC or at least to a part of the SDLC that is specific to their work. A key tenet of any good SDLC is that it both enables and creates a control framework for software development, which is obviously important for citizen developers as well.

Training Citizen Developers

Finally, the key to all of this—and the point of this chapter—is the knowledge needed to solve complex business problems using technology. Training programs often begin with a coding course in Python or SQL (common programming languages for scripting and accessing data). These can be bespoke courses developed by the company or courses that leverage the myriad online training content and coding boot camps that have emerged. In addition to the formal training, having a coding "buddy" is usually an essential ingredient in enabling successful development since a well-timed tip or trick is often the difference between successful deployment and giving up. Finally, training in analytic and conceptual thinking is foundational to successful software development.[12] This often comes with broader coursework in computer science or engineering and should be infused into the training of citizen developers.

The Role of the University

In 2010, Harvard University's president, Drew Faust, gave a speech at Trinity College in Dublin where she described the role of higher education as follows:

> When we define higher education's role principally as driving economic development and solving society's most urgent problems, we risk losing sight of broader questions, of the kinds of inquiry that enable the critical stance, that build the humane perspective, that foster the restless skepticism and unbounded curiosity from which our profoundest understandings so often emerge. Too narrow a focus on the present can come at the expense of the past and future, of the long view that has always been higher learning's special concern.[13]

Higher education plays a critical role in developing the perspectives and curiosity to drive a deeper understanding of the world around us. There is almost a moral obligation in that mission and one that should be guarded preciously. However, the reality for many graduates is that, in addition to perspective and curiosity, they need to work. As Dr. Faust warned, however, we should guard against too narrow a focus in how our colleges and universities educate their students. So how do we ensure that a vocational education is infused in the broader curricula in higher education? Elsewhere in this book, other authors offer their own ideas. Matthew Pittinsky, for example, advances a model in which technical skills are continually updated through certificate and other nondegree training. Similarly, Anne Trumbore also describes the value of alternative credentials. In separate chapters, Mary Alice McCarthy and Daniel Kuehn describe apprenticeship models as paths to skill building. Although there are many ways to approach this question, what follows are a few ideas.

Corporate Training Programs

Many large companies today have training programs for new college graduates that are intended to take a base of knowledge in a specific major and enrich it with the practical tools that employees need to be successful in a given corporation's workplace. That typically includes organizational and networking skills, an understanding of the firm's mission and strategy, and, increasingly, a foundation in technical methods that the company uses.

As firms develop a greater interest and capacity to support citizen developers, these training programs will likely evolve into more technical curricula that could be delivered in partnership with colleges. For example, the idea that a recruiter should be able to source data from social media outlets and write software to scan for the best-suited candidate for a job opening should not be daunting but a matter of course in our training programs. As colleges and professional schools develop courses and curricula, an acknowledgment of this need may manifest itself as a course in Human Resources Data Methods or Data Techniques in Talent Management. These courses should provide practical methods for data management but also the abstract principles in data structures that lead to sustainable solutions. Other authors in this book, including Jason A. Tyszko and Robert G. Sheets and Brian Fitzgerald and colleagues from the Business–Higher Education Forum, frame interesting models for how the private sector and higher education can partner to support future workforce training needs.

Community Outreach

There are many people who may be interested in a corporate career but do not have access to a degree program or the means to pay for it. There are a number of avenues, including technology boot camps, that they could take, but these may also be out of their reach. Universities could assume some responsibility for including these people in their training programs. There are a number of examples of groups like YearUp and NPower that target historically underrepresented groups in training programs that lead to internships or degrees. Structuring such a partnership, or even creating a program to bring new populations into the workforce, would be incredibly powerful.

Degree Programs

Perhaps in slight opposition to Dr. Faust's caution is the idea that degree programs must account for the digital transformation every industry and profession is undertaking. Just as we would not want any college graduate to receive a degree without being able to construct a coherent essay or do basic mathematics, some understanding of coding and data is the new literacy. We shouldn't dilute the primary purpose of higher education, but at the same time we should ensure that students in colleges and universities are prepared in a vocational sense for the digital landscapes they will be navigating after graduation.

3 THE FUTURE OF WORK

Four Difficult Questions I Ask Myself as an Employer

Matthew Pittinsky

ABSTRACT

This chapter explores the relevance of academic credentials for employers. As an employer, the author shares reflections on critical questions about the value of academic credentials in the workplace and explores logistical issues around designing alternative systems for documenting and communicating employees' skill sets in lieu of traditional degrees and credentials.

IN THIS CHAPTER, I bridge the perspective of universities working to innovate their credentials for employer audiences with my own as an employer and as a technology provider to universities to enable credential innovation. I argue that higher education efforts at credential innovation are about universities responding to employers as a more coequal audience and stakeholder, alongside other academic institutions, for their credentials.

Employer Needs for Skills

The socially defined charter of a degree-granting institution is its ability to provide the key—a degree—that unlocks opportunities. But how relevant is the academic degree in general today, and how relevant are academic credentials to employers? These are uncomfortable questions for higher education. The answers to these questions are both multifaceted and profoundly consequential.

Colleges and universities need to think critically about what employers are looking for in terms of learning experiences and outcomes and the credential records that communicate them (e.g., transcripts, certificates, diplomas). At the same time, employers need to be much more articulate and engaged with higher education to inform these efforts.

Contrary to the popular view that the traditional liberal arts degree is outdated or less than useful, the skills developed in a liberal arts field of study—which, in essence, constitutes a unique and valuable way of learning—are highly aligned with the needs for skills in many of today's workplaces. In fact, precisely because applied competencies are highly dynamic, changing with technology in particular, the value of a liberal arts degree in developing "evergreen" human capital is only reinforced.

Although colleges can chase the skill set of the moment with nondegree programs, the ever-contracting "half-life" of these skills reinforces the unique foundational position and value of the degree. As an employer, I care about an employee's ability to write well, speak well, think analytically, and be comfortable with numbers. Those are skills that employees typically gain through pursuit of a liberal arts degree. At the same time, I also care about that employee's ability to code, implement software, manage projects, and run a digital campaign. In that regard, for example, we seek individuals with role-specific, stage specific, more directly measurable skills, such as pragmatic marketing, scrum master, PMI/PMP certifications, and Dale Carnegie training. We have learned in our own studies and from other industry research that other companies feel the same way about the mix of skills we seek as employers.

Precisely because I value the liberal arts degree, I remain frustrated with academic credentials due to the limited extent to which the academic credential *record* gives me an understanding of how skills are developed, not just through the curriculum but also from cocurricular (experiential) learning and extracurricular activities. And because most students are not very good at communicating these skills themselves, their credential records must help speak for them.

Making Academic Credentials More Valuable

Today, credential innovation is on the collective minds of many, if not most, leaders in higher education, driven by the increasing focus on a specific type of outcome: employment. Credential innovation can take many forms, but the two primary ones are, first, innovating programs to provide new types and levels of credentials (e.g., short courses, micromasters, and certificates) and, second, innovating the credential record itself to better communicate learning outcomes (e.g., competency, cocurricular, and clickable digital diplomas). In other chapters in this book, Mary Alice McCarthy and Daniel Kuehn suggest yet another channel to skills development: apprenticeships.

Collectively these innovations are about providing better signals and measures to employers about what graduates know and how well they know it. Additionally, they provide today's lifelong learners with clearer pathways to translate their education into employment opportunities and to stay relevant in the workplace.

To the extent that credential innovation is driven by a desire to better align postsecondary education with the needs and interests of employers, implicit in that is a critique we must acknowledge: the four-year degree is misaligned with the actual training employers need. What students study is not dynamic enough to develop the skills needed in the workplace. What's more, skills and competencies that are earned are not communicated clearly.

Thus, helping make academic credentials more valuable to employers and expanding the types of credentials universities issue pays service to the idea that employers (and learners) want a better credential. They want the flexibility of not having to recruit just degree graduates but also more targeted types of credential earners. They also want more detailed skill and experience information about prospective employees who are recent graduates.

What Employers Want

Findings from two online surveys of business executives and hiring managers showed that the skill and knowledge areas of greatest importance to both respondent groups when hiring include oral communication, critical thinking, ethical judgment, working effectively in teams, working independently, self-motivation, written communication, and real-world application of skills and knowledge.[1] Note that most of these are broad skills that apply across multiple disciplines.

The survey also revealed that slightly less important outcomes, while still rated highly, include locating, organizing, and evaluating information from multiple sources; analyzing complex problems; working with people from different backgrounds; being innovative and creative; and staying current on changing technologies.[2]

Both business executives and hiring managers indicate that participation in applied and project-based learning experiences, particularly internships or apprenticeships, gives recent college graduates an edge.[3] In addition, respondents favored electronic portfolios that summarize and demonstrate a candidate's accomplishments in key skill and knowledge areas as more useful than college transcripts alone in evaluating recent graduates' potential to succeed in the workplace.

For a recently commissioned Parchment market study, we asked employers who collect transcripts about what information they would ideally get and how they would get it.[4] Employers polled in the Parchment survey said that the key information they want includes the following (data points are shown first for interview screenings and second for job offers, both using a scale of 1–10):

- Past work experience/internship: 8.3 (interview screenings), 8.1 (job offers)
- Leadership experience: 7.7, 7.7
- GPA: 7.6, 7.4
- Writing or coding samples: 7.0, 7.0
- Volunteering experience: 6.8, 6.9
- Graduation year: 6.8, 6.7
- Extracurricular activities: 6.5, 6.5

"When we make hiring decisions, we try to make them based on data as much as possible and based on instinct or gut-feel as little as possible," said one respondent, a human resources officer for a large company. "Getting more data in machine-readable format helps us do this. The more data we get in machine-readable format, the more analyses we can conduct on our end. We try to identify specific correlations (e.g., holding a certain credential being correlated with success in a certain role), and the more data we have available, the more new correlations we can identify, which further helps us refine our targeted recruiting efforts."

"We care a lot about credentials," another survey respondent said. "We've identified some correlations between strong performance on the job and holding a specific credential. As such, we tend to focus our hiring efforts on those that hold these specific types of credentials. Also, when it comes to the actual work they do when they start their job, we tend to assign them the tasks that others holding their credential have historically performed strongly on."

The Liberal Arts Degree: From Not to Hot

The liberal arts may well have added value in the sense that, as Wesleyan University President Michael Roth observed recently, the liberal arts is more a way of learning than it is about gaining specific abilities in a particular major.[5] There is always a risk of predispositions being confirmed, but communication, collaboration, and critical thinking skills are precisely what I value as an employer. That doesn't contradict the relevance of nondegree, skill-based programs. It frames them as an addition, not as a subtraction or replacement.

In an op-ed, George Anders argued that the "useless" liberal arts degree has become tech's hottest ticket.[6] Throughout the major US tech hubs, whether Silicon Valley or Seattle, Boston, or Austin, he says, software companies are discovering that liberal arts thinking makes them stronger.

One employer survey revealed the top implications for colleges and universities in strengthening outcomes for recent graduates:[7]

- Seek to break down the false dichotomy of liberal arts and career development. They are intrinsically linked.
- Support rich experiential opportunities that truly integrate the liberal arts with real-world learning as communication skills and problem-solving skills. These are in high demand, seen as lacking, and believed to be higher education's responsibility to teach.
- Go beyond a vision of majors articulating to specific careers. Majors matter to some extent, but in many cases, college major is not the determinant of career entry. A college should approach career development as career exploration for a great many of its students, guiding and supporting them with the right mix of solid liberal arts skills and content knowledge.

Business executives and hiring managers concur, citing the accumulation of knowledge, development of critical thinking and analytical skills regardless of profession, potential for increased earnings, and focus on a goal as factors that make it useful or important for an individual to obtain a college degree today.[8]

The Future of Work: Joint Responsibility of University and Employer

Much of the critique of how colleges prepare students in the eyes of employers is overdone, or at least one-sided. While many employers feel that today's college graduates are not particularly well prepared to achieve the learning outcomes that they view as important, the conversation often focuses solely on just the supply side: What do universities need to do? But the role of the employer is also critical: What do employers need to understand? How do they want to know it?

This conversation needs to be more mutual and bilateral in the sense that we cannot expect credentialing organizations, especially universities, to innovate their credentials on behalf of employers when employers are not able to articulate what they are looking for. Other authors in this book also see the need for business and higher education to find richer ways to communicate. Jason A. Tyszko and Robert G. Sheets, for example, describe a job-data exchange where information on skills and competencies could be shared between the private sector and higher education. In another chapter, Brian Fitzgerald and colleagues from the Business–Higher Education Forum outline a different model for sharing relevant information across multiple corporations and multiple sectors.

Reflected in these chapters is the common idea that we need employers to be more active, reflective, thoughtful, and articulate about what skills they need and in what format they want those skills measured and communicated. This is true for employers of all sizes, not just for large corporations.

As an academic and entrepreneur with one foot in the credential world, I believe that academic institutions must improve credentials and communicate more data while simultaneously developing new kinds of credentials. Outside of the degree, lifelong learners continue to add credentials that more directly index particular skills in particular trades, industries, and technologies.

As a CEO with the other foot in the employer world, I want our employees to have a liberal arts education with evergreen skills because we want people to play many different roles over time. At the same time, there are specific roles with specific skills and competencies that we look for, with credentials that are university or industry based meeting this need. What both have in common is the need for an effective credential record, one that communicates the learning experiences, assessment criteria, and outcomes that help me understand the substance of the credential claimed by a candidate.

4 WHY GEOGRAPHY IS SO IMPORTANT

Michael L. Ulica

ABSTRACT

Geography is much more than knowing where things are located. Without basic geographic knowledge, it is impossible to make informed decisions in our personal, professional, and civic lives. Geography is critical to our natural world and the health of the environment, to our culture and other cultures around the globe, and to the very future of humankind and our planet. Understanding geography helps us be better global citizens. Within those contexts, geography also has a vital role to play in the workplace. Geographic knowledge, skills, and technology provide a means to comprehend the rapidly changing physical and cultural environments of the world. Further, understanding geography is essential for a workplace that is characterized by economic globalization, diversity, and job mobility and that requires a sophisticated understanding of cultures other than our own.

GEOGRAPHY IS MUCH MORE than places on a map or memorizing state capitals. It is the foundation on which all other social sciences are based. Without basic geographic knowledge, it's impossible to make informed decisions in our personal, professional, and civic lives. Geography is critical to our natural world and the health of the environment, to our culture and other cultures around the globe, and to the very future of humankind and our planet. Many economic, political, and personal decisions rely on sophisticated networks. An understanding of climate and the environment, for example, enables good decision making by informed and responsible global citizens.

Multinational organizations are facing a new era of globalization, characterized by the polarized forces of cooperation and competition. As globalization becomes more prevalent, companies will have to deal with increased cultural diversity within the workforce. Economic globalization, diversity, and job mobility require that we understand the nature of the foreign cultures that we represent. A foundation in geography is important for understanding the world, cultural diversity, the environment, society, and globalization.

Geography is not a passive subject. It cannot be simply absorbed or memorized. A geographic education is a necessary part of a complete education. This is becoming more apparent as geospatial technologies, including remote sensing and mapping tools, have become critical to our economic success and governance in areas such as natural resource management, international commerce, transportation, risk management, and national defense and security.

The Stories Geography Tells

So what does geography mean today? Geography can mean the natural landscape and all its majesty—imagery, such as a breathtaking view of Big Bend National Park, the largest protected area of Chihuahuan Desert in the United States. Likewise, when we talk about geography, we sometimes think about the challenges facing our natural world. For instance, we witnessed the devastating impacts on communities and people in the aftermath of Hurricane Harvey in 2018. Sometimes geography is just a simple map, of course, but every map holds a million complexities and tells a million stories. Stories like Pulitzer Prize–winning journalist Paul Salopek's 21,000-mile odyssey, walking the pathways of the first humans who migrated out of Africa in the Stone Age and made the Earth ours.[1] Along the way he is covering the major stories of our time—from climate change to technological innovation, mass migration to cultural survival.

Geography tells the story of what is happening on our planet. Take eight-year-old Delagha Qandagha, a shy, skinny boy with tired eyes interviewed by a reporter from the *National Geographic* magazine. Delagha is stranded by himself in a refugee center near Serbia's border with Croatia, thousands of miles away from his parents and four younger siblings. He fled his home in Afghanistan more than two years ago with his ten-year-old-cousin and a fifteen-year-old uncle to escape the Taliban and ISIS on a journey to get to France. Forced to rely on smugglers, they traveled nearly 4,000 miles, only to have their path obstructed in Serbia due to border crackdowns. Now, he lives with a group of other children left to fend for themselves and trying to survive in a canvas-covered hangar, with no school to go to and nothing to do but mark time. He is hungry. It's freezing cold, and he has only a T-shirt to wear. The reporter writes that Delagha has goosebumps from shivering, and his skin is covered in scabies. The boy tells our reporter, "There is nothing here." He says that misses his parents and doesn't know what to do.[2]

Delagha is one of 300,000 refugee children who fled their homelands without an adult with them in 2015 and 2016—a fivefold increase over previous years.[3] This, too, is geography. The men, women, and children around the world who are suffering because of where they were born or the circumstances they were born into or because of the danger and violence inflicted on them by the people around them. The lives and fates of others like Delagha depend on whether the rest of the world is aware and understands the plight of those in need, whether they live a continent away or in the next county.

Geography: Raising Consciousness and Driving Progress

Geography raises consciousness and connects people, no matter the distance. It creates empathy and engagement. As Gil Grosvenor, former editor in chief of *National Geographic* magazine and president of the National Geographic Society, said, it allows us to analyze the past and anticipate the future.[4] Geography drives progress, as our world is growing more complicated by the day. Understanding geography will help future generations become more socially conscious and to be informed change makers.

Today, the latest technologies are creating amazing new ways to engage and interact with one another, but they can also cause disruption. True connection, human connection, is being lost. At the same time, overpopulation threatens our very existence. By 2050, we will have more than nine billion people on the planet, and we will require the equivalent of almost three planets' worth of resources.[5] From population explosion, to damage to our environment, to rising geopolitical tensions, we need younger people around the globe to be more aware to take on these enormous challenges.

Geo-literacy Today

According to the National Geographic Society, geo-literacy is "the ability to use geographic understanding and geographic reasoning to make decisions."[6] National Geographic highlights the importance of geography in our daily lives, contending that we all use geo-literacy on a regular basis to make decisions about where to live, travel, visit, and more. But the stakes of a lack of geo-literacy go far beyond our daily lives.

Research shows that a basic understanding of the world and geography is dangerously lacking. A survey of young Americans we fielded with the Council on Foreign Relations found that many in their teens and twenties are simply not prepared to understand the world they will one day lead:

- Nearly half could not identify that Sudan was on the African continent.
- Only about a quarter knew the United States is bound by a treaty to protect Japan if it is attacked.
- And less than a third knew that Congress has the constitutional authority to declare war.[7]

Another survey, this one by the *New York Times*, showed that only 36 percent of Americans are able to locate North Korea on a map.[8]

Automation and Other Technological Developments[9]

The practice of geography through GIS (geographic information system) and mapping has undergone revolutionary change in the last decade due to technological advancements in software and hardware tools. The automation of earth-sensing devices from multiple platforms (satellites, airplanes, drones, and even balloons) means that terabytes of near-real-time mapping data is available through cloud-based systems. Combining this powerful stream of geospatial data with new software tools that integrate artificial intelligence and machine learning means we can derive insights about changes to the world that were just not possible in the past.

In terms of cartography and visualization new tools allow integration of vast amounts of data into digital displays and the ability to scan through many years of information. The ability of users to access maps and graphics on mobile devices has meant an ability to reach large audiences quickly.

Technological advances have influenced geospatial data collection, data processing and analysis, and geo-visualization in wide-reaching ways. Those advances notwithstanding, the core skills of a geographer—pattern recognition, knowledge of place, integration of human and physical earth processes—are still required to apply the new tools in the practice of better understanding of the nature of the world.

Implications for the Future of Work

Geographic knowledge, skills, and technology provide a means to comprehend the rapidly changing physical and cultural environments of the world, and the future needs talented educators and geographers, and educational institutions with a commitment to geographic education. Nearly every profession uses geography to solve problems, create opportunities, and build relationships. Linking location to information is a process that applies to many aspects of decision making in business and the community. Choosing a site, targeting a market segment, planning a distribution network, zoning a neighborhood, allocating resources, and responding to emergencies—all these problems involve questions of geography. Where are my customers and potential customers? In which neighborhoods or ZIP code areas do consumers with particular profiles live? Which areas of a city are most vulnerable to seasonal flooding or other natural disasters? Where are power poles located, and when did they last receive maintenance?

Geography is helping people make better decisions in many disciplines. Geographic data can be gathered and organized to support the generation of information products that are integrated in the business strategy of any organization.

Career and job opportunities for those with an interest in geography are widespread and challenging. Geospatial technology is one of the most dynamic and rapidly expanding workforce categories identified by the US Department of Labor.[10]

According to the National Geographic Society, a geographic information system (GIS) is a computer system for capturing, storing, checking, and displaying data related to positions on Earth's surface.[11] The use of GIS, the global positioning system (GPS), and other mapping technologies gives access to a world of geospatial information. GIS can show many different kinds of data on one map, such as streets, buildings, and vegetation, but a geographic information system is not an end in itself. It is used to create useful informational products that help organizations run better. It has saved hundreds of millions of dollars through increased productivity and efficiencies. Geography matters in every business and every discipline—wherever you turn, geography helps people do a better job and make a difference. GIS is helping thousands of organizations around the world.

ESRI, an international supplier of geographic system software, further states that GIS enables people to more easily see, analyze, and understand patterns and relationships.[12] GIS is used on the internet in places such as Sacramento County to organize its government for constituents. Simply touch a parcel on an online map, and the information for that location is available to you. The City of San Diego is helping people find resources by providing maps that allow them to find a job, find a park, or find a day care center and then show them how to get there. Nashville Electric is using GIS to automate all its electrical facilities for asset management.

GIS is being used to study the effects of global warming using maps to study the inundation from sea-level rise occurring off the coast of Delaware and the melt of glaciers in the Himalayas. Florida Power and Light is using GIS to track weather fronts and hurricanes. In Mississippi, people are using GIS for land-use planning. In Kentucky, the northern state's regional planning agency is using GIS to support and update its general plan. In Canada, Timberline Inc. is looking at sustainable forests and the visual and biological impact of forestry. Nongovernmental organizations (NGOs) are looking at saving some of the last unprotected wilderness in California.

GIS is also at work in transportation, looking at travel times in Baltimore, Maryland, and environmental impacts of transportation systems in Latvia. In New Zealand, GIS is being used to automatically generate aeronautical navigation charts. In the United States, the Air Force is defining obstruction zones around all of its major airports.

The National Geospatial-Intelligence Agency, the largest provider of geographic data in the world, is building databases, automating its charts and mapmaking process, and distributing these charts around the world to its users and customers. GIS software is also being used for "business geographics." In Norway, GIS is being used to find new sites for stores. In Germany, GIS is assessing markets for new commercial activities. In Ecuador, automated maps are being used to show where milk delivery trucks go, saving millions of dollars in logistical costs.

Conclusion

Geographic knowledge and skills are essential for us to understand the planet and better interact with people. Communication is global, as is the diversity of the workforce. Individuals who have a foundation in geography education will be open to opportunities to be future leaders of our society. This is why geography matters more than ever!

5 ENABLING A HIGH-PERFORMING, HUMAN-CENTERED ORGANIZATION IN PFIZER'S UPJOHN DIVISION

Amrit Ray, Lu Hong, and Trish White

ABSTRACT

Work will look distinctively different in the future, due in part to rapid advancements in technology and automation. With many future-of-work discussions focusing on the impact of digital advances, the significance of human experience often receives less attention. Leveraging technology will be essential, but so too will be facilitating an organizational culture that successfully galvanizes individual and team efforts around a worthy mission. In Pfizer's Upjohn division, we recognize that the digital revolution renders the "humanity" of the workplace more critical than ever, and we have kept this at the forefront while establishing our new organization. We are paying careful attention to the assumptions and intentions that make up our compelling sense of purpose as well as the practices that contribute to shared experience of a positive culture. In the context of individual and team development, we're replacing a reflexive preoccupation with weaknesses with a focus on growing and leveraging naturally occurring talents. We're experimenting with novel ways to simultaneously maximize global scale and empower local teams, and we're committed to learning together so that we may continually evolve at pace. We believe that a next-level, human-centered workplace will be the true differentiator in an increasingly digital world.

IN THE PAST, fundamental human desires such as the need to belong, work with people we enjoy, and pursue a meaningful purpose were met by extended family and close-knit communities. That was before what some observers consider to be the collapse of social capital, a disturbing trend well described in the 2000 book *Bowling Alone*.[1] Data from the Organisation for Economic Co-operation and Development (OECD) suggest that, in nearly every OECD member country, the share of fifteen-year-olds saying they feel lonely at school rose between 2003 and 2015.[2] This finding suggests that the digital revolution, with technologies that boast of connecting people in unprecedented ways, may paradoxically be contributing to an increased perceived sense of isolation. What impact will this growing development have on the workplace?

The psychological (and actual) contract with the workplace is changing. A survey of LinkedIn sample users across more than twenty countries found that as many as 90 percent of the workforce is open to new opportunities.[3] Few would argue with the assertion that commitment to one company for even a decade (let alone a lifetime) is fast becoming an archaic notion. Further, it doesn't seem to matter whether we're Baby Boomers, Generation X, Millennials, or younger; expectations of work today extend far beyond the aspiration to make a living. According to Tracy Brower, a sociologist for *Fast Company*, we're no longer content even when we achieve good work-life balance; rather we seek work-life *fulfillment*.[4] The publication *It's the Manager*, summarizing Gallup's most recent research, identified the changing demands of the workforce as shown in Table 5.1.

Table 5.1 Workforce Demands: Past versus Future

PAST	FUTURE
My paycheck	My purpose
My satisfaction	My development
My boss	My coach
My annual review	My ongoing conversations
My weaknesses	My strengths
My job	My life

SOURCE: J. Clifton and J. Harter, *It's the Manager: Gallup Finds the Quality of Managers and Team Leaders Is the Single Biggest Factor in Your Organization's Long-Term Success* (Omaha, NE: Gallup Press, 2019). Republished with permission of Gallup, Inc., from *It's the Manager*, Gallup, 2019; permission conveyed through Copyright Clearance Center, Inc.

Gallup claims that lack of development and career growth is the top reason employees leave a job. Development, they find, is the most important element of the unwritten social contract between employees and employer.[5] Gallup research finds that only one in three employees strongly agree that they have the opportunity to do what they do best every day. By doubling that ratio, organizations could reduce turnover by 30 percent.[6]

These observations are consistent with our experience at Upjohn. Colleagues[7] who have been with the company a long time are increasingly reconciled with the reality of accelerated change. Newer colleagues have even less expectation of stability. The trade-off expectation, however, is for Upjohn to provide meaningful work, growth, and development *today*.

Among other factors, our colleagues want to know that we put patients above profits (*purpose*), that we're dedicated to growth of individuals (*development*) as well as our business, and that we're capable of creating an environment where work is fun and life-enhancing. This chapter expands on our interpretation of these escalating expectations and the view we take that, above all else, it is organizational culture—especially local, emergent culture—that will determine our success as a workplace and, by extension, our impact as an organization on world health.

Being a start-up business division within a successful global pharmaceutical company that is more than a century old, we at Pfizer Upjohn put considerable time into determining how best to honor the Pfizer legacy and constancy of purpose that allows us to exist, while simultaneously pushing the boundaries necessary to pursue a highly distinct mission. The legacy we build on is one that puts patients first, practices unwavering commitment to quality, and measures its impact in results, including both business results and the number of new medicines brought to the world.

On the face of it, our Upjohn business does not need to be innovative like a traditional biopharmaceutical company: we are not in the business of new medicine discovery. One could suggest that our patients can be well-served by trusted, quality medicines that have existed for many years. In point of fact, however, Upjohn has declared its commitment to the ambitious goal of relieving the burden of noncommunicable diseases (NCDs) for every patient, everywhere, and we have directed our focus accordingly. That requires a reimagination of innovation itself. We are challenged to understand the complex and diverse health ecosystems that have led to today's growing and global epidemic of NCDs. To meet our goals, we will need to forge new partnerships with a multitude of stakeholders, including governments and civil society organizations, to shape those ecosystems so that medicines can reach the vast numbers of patients at risk or currently suffering from untreated NCDs.

In this context of a changing contract with the workplace, a reimagination of innovation itself, and the urgency of our mission, we concluded that it will not suffice to create a traditional organization with centralized leadership and top-down innovation. Rather, we need empowered, dispersed leadership and innovation in every local market. Beginning with that end in mind, we describe our aspired-to culture in the simplest possible terms as follows: our organization needs to be "Fast, Focused, and Flexible," defined as shown in Figure 5.1.

Understanding that culture is not something that can be designed from "on high" and cascaded throughout a global organization, we began discussing with extended leadership how we all might make Fast, Focused, and Flexible a reality at every location and in every team. We invited our leaders to engage in these discussions by drawing on their distinctly human capacities of curiosity, generosity, and courage. Through those early explorations, we quite quickly noticed emergent patterns of belief, feeling, and certain practices that seemed to support our shared ambitions. Ultimately,

Figure 5.1   Fast, focused, and flexible

we speculated, these patterns might be the best and most relevant descriptions we have of actual, lived culture today, with Fast, Focused, and Flexible being the ultimate outcome to which we aspire and that we are already realizing in certain business outcomes (e.g., in big decisions being made in record time).

Although we do not expect the aspirations of Fast, Focused, and Flexible to change, we do recognize that emergent patterns are not static and are descriptive, *not* prescriptive. In keeping with the reality that culture is something that unfolds through our interactions, we expect these patterns to evolve, just as we do, and as we continue to cocreate this culture. With this understanding, leadership is less about designing and cascading culture and more about paying close attention to our intentions, assumptions, and emergent patterns in our interactions; amplifying positive patterns; becoming aware of our responsibility as "culture carriers"; and interrupting less desirable patterns before they gain momentum. Figure 5.2 encapsulates seven welcome cultural patterns that we currently observe.

We are beginning to derive a great deal of meaning from each pattern.

1. *We mean what we say.* First articulated by an Upjohn executive, this has become a powerful and often repeated catchphrase. It powerfully reminds us to "be" and not merely describe the patterns we aspire to. We talk

1 We mean what we say.

2 We're unified by an ambition to become a **Fast, Focused, Flexible** (and fun) organization.

3 We maximize strength in teams by growing diverse talents and supporting individuals to do their best work.

4 We realize the potential across teams by minimizing all barriers to genuine dialogue in pursuit of our shared mission.

5 We know how fast, quality decisions get made, and we follow through.

6 We're willing to explore novel ways of working together that unleash the full potential of our organization.

7 We're not aiming for perfection; when it's challenging and we're learning from mistakes, we know we're on the right path.

Figure 5.2   Upjohn's emerging cultural patterns

a lot about the fact that culture does not live in slogans, posters, PowerPoint decks, or anything else outside of us and our own practices. Such examples of so-called culture collateral are merely props—they help remind us of our aspirations, but they are not a proxy for culture. Culture lives in our daily interactions with one another, including those that are both important and mundane. We shape and are shaped in turn by our culture. In this context, the "we" that we refer to includes colleagues at every level, together with external stakeholders, who are bound together on a shared mission to achieve our company purpose of relieving the burden of NCDs globally.

2. *Fast, Focused, and Flexible organization.* We have intentionally and actively promoted attitudes and practices that reinforce being a Fast, Focused, and Flexible organization. That has quickly become the reputation of the Upjohn division across the broader organization. The "fast" component of the culture represents our bias for action, being empowered and learning together. One example is represented in our process for making strategic funding decisions, which are often made in a single meeting with key stakeholders, as opposed to a longer, drawn-out traditional budget approval process. "Focused" refers to placing our attention on what matters most for the business and to keeping our commitments to stakeholders and colleagues. This focus is particularly critical as Upjohn builds a new business strategy and operating model at a time when the number of priorities could quickly exceed capacity to complete them. "Flexible" represents our aspiration to be a dynamic, open-minded, and creative organization. This is reflected in our objective-setting process, in which we have replaced privately and individually established SMART goals (widely applied since the 1980s) with team-located FAST objectives (frequently discussed, ambitious, specific, and transparent) that deliver the transparency needed for collaboration and also enable calibration and recalibration of priorities in teams throughout the year. Finally, an informal addition came in calling out the spirit of "fun" and how important it is to enjoy lighter moments together at work amidst the serious world of health care.[8]

3. *Maximizing strength in teams.* The rise of individualism is well documented. Growing freedom of choice is eroding the now-outdated notion of loyalty and forcing organizations to respond to diverse needs.[9] Our response to this macro trend is to dispense with one-size-fits-all competency and behavior models and create instead a development ecosystem that begins with an individual's talents. We subscribe to the enduring wisdom

of Peter Drucker, who wrote, in his classic book *The Effective Executive* (originally published in 1967), "The effective executive makes strengths productive."[10] To that end, more than 800 of our managers, and many of their teams, had by the time of this writing completed an assessment of their naturally occurring talents (Gallup's StrengthsFinder) to better understand and leverage their individual and team strengths. This strengths-based development foundation creates a shared vocabulary for discussing performance from strengths. Insights from the assessments can be used at the individual and team levels. Gallup argues strongly that our greatest room for growth is, counterintuitively, in our areas of naturally occurring talent. Developing our weaknesses may prevent failure, but it will not deliver the excellence that refining our unique combinations of talent can. When the most senior leadership team at Upjohn explored its team profile, they discovered that the Responsibility strength was one of the most frequently occurring dominant talents in the team. This prompted the insight that while the team would be dedicated to fulfilling its promises to stakeholders, one of those promises, the promise to empower all leaders throughout the organization, might be more challenging than the others. At the individual level, leaders across the organization are developing individual growth plans that focus on how they can apply and build on their natural strengths to continue their professional improvement, contribute their best performance, and accomplish their career aspirations.

We also recognize that the benefits of diversity are realized only if we capitalize on varied talents, perspectives, and ways of thinking in a team context. We see a need to maintain a careful balance between the individual and team at all levels, honoring the unique talents of team members while nurturing the team climate within which the most impactful growth and work take place.

4. *Minimizing barriers to genuine dialogue.* It could be argued that most of our collaboration and resulting innovation happen when we meet, within and across teams. For this reason, we are placing considerable emphasis on upgrading our meetings in terms of both efficiency and effectiveness. We are adamant that "death by PowerPoint" become a historical artifact. Instead, thinking-together time is maximized.

We conducted much of the earliest meetings of 100+ extended leadership seated all together in a single set of concentric circles. This configuration signaled a departure from the more familiar rows or small group tables facing a presenter on stage. In place of a presentation, the senior leadership team began an exploratory dialogue on their vision for the organization that radiated from the innermost circle out to include the entire gathering. This meant the extended leadership were not being asked to simply "buy in," but, rather, they were building on and adding their fingerprints to an emerging vision of the future. Such was the enthusiasm for this new way of working that many of those leaders similarly dispensed with tables and minimized PowerPoint in their follow-on regional and local market meetings. This approach has become affectionately known as the "fishbowl," implying that nobody is invisible and everyone is a participant. The result is a growing and palpable sense of ownership and vitality for which this young division within Pfizer has already become renowned.

5. *Making fast, quality decisions and following through.* In our fast-moving industry, we know that we must empower our colleagues to make quality decisions rather than create unnecessary structures that restrict autonomy and slow things down. We have created a much flatter organization, moving from twelve organizational layers to six in most parts of the organization. That has effectively eliminated unnecessary hierarchy and enabled connections between employees at different levels of the company that would have been more difficult previously. For potentially complex and high-stakes decisions, we are taking time up front to clearly establish and communicate relevant roles, such as distinguishing clearly between who is charged with making a recommendation and who has ultimate decision rights.

6. *Exploring novel ways of working together.* To be an effective global organization in the future, we know that we will need to be open to new ways of collaborating across functional and business lines. For instance, rather than the traditional "matrix" operating model, in which functional leaders have centralized funding and primary decision-making rights, we are experimenting with an operating structure in which business leaders own the funding for their country or region and are empowered to allocate *globally sourced* enabling resources as needed for their local business. This new operating model has the potential to improve alignment of resources at the local level while continuing to benefit from global standards and expertise.

7. *Not aiming for perfection.* "Not aiming for perfection" is currently the bookend catchphrase to "we mean what we say." If we are to venture into unchartered territories, we must be prepared and willing to make mistakes and to fail. Our ultimate success depends on a capacity to do

so transparently and to learn together from every experience. We aim to process all results, welcome and unwelcome, through the lens of culture first by asking pertinent questions: What were the patterns of engagement that contributed to this result? What was our part in them? What patterns do we wish to interrupt, and what do we want to reinforce?

Those seven patterns are the beliefs, feelings/attitudes, and practices that are creating the early culture contours enabling Upjohn to be Fast, Focused, and Flexible in pursuit of our mission.

Many organizations today focus on maximizing the role of technology. We embrace technological change but also see it as a given. In an era when technology is increasingly ubiquitous and ever improving, we see a growing premium and value being placed on the human aspects of work life. It is these human aspects that are emphasized in our organizational culture. In the end, it is human capacities, such as curiosity, generosity, and courage, that will determine our impact on health care. Our culture—or, more precisely, our colleagues' subjective experience of their culture—will determine the extent to which those most valuable human capacities are unleashed on the world's most pressing health challenges.

Other authors in this book also consider the human perspective in the era of technology, albeit from different angles. Mike Ulica from the National Geographic Society argues, for example, for the importance of geographical knowledge, particularly in the context of understanding other cultures. Stephanie Bell-Rose and Anne Ollen focus on the importance of diversity and inclusion in the workplace.

Postscript

Since writing this chapter, an agreement to combine Upjohn with Mylan has been announced, creating a new champion for global health. A prominent question from Upjohn colleagues is "Will we get to keep our culture?" Our belief remains that culture is not static and therefore not a "thing" we ever get to keep. We do, however, intend to scale our understanding of how a positive culture is continually generated. Beginning with integration planning, we look forward to cocreating patterns of working together worthy of a greatly expanded opportunity to fulfill the world's need for trusted medicine.

6 HOW THE FUTURE OF WORK IMPACTS THE WORKFORCE OF TECHNICAL ORGANIZATIONS

Gregory L. Robinson

ABSTRACT

How will we work in the future? This chapter discusses how we worked over the past twenty years and how we transitioned to how we currently work. The chapter examines the way that automation, robotics, and artificial intelligence have changed the way we work. The focus is on how we prepare the future workforce based on innovative and advanced tools and processes. We are most interested in the "way" that we will work. Examples illustrate workforce training and development. The focus is on training and development, as learning is the key factor in competitive advantage for the future of work. Continued innovation, although currently at accelerated rates, will always have an impact on the evolution of work because of enhanced efficiency and productivity.

THE THEME "THE FUTURE OF WORK" has been around for many decades.[1] As industry continues to implement long-term strategic planning, it is important to both plan for the future and adapt to current challenges. First, we must establish a good understanding of what the future is most likely to be, and then we must align capabilities to continue current execution, while developing institutional transitions to meet future needs. These capabilities generally revolve around people, processes, tools, and environment/culture.

As a case in point, the aerospace industry has experienced a tremendous increase in efficiency and productivity over the past two decades due to leaps in innovation.[2] Compared to twenty-five years ago, work improvements include innovative engineering, design, manufacturing, and testing tools. The industry has experienced numerous innovations in materials and processes, including additive manufacturing. Data rates are raging at gigabit speeds, and data processing (Big Data) is allowing for superfast decision making. Virtual reality and telepresence facilitate a record number of transactions in remote commerce.

An area that is generally not considered when we discuss innovation is leadership and organization behavior. With a global marketplace, multi-national companies, and complex global partnerships, leadership is more important than ever before.[3] Leadership and organizational structures and norms have also transformed to maximize the benefits of technological innovations.

As we reflect on the past twenty-five years, certain key questions are particularly important to consider: How did we know and anticipate these changes in the workplace and the workforce? How did we prepare for change? Who filled those preparatory and transitional roles? Even more important, how do we see the future of work over the next decade, and how will it affect the workforce? Who has the foresight and responsibility to facilitate an efficient and effective transition to that future, and how do we make that happen?

The observations that follow stem from my experiences in the aerospace industry. Elsewhere in this book, Earl Lewis and colleagues examine the effects of disruptive change in the manufacturing economy and Susan Lund and Bryan Hancock explore the effects of automation writ large on the demand for advanced technical skills.

The Way We Worked

During my high school years in the late 1970s, students were encouraged to take an elective typing class because people were thinking about the future of work. Of course, most boys, like me, turned their noses up at the class because that was for future secretaries—and, therefore, for women. In practice, I later found out, that skill would have been very helpful when I was typing papers in college. When I started my career as an engineer, I had a secretary who typed everything for me. A few years later, word processing became popular, which made the secretaries' work more efficient with higher productivity (and reduced the number of secretaries required). As computers became available for all individuals in the workplace, there was a mandate for employees to perform their own typing.

What happened to most of those secretaries? Many were phased out via natural attrition, many lost their jobs, and some others were retrained for new jobs, which required them to receive external training. That training included college and university classes to obtain associate and bachelor's degrees, and certificates. The local colleges and universities designed adult learning programs to help prepare working professionals for the future. As secretarial and administrative jobs decreased, information technology (IT) support jobs increased significantly, including help-desk support, IT training, and training and support in the use of applications tools such as Word, Excel, and PowerPoint. Many organizations trained their employees for these new jobs and roles, which helped with the transition. A large number of employees lost their jobs and pursued training on their own. Hundreds of small companies popped up across the country to provide IT certification training.[4]

The way that we worked in the aerospace industry in the past required more technicians to perform "touch labor" than it does today because there was much less automation. This was the same for engineering. One reason that it took more time to do engineering design and analysis was because engineering tools could not "talk" to each other (integration and translation), whether they were different brands or different versions of the same brand. Integration of data, drawings, and designs was mostly performed manually, which also required lots of checking and verification. This is commonly referred to as product and data management.

Manufacturing floors were crowded with hardware, machines, and manufacturing and inspection personnel. Innovative automation tools and techniques rapidly flooded manufacturing floors over a few short years, which substantially decreased the manufacturing workforce and significantly increased production. Printed wiring boards (PWBs) were received as bare boards and required visual inspection by a quality control technician for compliance to requirements. The electromechanical, electrical, and electronic (EEE) parts were hand-placed on the PWB, and then a manufacturing technician soldered the parts to the board. Then, a quality control technician inspected the fully populated printed circuit board (PCB) prior to testing.

Work Today

Today, PWBs are manufactured directly via computer-aided manufacturing (CAM) from a computer-aided design (CAD), and they are often 3-D printed in real time via numerous methods of additive manufacturing, followed by automated inspection. The EEE parts are autonomously loaded into the automated PCB packaging machine, which places those parts in the correct circuit locations and solders all parts with very few defects or noncompliances.

Something that we take for granted today, the taking and sharing of photos of technical products, was effective then but with considerable time latency, which affected decision making. We often needed to take photos of the hardware in a manufacturing and/or integration and test facility (clean room) with a Polaroid camera and send the photos overnight to engineering in another geographic location to help troubleshoot a problem. This would always cost a minimum of one day, while the development team waited for a response from engineering. Today, photos are taken with digital cameras, including iPhones, and the photos are transmitted in real time anywhere in the world for inspection, analysis, and troubleshooting. This facilitates more efficient troubleshooting and faster decision making, which increases productivity and reduces technical and product risk.

As these and numerous other innovations flooded the aerospace industry, organizations transitioned to more automated manufacturing and engineering environments, and the technician workforce dwindled rapidly. Some engineers, for example, had to prepare for careers in other technical areas such as going from mechanical to electrical engineering (and vice versa), from discipline engineering to systems engineering, and from engineering to program and project management. One of the larger transitions was to software, computer science, and information systems and information management.

The National Aeronautics and Space Administration (NASA), like numerous other organizations, developed a learning academy (the Academy of Program/Project Engineering & Leadership, or APPEL) to cross-train engineers to transition to systems engineering and project management.[5] Project leadership of large complex missions was the primary focus, since a large and strong cadre of discipline engineers already existed. Forming and leading teams was a growing workforce gap because the number of large complex projects with global partnerships was increasing rapidly. APPEL was a primary leader in developing the strategy, scope, and content, and in implementing the transition. APPEL covered developmental programs, internal training, and university training. Over the past twenty years, however, other organizations and corporations have abandoned long-established formal development programs, leaving employees on their own to prepare for the future.

Looking Ahead

In the years to come, the nature of work will continue to change at a rapid pace with advancements in digital technology, advanced materials, engineering and manufacturing tools, processes, and a more global and mobile workforce. In the aerospace industry, everyone is clamoring for lighter weight, faster speeds, less noise, a smaller carbon footprint, faster data processing and analysis, and faster transmission rates.[6] Similar interests and needs are quite prevalent across other industries. We should expect to experience organizational and leadership changes to accommodate global partnerships, a mobile workforce, transparent borders, and more company entrants into the marketplace.

The nature of work has fundamentally changed with the advent of telework, remote medical care, global organizations and partnerships, supply chain, the proliferation of data (Big Data), and so on. With these changes, there is a need for accelerated learning and workforce engagement. As more jobs are performed via AI/automation, the workforce will require retraining and development for increasingly higher-functioning jobs that require critical thinking and the human element in general. It is critical to start transitioning long before these changes are needed, which allows for more efficient and effective workforce planning.

One example is that hands-on technicians are already very highly functioning; hence, they often experience a natural transition to engineering, where more formal training and critical thinking is required. As one example of such a transition, Roger Forsgren, the NASA chief knowledge officer and director of the Academy of Program/Project & Engineering Leadership (APPEL), outlined the path he took to gain advanced skills:

> There wasn't an agency-wide program to help transition into engineering roles, but several centers helped technicians who wanted to go to night school to get an engineering degree. The Glenn Research Center (GRC) had a forward-looking director of engineering who supported technicians, but legal problems arose because the government won't pay for a degree but will pay for job-related courses. So any technician who wanted to get a degree at night had to justify how the course was going to help their work as a technician. It's hard to justify how calcu-

lus is going to help a machinist become better running a mill. So this regulation weeded out a lot of folks (so did calculus).

I was fortunate that most of my supervisors were real supportive. One even let me use his office to study for final exams. But some folks ran into supervisors who tried to stop them from getting a degree. The branch chief of the machine shop once said, "My best technicians are the ones wanting to get an engineering degree. Why should I permit my best people to leave?"

In the end, at GRC, I think a handful of techs, maybe 10–12, actually graduated and got promoted to engineering. The rest went back to their trades. . . . I do know that once a tech graduated he or she was a hot commodity at GRC because a lot of managers wanted them in their orgs because of their experience.

I did it the hard way, 10 years of night school to get an undergraduate degree and then a MS, but it was well worth it. Once I was an engineer I could look at a drawing and ask the right questions, like "Why are the tolerances so tight?" and "How will anyone reach that fastener with a tool with all this stuff blocking it?" I could point out a tubing bend that would be impossible to fabricate. I wasn't intimidated by hardware and fabrication like so many fresh-outs who spent so much time behind a computer screen rather than on the shop floor.[7]

Employers, colleges, and universities must be prepared to facilitate a growing need for these professional studies. Subject to debate, of course, is who should provide the necessary training, how to deploy it, how to package it, and, more fundamentally, whether more training is even required or necessary.

In contrast to my precollege years, my kids learned IT naturally and organically by doing homework on the computer and playing games on the computer and small personal devices. Schools have integrated IT into the teaching curriculum. Numerous colleges and universities teach software languages (e.g., C, C++, Python). In that sense, my children and their peers are already prepared for the future of work as new entrants and early career employees in the workplace.

Colleges and universities have historically provided a solid "technical" base for undergraduate and graduate degree programs such as engineering, accounting, finance, nursing, economics, human resources, chemistry, and marketing. This type and level of academic training will always be required regardless of the future of work in the coming decades. The early-career workforce training and learning for the future is organic to my kids' high school and college training because many/most emerging and future innovations, technologies, and processes are taught and learned during that phase of their careers. They are similarly influenced by new products and methods in all aspects of their lives. Although my personal bias is that on-campus classroom settings are generally more effective than distance learning for undergraduates, after extensive research I did not find studies that support my bias. Distance learning programs for graduate and adult learning are common and are proliferating rapidly. I suspect distance learning will make huge inroads into undergraduate programs as well. Learning institutions must prepare for that trend.[8]

Some technical careers such as engineering tend to foster seamless transition to other related careers. At NASA, it is quite common for engineers to expand their discipline engineering training into multiple disciplines. During my time at the NASA Goddard Space Flight Center during the 1990s, engineers were highly encouraged to mix disciplines and, in some cases, actually change disciplines because there were growing concerns that the need for some disciplines was increasing rapidly while it was dwindling for others. These changes supported new assignments with on-the-job training, additional formal training, and more schedule and technical flexibility to get up to speed. Additionally, within the aerospace industry, it is the norm for engineers to progress to systems engineering and program and project management. Generally, organizational and industry training is required. There are numerous avenues to obtain the additional training, including degrees, certificates, audited classes, in-house training, and university on-site training.[9]

Trends in IT jobs and career growth since 2000 have resulted in exponential changes in software, networks, computer processors, applications, and help-desk support.[10] Today, change continues at an exponential rate in such areas as cybersecurity, social media, and demand for programming. Although college- and university-level training is instrumental in developing this workforce, much of today's demand for training in some fields is being filled via certificate programs.[11] The demand for certificate programs in IT, human resources, project management, and medical technology, for example, will continue to increase due to an experienced workforce shifting careers.

The late-career workforce is only minimally affected by the next wave of workplace changes because they will transition to retirement, Nonetheless, such employees face the challenge of maintaining their technical, industry, and corporate knowledge until they retire. The early-career workforce is affected only minimally because they are organically trained for the next ten to fifteen years. Midcareer is where the huge impact and challenge lie, because technologies and methods will change rapidly within the five to ten years after younger employees complete their college education and start their career. Hence, retraining will benefit the employees and their organizations for many years into the future.

7 CORPORATE LEARNING AND DEVELOPMENT HAS A VITAL ROLE TO PLAY IN THE ROBOTICS REVOLUTION—IS IT READY?

Uli Heitzlhofer

ABSTRACT

Artificial intelligence and robotics are affecting today's workforce, and further changes are anticipated for the near future. The current education system, however, is not set up to successfully reskill the workforce for tomorrow's job market. Weighing those trends, this chapter considers what a single company can do to prepare for the shift in workforce needs and how a collaborative effort across multiple companies and industries can have synergistic effects, looking at efforts already in place and making recommendations for next steps for further improvements.

THE WORLD, and especially the world of work, is being upended by technology, with much of the disruption arriving in the form of artificial intelligence (AI) and robotics. Across all occupations, more than half (61 percent) of the US workforce will experience at least a medium level of exposure to automation by 2030.[1] Individuals with a high school diploma or less are most vulnerable; they will be four times as likely to be displaced as those with a bachelor's degree.[2]

Although these numbers may seem like something from the distant future, the reality is that the AI revolution has already begun. In 2018, US companies acquired more robots than ever before, with shipments increasing in nearly all sectors of the economy.[3] One of those companies was DHL Supply Chain. After piloting AI in its warehouses—and seeing productivity increase by more than 100 percent—the company invested $300 million to quadruple its cadre of robots, with plans to employ them at

80 percent of its facilities.[4] A much smaller-scale example comes from the UCSF Medical Center at Mission Bay. The San Francisco hospital is now using robots to transport food, linens, specimens, and medications around its 600,000-square-foot facility, thereby allowing employees to devote more time to patient interaction.[5]

These types of human-to-robot transitions will only increase as AI inevitably improves. That does not mean, however, that humans will become obsolete. The World Economic Forum estimates that, although 75 million jobs may be displaced in the future, 133 million new jobs could emerge—potentially creating a net positive of 58 million jobs globally.[6] The challenge, therefore, will not be a lack of jobs, but a lack of workers qualified to fill them, given that nearly half (42 percent) of the core skills required to perform these jobs will change.[7] In the future, we could witness a previously unseen situation: high unemployment accompanied by a deluge of open positions.

Meeting Future Demands

To avoid this paradox, action must be taken now to train the workforce in the skills of the not-so-distant future. Nearly three-quarters of Americans do not believe government, higher education, or large businesses are "doing enough to address the need for lifelong learning"—and 36.3 percent believe employers are best equipped to remedy that.[8] Perhaps that is because, although the American education system will undoubtedly play a central role in shaping tomorrow's students, it will take many years, and potentially decades, for it to transform to the degree needed to meet the future's demands. The onus, therefore, falls on corporate America to do its part—but it has yet to wake up to that fact.

As of today, only 3 percent of American executives plan to "significantly increase investment in training and reskilling" over the next three years,[9] and only 29 percent of executives at American companies with more than $100 million in revenue cite "addressing potential skills gaps related to automation/digitization" as one of their top five priorities.[10] This is far from ideal. The average employee will need 101 days of retraining and upskilling in the years leading up to 2022—and it will be up to their employer to provide it.[11]

To be clear, an employer's creation of upskilling and reskilling programs should be seen not as an act of altruism but as an act of self-preservation. "[A]s digitization, automation, and AI reshape whole industries and every enterprise, the only way to realize the potential productivity dividends from that investment will be to have the people and processes in place to capture it," stated a McKinsey report. "Managing this transition well, in short, is not just a social good; it's a competitive imperative," it continued.[12] If companies want to remain relevant amidst advancing technologies and an increasingly ruthless talent war, the answer is evident: they must train the workers they need. This chapter will reveal strategies for doing so.

What Can a Single Organization Do?

When it comes to upskilling one's own staff, leaders can look to two different models: AT&T, a legacy company striving to stay abreast of constantly evolving technologies, and Amazon, a business that developed during—and due to—the technological revolution. Both have launched company-wide upskilling programs to prepare their workforces for the decades ahead.

When AT&T assessed its workforce in 2008, and realized that only about half of its 250,000 employees had the science, technology, engineering, and math skills needed for the future, it committed $1 billion to a massive reskilling project.[13] Its efforts are entirely web based: On AT&T's job search platform, employees can quickly see a position's salary and growth prospects, determine which skills are needed, and then click directly through to a relevant online training. Once completed, employees can add the training to their internal career profile, where managers can flag them as promising candidates for current vacancies. In 2018, more than 200,000 AT&T employees utilized the job search platform more than seven million times, and 4,600 employees have transitioned into new roles after receiving training in AI and machine learning.[14]

In July 2019, Amazon followed suit by announcing a $700 million investment in retraining its workforce. Known as "Upskilling 2025," the initiative promises to reach 100,000 employees—one in three staff members across the US—over six years.[15] It includes job placement programs, prepaid tuition opportunities, apprenticeships, and academies that train nontechnical employees in growing sectors such as software engineering, machine learning, robotics, and cloud computing.

Upskilling 2025 is not only a wise investment on the part of Amazon but also a call to action: if the world's largest retailer is prioritizing retraining, other companies should do the same.[16] As a Brookings Institution report stated: "[E]mpirical studies have shown that firms frequently recapture the costs of training workers, in particular through increased worker productivity. Employer-led trainings can improve firm output, enhance workers' career prospects, and help companies fill emerging critical needs."[17]

For a larger-scale example—one that affects an entire country's education-to-career pipeline—leaders should consider Germany's apprenticeship model. There, apprenticeships generally begin at age sixteen, last three years, and are funded by the company. They funnel approximately half a million youth into the economy each year,[18] providing an effective combination of theoretical and practical education, and paving the way for fulfilling careers for blue-collar workers. Though frequently discussed, apprenticeships have failed to become popular in the United States because American companies are reluctant to pay individuals who are not yet trained. That perspective is shortsighted. Since apprentices can do 60 percent of the tasks of a fully skilled worker by their second year, training costs are estimated at just $10,000 per worker[19]—nearly 50 percent less than the cost of one bad hire.[20]

An Opportunity for Cross-Company Collaboration

Although the isolated efforts of the aforementioned companies are welcome and necessary, they will not be enough to meet the macrolevel demands of the future. Scaling the upskilling movement requires cross-company and cross-industry collaboration—a paradigm shift. If corporate America hopes to play its part in preparing the global workforce, in other words, it must move from a culture of clandestinity to a culture of candor.

As a leader at Lyft, I have seen these types of transitions firsthand. Several years ago, it was taboo to get into a stranger's car; now, with the advent of ride sharing, it happens every day across the world. A similar revolution must extend to the entire business sphere: we must progress from sharing rides between strangers to sharing knowledge between organizations.

As noted earlier, this does not require any degree of altruism; it simply requires an interest in self-preservation. If we do not have the individuals needed to fill the roles of the future, the struggles will ripple beyond a single company or industry and outward to the entire economy. To avoid a failure of global magnitude, organizations must synthesize their efforts in fostering engaged and hirable employees. They must start unifying to deliver the workforce of the future—for both their companies and the world. I am not alone in this thinking: in another chapter in this book, for example, Jason A. Tyszko and Robert G. Sheets describe a job-data exchange where business and higher education could share information on skills and competencies. The chapter by Brian Fitzgerald and colleagues from the Business–Higher

Education Forum outlines a different model for sharing relevant information across multiple corporations and multiple sectors.

While at first this type of cross-company sharing might be uncomfortable, I am confident it could soon become the new normal. So get in and enjoy the ride!

The Role of Learning and Development

In Silicon Valley, where Lyft is headquartered, the majority of companies have distinct learning and development (L&D) departments—and therein lies an untapped opportunity for orchestrating cross-company collaboration. At the moment, few L&D units act as a bridge between companies; instead, the majority are separate and secretive, dedicated to keeping their processes and observations proprietary. This leads to redundancies in the system—when, for example, we all teach new hires very similar baseline skills—and wasted time and money for both companies and employees. That is amplified by the fact that decade-long, loyal stints at a single organization are a relic of the past, as today's employees are constantly seeking better opportunities. This applies especially to the tech industry, where tenures have reached new lows: an average of 1.8 years at Uber, 2.5 years at Facebook, and 3.2 years at Google.[21]

Imagine a world in which corporate L&D teams share best practices, materials, and trainers with one another—and maybe even cocreate learning programs. If L&D widened its scope of practice, economies of scale could come into play, thus accelerating the rate of change and significantly augmenting the economy's level of preparedness.

In this vein, potential solutions include the following:

- Creating a consortium of L&D departments, through which leaders can share learnings and strategies, as well as proposals for future collaborations.
- Developing a certification model, wherein employees can receive training from one company and then bring that certification to their next employer, thereby reducing redundancies. One way to start experimenting with this process would be through simple trainings, such as those surrounding unconscious bias, interview, or feedback skills.
- Launching a task force of professionals in AI and robotics to consult and cocreate learning materials and share those with individuals interested in beginning their upskilling journeys.

To enable any of these proposals to come to fruition, it is essential for companies—and L&D departments especially—to break down silos and start sharing their efforts in the name of "noncompetitive" advantage. We must give ourselves permission to discuss what we are teaching our employees, how we measure competencies, and which tactics are resonating. With the future looming, cooperating to develop our people is more than a smart business strategy; it is the only route to elevating our workforce as a whole and to helping countries and the world transition to Industry 4.0.

It's Time for an Upskilling Revolution

We cannot rely on any one sector—be it education, industry, or government—to prepare the global workforce. The future is arriving too quickly, and its needs are too great. To achieve change at scale, we must collaborate to train current employees and educate the next generation.

The upskilling movement is no longer about one particular company, industry, or country; it is about global progress—and it is a transformation that all companies have an obligation to support. For L&D leaders especially, the first step is realizing that our responsibility is not to educate people only for our organizations but to educate people for the world.

PART II

HIGHER EDUCATION

Still the Solution for a Workforce in Flux?

BUILDING ON THE EMPLOYER-DRIVEN discussions in Part I, Part II turns to leaders and researchers from the higher education sector who discuss the myriad ways that higher education imbues students with the skills and knowledge needed to craft successful careers over their lifetimes. The contributors in this section focus on how higher education helps students to establish their careers and to adapt over their lifetimes as careers change. They address both the strengths and shortcomings of current educational approaches and their perspectives on how higher education should change to meet these challenges more successfully. Dede examines the importance of unlearning deeply held identities in order to induce transformational change in learners, and he advocates for incorporating tactics for unlearning into continuing education programs. Gazi and Baker describe the growing need for continuous learning in STEM fields, drawing on their experiences at the Georgia Institute of Technology to illustrate the importance of professional, continuous, and online learning programs as a central component of STEM higher education. Trumbore shares research on a microcredential program at the Wharton School at the University of Pennsylvania, showing the value of such courses. Lewis, Young, Schaffner, and Arbit turn to the experiences of "fragile workers" who do not typically enroll in college and who have a tenuous relationship with the working world, yet whose needs for education and training present an opportunity for higher education to enhance their employment prospects. The chapters by Mayer, Otter, and Schejbal all address the value of the liberal arts education model. Mayer examines approaches taken by a number of institutions to balance traditional liberal arts education with the acquisition of practical knowledge and skills that prepare graduates to transition easily to the workforce. Otter reinforces the importance of the liberal arts and their interdisciplinary perspective for preparing graduates to meet the demands of a global and interconnected world. Schejbal questions the value of the liberal arts for adult and nontraditional students who seek curricula that have practical and clear-cut connections with their lives; his discussion assesses the organizational barriers that prevent higher education institutions from developing coherence across the curriculum. Rascoff and DeVaney make a case that higher education should invest in the success of their alumni across their lifespans, drawing on their experiences at Duke University and the University of Michigan. Supporting the continuous learning needs of alumni is one way that colleges and universities can contribute to the larger societal need for workforce training and upskilling.

INTRODUCTION

Joseph Williams

MANY OF THE PEOPLE READING THIS BOOK were probably conditioned to think that one graduated from a four-year college and immediately began working on the path toward retirement, only to return to school perhaps for a graduate degree somewhere down the line.

That, increasingly, is no longer the case. The jobs of yesterday are changing rapidly. And it's not just blue-collar positions, which thrived over the past century, that have gradually disappeared due to the rise of automation and other new technology. Now, even skilled professionals like accountants and doctors are facing the potential for major upheavals as a result of artificial intelligence (AI) and other burgeoning tech.

Numbers vary wildly, but it's projected that as many as 75 million US workers could lose their jobs to AI. There's intense debate over those figures, however, with some observers even suggesting that the technology could spur job creation—although those jobs won't be the same positions we have today.

Amid the back and forth on the impact of AI on the workforce, another major trend is occurring: companies are vigorously trying to find the talent needed to support the push to adopt the advanced tech. In fact, two of the top three skills that job applicants are lacking are data science and engineering, according to a 2019 report from the Society for Human Resource Management.

These changes are putting immense pressure on the legacy higher education institutions to adapt to an environment in which a four-year degree is no longer sufficient—or even required. Instead, employers and employees are seeking continual, low-cost educational opportunities in specific skill sets that will allow them either to pivot to new careers or to stay relevant in their current roles.

That phenomenon has given rise to new, online-based platforms, such as OpenClassrooms, that partner directly with companies to craft educational courses based on the organization's needs, a method that corporate giants like McDonald's and Amazon are adopting.

Some companies are even crafting their own education-like pathways. Salesforce—the software giant with a market cap valued at over $142 billion—created Trailhead, a free online platform that allows anyone to take courses on topics such as data analytics. And Toyota recently took nationwide its own two-year apprenticeship program that boasts graduation rates significantly higher than those of rival community colleges.

I've spoken to numerous executives, professors, and deans about these threats. The resounding belief is that higher education will remain as relevant as ever, but it's going to take significant—and occasionally painful—overhauls to make that possible. Leaders will need to rethink the way they interact with students, the populations they aim to target, what courses they offer, and the medium in which students take those courses.

One key way that colleges are responding is by offering their own online learning opportunities outside the core curriculum. The Wharton School, for example, runs four-week courses that result in microcredentials on topics such as data literacy and computational models, as Anne Trumbore, senior director at Wharton Online, discusses in greater detail in this part.

The switch to online is not only a necessity to match the needs of the changing workforce; it's also a method for survival for many institutions. As David Schejbal outlines in his chapter, online courses are a way to bring in more nontraditional students, namely, those over the age of twenty-five. But the changes on the horizon are broader than just how courses are offered. Universities, argues Schejbal, will need to completely revamp their cultures and curricula to cater to these older enrollees.

And there's ample reason to think that these nontraditional students are the wave of the future. Companies and employees alike are progressively pushing for continual educational opportunities, which allow former graduates to return to school either to reinforce their current skill set or to develop a new one.

That doesn't mean universities can eschew their current alumni and focus exclusively on this new market. Instead, Duke University's Matthew Rascoff and the University of Michigan's James DeVaney argue that institutions need to rethink their relationships with graduates. Colleges, they say, can serve to help alumni pivot after major life events—like returning to the workforce after starting a family or undergoing a complete career shift—by allowing them to tap into the often vast network of other graduates located around the world.

Ultimately, universities will need to focus on both markets to remain relevant and successful. The good news is that major investments are being made across corporate America that academia can benefit from. Behemoths like Amazon, PricewaterhouseCoopers, and Microsoft are collectively spending billions of dollars to upskill or retrain their current workers as a way to mitigate the talent shortage plaguing corporate America.

The federal government recently projected that US companies will need one million additional science, technology, engineering, and mathematics (STEM) professionals. This forecast offers universities a prime opportunity to rethink their educational pathways. While colleges are expanding their curricula to include more tech-focused courses, that doesn't address the continual learning needs. As Georgia Institute of Technology's Yakut Gazi and Nelson Baker point out in this section, even those with STEM degrees need a refresh as often as every five years.

But that's only part of the problem. Companies regularly bemoan the lack of "soft skills" among current graduates, some even going so far as to label it a crisis. The result is a push among academics to modernize liberal arts majors.

For one thing, although new tech will be able to automate traditionally human-centric tasks like reading X-rays, it will be unable to replicate skills like leadership, creativity, and critical thinking—all of which can be honed through a liberal arts concentration. Christopher Mayer, the associate dean for strategy and initiatives at the United States Military Academy, presents an excellent analysis of this phenomenon in his chapter.

Overall, the chapters you are about to read paint a vivid picture of the struggle that universities, employers, and employees alike are facing. The message can be quite sobering, but the key takeaway is that higher education is more important now than it has ever been. But the pressure is on those institutions to respond to both the workforce needs and the looming threat that new educational pathways pose.

Ultimately, I believe you'll come away with the view that colleges are on the right track. There is still substantial work to be done, but the first steps are often the most difficult ones and you'll find that many top institutions have already moved well beyond their initial efforts.

That being said, the chapters in this part should still serve as a stark reminder. The world has changed and with it so must the institutions that so many of us hold closely as places that gave us the skills, experience, life lessons, and other invaluable learnings that made us who we are today.

8 SUPPORTING UNLEARNING TO ENABLE UPSKILLING

Chris Dede

ABSTRACT

The average lifespan of the current generation of students is projected to be 90–100 years,[1] so many of these students will need to work until their mid-seventies. In progressing through about sixty years of iteratively preparing for employment and then working, they will face evolving jobs requiring expanding skill sets and multiple careers, as some occupations disappear and new roles appear in workplaces shaped by globalization, environmental crises, and artificial intelligence.[2] As a result, society must help people of all ages through six decades of career growth and change—followed by retirement. Continuing education is faced with developing students' capacities for unceasing reinvention to take on many roles in the workplace, including occupations that do not yet exist. A major barrier in helping students repeatedly upskill for new occupational roles—and in reinventing continuing education's models for adult learning—is unlearning deeply held, emotionally valued identities in service of transformational change to a different, more effective set of behaviors. This chapter focuses on ways to integrate unlearning into occupational upskilling and into the transformation of continuing education.

Letting Go of Deeply Held Identities

To cope with the uncertainty and disruption characteristic of the twenty-first century, we and our students have to let go of deeply held, emotionally valued identities to achieve transformational change to a different, more effective set of behaviors. This has to happen at both the individual level (an instructor transforming instructional practices from presentation and assimilation to active, collaborative learning by students) and at the institutional level (a higher education institution transforming from degrees certified by seat time and standardized tests to credentials certified by proficiency on competency-based measures). These examples capture the situations I find of interest. They involve transformational shifts (i.e., second-order, double-loop, deep) based on a reconceptualization of assumptions, beliefs, and values. Often, this means that individuals and organizations shift to behaviors that are more time consuming, expensive, and difficult—but more effective based on a new frame of reference. At times, this form of change also involves difficult situations (i.e., wicked, intractable) with multiple stakeholders, competing perspectives, and an absence of obvious resolutions that leave many dissatisfied with the new status quo.

Unlearning requires not only novel intellectual approaches but also individual and collective emotional and social support for shifting our identities—not in terms of fundamental character and capabilities, but in terms of how those are expressed as our context shifts over time. My interest centers on volitional change (i.e., not based solely on compliance with organizational mandates and not based primarily on fading old practices) that is relatively swift. A powerful, negative emotional overlay (on intrapersonal and interpersonal dimensions that are not necessarily conscious) usually undermines rational, cognitive drivers to the point that transformation is, at best, temporarily and partially accomplished before involuntary, automatic reversion to standard practices and policies. This type of response to change is documented in a variety of contexts; as one example, Thomas Kuhn discussed how emotions can undercut scientific rationality in his book *The Structure of Scientific Revolutions*.[3] Another example can be found elsewhere in this book, where Susan Zhu and colleagues from the Society for Human Resource Management discuss research on why individuals may be resistant to technological change and retraining for the jobs of the future.

Upskilling and Unlearning

I am interested in the type of unlearning that can overcome or undercut this emotional resistance. My hypothesis is that the affective response is based on a perceived threat to personal identity. By this, I don't mean simply what people will intellectually describe when asked, "Who are you?" I include deep, unconscious assumptions, beliefs, and values distributed throughout the mind/brain, including preconscious processing in the limbic system. In the case of upskilling, unlearning would become important individually when the new role involves abandoning prior skills and identities (e.g., a teacher or professor transforming instructional strategies from presentation and assimilation to active, collaborative learning by students) to use new practices opposite to automatized and identity-defining prior behaviors.

However, describing this as a shift from one well-defined state to another is too simplistic. I am influenced by the arguments of Brook, Pedler, Abbott, and Burgoyne that the result of unlearning may be moving from knowing to not knowing and from action to nonaction, as a transitional step toward developing some transformed form of knowing and acting.[4] In such a process, support for an "intermediate" identity that is based on not knowing and not acting as a form of exploratory deliberation may be valuable, so that unlearning does not fail through existential crisis when one's new identity is unclear.

I hypothesize that individual unlearning could be based on a series of powerful experiences that influence the mind/brain cognitively and affectively, intrapersonally and interpersonally.[5] As a scholar of immersive learning (i.e., virtual, augmented, and mixed realities), I believe these media hold promise for investigation of what they might accomplish.[6] In particular, 360-degree video and sound systems are now inexpensive and have high quality; used with powerful authoring systems like Uptale (https://www.uptale.io/), these provide a practical way to create authentic learning experiences without the cost and expertise required to design immersive graphical environments (e.g., Minecraft). Further, mixed-reality systems like Mursion (https://www.mursion.com/) enable puppeteering: the learner is in the real world interacting with a virtual environment populated with digital people, whose behaviors are controlled by a skilled actor behind the scenes (like in the *Wizard of Oz*). With support from the Chan Zuckerberg Initiative for the Reach Every Reader project (https://www.gse.harvard.edu/reach-every-reader), my colleagues and I are conducting design-based research to devise effective methods for unlearning and upskilling using these two immersive media.

One area of our work involves identifying barriers that keep adults from building early literacy in the most effective ways, then designing experiences that can mitigate those factors via upskilling that involves unlearning. One barrier on which we are focusing is lack of empathy. Adults (parents, teachers) who have high literacy often cannot relate to the experience of a struggling reader. They no longer identify with how hard it is when one is starting out reading, or what it feels like to have certain reading difficulties. Through narrative-based 360-degree video experiences like the ones shown in Figure 8.1, we aim to build empathy in adults for the children in their lives, helping them to be more patient and understanding around the challenges of early literacy.

In our pilot study, we found that most participants express feelings of empathy, anxiety, and sadness for the child, as well as empathy for the struggle that the parent is facing. As one parent-participant said, "I knew about dyslexia from a research standpoint so it didn't teach me much about the problem, but it helped me understand what it's like as a child and as a parent."

Based on this early study with small samples, we see suggestive evidence that, using longer-duration experiences than our intervention, some adults may experience increased empathy for children who struggle with reading and for their parents. A challenge we are facing is that standard paper-based survey measures of empathy have problems with validity and sensitivity to change. The field needs to develop behavioral measures that can be assessed through immersive experiences.

Figure 8.1 Screen shots of the immersive experience in Project Empathy

Figure 8.2   Learner interacting with virtual students controlled by puppeteer

A second barrier on which we are focusing is bias. Many teachers carry an implicit bias into their teaching and often don't realize that it is influencing their teaching practices. Using Mursion (Figure 8.2), teachers are placed within a virtual classroom setting with students of varying backgrounds. In our pilot study, many participants exhibited biases about how perceived socioeconomic status influences their assessment of students' literacy.

In our pilot study about bias, none of the participants believed they were influenced by student background or appearance. However, for simulated students who were making identical progress, teachers often perceived that students labeled as being of low socioeconomic status (low-SES) were making more progress. Yet they also expressed some disbelief that low-SES students could perform as well as they did. Such perceptions were reflected by one teacher-participant who noted, "Based on the background, at least Veronica (high-SES) has so much exposure. Maybe that is where her ability comes from. But Betty's case does not make sense, because Betty (low-SES) has no family support."

Based on this early study with small samples, we see suggestive evidence that some teachers have unrealized biases for which unlearning could be helpful. Further work is needed to clarify the extent to which these types of immersive experiences can assess and remediate instructional biases. More generally, we hope through these studies to develop design principles and competency-based assessments for immersively enabling transformative upskilling that requires unlearning.

Organizational unlearning is parallel in its challenges but more complex because it involves an added level of collective unlearning, mutual reinforcement of transformed roles, and policy shifts that reform institutional identity. To transform current models of continuing education into a six-decade pipeline of adult upskilling requires organizational unlearning at each institution as well as in field-wide associations like the University Professional and Continuing Education Association (UPCEA). Adult learners need educational opportunities and stackable credentials not limited to formal degrees and certifications. Further, the instructional emphasis shifts to acquisition of competencies (skills, knowledge, and abilities) rather than disciplinary topics and knowledge communication—the student's goal is to develop a suite of skills and strategic attitudes to make a difference in the world rather than just attaining formal academic certification to meet the immediate requirements of a particular occupational role.

Beyond these models of how universities might help, partnerships with employers are important in recognizing the value and complementarity of situated workplace learning and acculturation. A coalition of extension schools might accomplish this broader task by working together to extend their mission, moving beyond episodic "continuing education" to sequential, continuous adult learning. Another organizational model could be regional higher education coalitions parallel to Western Governors University in their cross-institutional cooperation. All of this will require organizational unlearning.

9 HIGHER EDUCATION'S CHANGING FACES

Serving STEM Learners for a Lifetime

Yakut Gazi and Nelson Baker

ABSTRACT

This chapter explores the shifting role of higher education as a response to the changing STEM workforce needs. New knowledge, especially in STEM fields, is being created at an increasing rate. Accordingly, STEM professionals, just as in many other fields, need to continuously engage in learning to stay employed. This renewed need for lifetime professional, continuing, and online education (PCO) moves PCO operations and capabilities from the fringes of higher education to center stage. This chapter explores efforts to deliver relevant, valuable, affordable education for the future of work and provides current examples from higher education STEM institutions.

PROJECTIONS THAT ANTICIPATE a 60-year curriculum, coined by Matkin[1], and a 100-year life[2] call for a lifetime vision of education that suggests that higher education institutions need to dramatically refocus from just providing foundational academic programs that enable graduates to enter the workforce to providing ongoing preparation for career-long learning journeys.

Unprecedented changes in the US workforce are expected. By 2035, the number of Americans of retirement age will, for the first time, surpass the number of Americans aged eighteen or under.[3] We will soon be functioning with a workforce that employs five generations of people, ranging from teenagers to people in their eighties. With these changes will need to come a parallel shift in higher education's understanding of fundamental aspects of work—such as the work week, work location, and workspace—because colleges and universities will need to reimagine these factors through education that accommodates the needs of an aging population and longer careers. Some academic programs are already seeing enrollments across many generations, so these trends are having an effect even now.

Shifting Needs of the STEM Workforce

New knowledge, especially in STEM (science, technology, engineering, and mathematics) fields, is being created at an increasing rate. Concomitantly, STEM professionals, just as those in many other professions, need to continuously engage in learning to stay employed. In their research with 11,000 workers and 6,500 business leaders globally, Fuller, Wallenstein, Raman, and de Chalendar identified seventeen forces of disruption that shape the future of work.[4] Ranging from "general increase in skills and formal education required to perform the work" to new "regulation aimed at controlling technology use such as robot taxes," these factors are grouped under six overall forces that shape the future of work:

- Accelerating technological change
- Shifting labor demographics
- Transitioning role models
- Growing demand for skills
- Evolving business environment
- Changing employee expectations

Fuller and colleagues further found that employees seem to be optimistic and ready to face the change that the future will bring. Many managers, however, lack confidence that their employees will survive what the future of work is bringing to them. This discrepancy is important for higher education leaders to recognize, especially since most of the interaction, collaboration, and program development that occurs in partnerships between higher education and business takes place at the C-suite level. Programs for reskilling and retooling as well as for "unlearning" and "relearning" that are created only with input from the C-suite risk not matching employee ambitions and resulting in the misallocation of resources, to say nothing of the potential impacts of lost time and employee dissatisfaction.

Some companies view this challenge as an opportunity to differentiate themselves from their competitors. Such employers may view their commitment to offer continuing opportunities for professional growth as going beyond the traditional sense of "keeping up with the field" and focusing more on transforming employee skills and capabilities as preparation for the workplace of the future. This continuing and growing need for learning while in the workforce results in a view that is a departure from the traditional view of spending the earlier years of life in the educational system toward a more commonplace swirling of life, career, and education.

Employer Perspectives

Through undergraduate and graduate programs, higher education has been reasonably successful in creating generations of people with new knowledge and skills. Today's employers, however, expect more from higher education than this initial imparting of knowledge and skills. Employers today have a pressing and ongoing need for continuous skills development for their employee base. That challenge is especially exacerbated by advances in STEM fields. Today's employers and employees alike cite fields such as cloud computing, analytics, cybersecurity, and machine learning as areas particularly in need of skills development.[5] The reality is that anyone with a degree older than five to seven years in these domains is very likely to need at least a skills refresh, if not reeducation or reskilling.

In 2015, corporations spent $160 billion in the United States and $356 billion globally on education and training.[6] Despite this huge investment, a Deloitte survey found that 39 percent of executives at large companies said they were barely able or unable to find the finance talent they need.[7] Companies like AT&T, with core legacy businesses that are becoming obsolete, have been investing heavily on training to reinvent themselves. At AT&T, for example, 130,000 employees have engaged in learning since the inception of a talent development initiative that began in 2013. Since then, employees who had been retrained occupied half of the jobs and received 47 percent of the promotions.[8] In July 2019, Amazon made experts in higher education, workforce, and training take notice when it announced a commitment to invest up to $700 million over the next six years for retraining 100,000 of its employees in the United States. That training focuses primarily on technical skills such as software engineering and information technology (IT) support.[9] Confirming Amazon's recognition of a high rate of churn in the knowledge necessary for successful operations, the announcement could also be perceived as a threat to higher education, which traditionally has supplied workforce training for professional and continuing development.

According to the US Bureau of Labor Statistics, in 2018, the median tenure for employees in their current job was 4.2 years.[10] That figure leads some companies to hesitate to invest in redeveloping talent in-house. Such companies may adopt the philosophy that employees should be CEOs of their own career and should regularly seek new skills and opportunities on their own. It will be interesting to see how these companies fare compared to those that invest heavily in their employees in terms of ability to retain their talent and their competitive advantage in the market. But in the meantime, employees who are seeking their own paths to retraining and upskilling constitute an important market for institutions of higher learning. Faced with the choice to retire when their skills become too outdated or invest in educational opportunities to remain viable in the workplace, older employees present opportunities that may be especially appealing to colleges and universities. The needs they have for further education, coupled with their ability to afford this learning,[11] should have a bearing on how universities and companies can and should think of the future learning landscape.

According to a Pew Research Center study, more than 80 percent of adults in the United States think that in around thirty years robots and computers will definitely or probably do much of the work instead of humans. Just 37 percent of employed adults, however, say that their own jobs are the kind of workplace roles that will be replaced by robots and computers.[12]

Employees in search of additional training are nontraditional learners in several respects. Needing to keep their jobs and work at the same time, most will be part-time learners. The learning content they seek might be different from that pursued by more historically traditional learners. Further, their needs for continuing education may not necessarily include pursuit of full academic degrees; they may be interested in shorter educational sprints in which they acquire stackable credits that build toward a credential rather than a full degree. In addition, these new learners may expect services beyond typical student services on campus. For example, they might make decisions about where to continue their education based on the availability of learning coaches, career coaches, and mentorship networks.

Higher Education's Response

Although the advent of digital technologies and online education has brought never-before-seen opportunities to adult learners over the past twenty-five years, many of these opportunities fell short of responding to the iron triangle of higher education: accessibility, affordability, and quality. The insufficient quality of some programs, sometimes correlating directly with the employability of their graduates, along with the high loads of debt that some students incurred, called some programs into question. But important innovations have helped mitigate some of those concerns. Within the past decade, for example, massive open online courses (MOOCs) and, most recently, MOOC-based (or at-scale) degree and certificate programs have been trying to further democratize and broaden the impact of affordable high-quality education. In general, MOOC activities of the past decade have accelerated the growth of online content delivery in STEM fields.

The importance of continuing education in the STEM areas cannot be overstated. Envisioning the research university of 2040, for example, the Commission on Creating the Next in Higher Education at the Georgia Institute of Technology (Georgia Tech) saw a strong need for lifelong education in STEM areas at research-intensive institutions.[13] That report is similar in its emphasis to the US National Academy of Engineering's *Lifelong Learning Imperative in Engineering* report, published in 2012, that recognized that engineers' careers will change rapidly as technology changes and called for engineers to be lifelong learners throughout their careers.[14]

A Harvard–Georgia Tech study found that by satisfying large, previously unmet demand for midcareer training, Georgia Tech's Online Master of Science in Computer Science program will boost annual production of American computer science master's degrees by about 7 percent.[15] As such, we expect Georgia Tech's at-scale programs in STEM areas to have a real impact on shaping the workforce of the future. Work at Arizona State University to collaborate with Starbucks to create a Freshman Academy and a growing number of similar programs also testify to changing needs for education and to the importance of innovations in higher education to meet those needs.

We have seen similar change in the context of microcredentialing. A quick search on higheredjobs.com in the disciplines where advocates of badging are in higher density (such as instructional technology/design and distance education) reveal no job postings with a mention of an alternative credential or badge. Similarly, in a search we conducted in 2016, Georgia Tech, an innovative powerhouse and a leading institution in its implementation of MOOCs, or Pennsylvania State University, known for its recent work with the University Professional and Continuing Education

Association on microcredentials, had no job postings with a mention of badges or microcredentials at the time.[16]

The future of work and everything it entails means that higher education needs to give credence and importance to flexibility, agility, learning, and adaptation in the employees that we hire. In trying to attract, hire, and retain this kind of workforce, we also need to be exploring distributed (remote) work, telecommuting, and flexible work arrangements that expand our talent pool beyond our local communities.

In light of these trends, how can higher education best serve the needs of the future workforce? One important asset at many colleges and universities—their professional, continuing, and online education (PCO) units—has considerable experience educating nontraditional learners and delivering lifelong learning. Indeed, PCO expertise in innovating to meet fast-evolving learner needs could be a model for other divisions and schools.

Other chapters in this book offer related perspectives. David Schejbal argues, for example, that institutions of higher learning need to help faculty overcome cultural barriers that necessarily lead them to focus on curriculum through the lens of their particular area of expertise; rather, Schejbal suggests, joint ownership of the entire curriculum will help faculty become better prepared to educate lifelong learners. Not unlike our suggestion that universities draw more definitively on expertise in their PCO units, Michael Rascoff and James DeVaney outline a model that proposes doing more to engage alumni networks in bolstering an institution's ability to serve lifelong learners.

Going the Extra Mile

In the age of free content, we advise institutions of higher education, especially those that focus on STEM, to concentrate their efforts and experimentations on certain activities to stay relevant and continue to provide value in the changing future of work and life by doing the following:

- Creating industry- and employee-demanded new credentials, inclusion of industry certifications within the curriculum to showcase the competencies of learners, or programs designed and assessed by competencies, not seat time
- Developing services for learners that will assist them for a lifetime of education such as career coaching and guidance on rebundling of credentials

- Exploring technologies and partnerships that help scale these educational solutions to maintain affordability and impact (delivery platforms, artificial intelligence, augmented learning, blockchain, Big Data, and analytics)
- Conducting applied research on effective learning approaches for digital and mobile learning environments, generational learning, as well as learning science for the aging population
- Examining intercultural, global, and ethical perspectives on the future of work

These activities are not foreign to some institutions that have been players in this field, but some may still be nascent efforts at many institutions of higher learning.

With the unprecedented change in demographics and technology that will increasingly impact the future STEM workforce, we are faced with serious and significant problems to which we must turn our focus:

- How will the constant need to educate a larger, aging group of people, for longer periods of time, impact learning and teaching strategies?
- How will universities prepare their faculty to respond to the needs of business and industry in an agile and relevant manner?
- How should K–12 systems, curricula, and teachers adapt to prepare learners for a 60-year curriculum and 100-year life?
- How will learner services be modified or adapted to serve such a broad demographic with varying needs?
- What new models for higher education will emerge?

These and related questions will be the focus of discussion for many years ahead.

The number of reports, conferences, thought leadership, and convenings on the future of work across the globe signals something is starting to happen and take shape. Employers, universities, and individuals who are following and creating discourse into these forums will be helping shape the future to come. We envision that this chapter, written in the middle of 2019, will likely change quickly, much like the landscapes around us are changing.

10 THE FUTURE OF BUSINESS EDUCATION

New Economies of Automation, Certification, and Scale

Anne Trumbore

ABSTRACT

The old way of offering business education to degree students and professionals costs a lot and benefits only a few. Yet the changing world of work will require workers to switch jobs and acquire new skill sets multiple times throughout an extended working lifespan. New models of delivering business education show promise for both serving the needs of learners and providing critical revenue to institutions, but the paths to successful execution of strategies that leverage these models are unclear. One such model, offering short, asynchronous, credential-bearing, online courses (microcredentials) at a low cost has been pursued by the Wharton School for the past four years. Learners are finding value in these microcredential-based courses, but little scholarship shows what the value of these courses are and whether the value is in the content or the credential. This chapter focuses on the results of a study-in-progress that investigates which in-course behaviors correlate to postcourse career advancement and whether these correlations are different for men and women.

The traditional brick-and-mortar way of offering business education to degree students and professionals costs a lot and benefits only a few. Yet the changing world of work will require workers to switch jobs and acquire new skill sets multiple times throughout an extended working lifespan. New online models of delivering business education show promise for both serving the needs of learners and providing critical revenue to institutions, but the most effective pathways to successfully leveraging these models are unclear. One such model, offering short, asynchronous, credential-bearing, online courses (microcredentials) at a low cost has been pursued by the Wharton School since 2015.

More than 100,000 learners have earned certificates from these courses, but little scholarship demonstrates the value of these courses for learners and whether the value is in the content or the credential. This chapter focuses on the results of a study-in-progress that investigates which in-course behaviors correlate to career advancement and whether these correlations are different for men and women.

The Problem and the Context

The future of work seems dim for humans and bright for machines. Predictions about the impact of automation and artificial intelligence on the job market are dire, with some reputable estimates at 75 million jobs displaced by 2022.[1] It is estimated that many of the jobs that will remain for human workers will require new technological skills, and it is also anticipated that traditional systems of higher education will be unable to meet this demand.[2] Even today, a majority of businesses report difficulties in hiring enough trained workers. Popularly dubbed the "skills gap," this challenge has been shown to be a skills mismatch between what employees know how to do and what businesses want them to do.[3]

Continuing education, or lifelong learning, is seen as the best response to this threat; workers will continuously learn new skills and evolve alongside the changing nature of their jobs.[4] The standard modes of education, however, are unlikely to adequately address these challenges. On-campus, residential degrees require substantial investments in time and money. Both corporations and workers are looking for effective, low-cost education that can be easily accessed while employees continue to work.[5] Business schools, which traditionally have a much more direct connection to employers than many other disciplines, face both a critical challenge and a tremendous opportunity in this new context. To thrive in this shifting landscape, business schools will have to evolve their definition of *learner* to include employees who want to remain hirable, corporations that want to provide education for their employees, and workers around the globe who want to remain competitive in their own job markets.

Technological advances in the past decade have provided business schools with the capability of scaling their content to reach these new audiences. Massive open online courses (MOOCs), especially those in business or technical fields, can provide reputable, accessible educational content at an affordable price. Initially seen as a technological disruption of higher education, they are now marketed as the solution to the ever-widening skills gap.[6] In March 2019, the largest MOOC provider, Coursera, published the "Coursera Global Skills Index," which "assesses the skill proficiency of learners in each country and industry (entity) and measures which skills are trending around the world."[7] Other major MOOC providers such as edX and FutureLearn also position their offerings as a way to advance one's career. The Wharton School was the first business school to offer MOOCs on Coursera, beginning in 2012,[8] and it now offers more than fifty courses on Coursera and edX.

In 2015, the school introduced Wharton Online as a strategic revenue-producing initiative. Wharton Online produces, develops, designs, and implements short (four-week), asynchronous, online courses on fundamental business topics. These courses are the next generation of MOOCs, which were initially designed on a model of "translating" an existing, semester-long, on-campus course into an asynchronous course environment where hundreds of thousands of learners could access content. Using data on learner behavior from these original courses, both at Wharton and elsewhere, Wharton Online developed the following standard design for open-enrollment course offerings: each course contains four modules, and each module contains sixty to ninety minutes of short lecture videos and an associated assessment. Individual modules, while thematically linked to other modules in the course, are created to stand alone, allowing for multiple course designs from existing modules.

As of this writing, Wharton Online offers sixty courses on multiple platforms that run continuously throughout the year, with more than 240 modules of interoperable content. Since 2015, we have seen more than 225,000 completions in these courses from more than 100,000 unique learners. More recently, Wharton Online has partnered with several large global corporations to provide customized curricula to support employee development at scale in key business topics. Although these efforts give Wharton an advantageous position to participate in the future of work, questions remain about why and how these courses are effective for learners and for companies. Recent scholarship from Hollands and Kazi shows that learners are reporting career gains from taking MOOC specializations and micromasters.[9] But as yet, no one has examined if learning behaviors in MOOCs are correlated to career benefits. To find out more about the link between career advancement and MOOCs, I developed a study that seeks to answer two related research questions:

- Which behavior variables in online courses correlate to postcourse career benefits?
- How do these correlations vary for men and women?

Methods

A survey about career advancement, based on the Hollands and Kazi instrument that measures career, education, and financial benefits from participating in specializations and micromasters,[10] was sent to random samples of learners who had completed at least one Wharton Online MOOC from 2015 to 2018. Course behavior data—which included videos watched, number of assignment submissions, grades on assignments, and forum posts—were linked to the survey results of 2,800 respondents who agreed to participate.

Survey Results

Learner-Reported Career Benefits

Seventy-nine percent of learners believed they definitely or probably experienced career benefits from taking the courses, while only 5 percent said the courses had no value for their careers. These results align with previous work that shows learners found MOOCs useful to their careers; further, the percentage of learners who report benefiting from MOOCs has remained in the range of 70–80 percent since the first study in 2015.[11] However, the benefits learners experienced from completing the Wharton Online business courses did not always align with their motivations.

Reasons for Enrolling in the Course/Benefits from the Course

Intention has proved to be a strong predictor of completion,[12] particularly for learners who take MOOCs to enhance their resume.[13] In our study, 43.7 percent of the Wharton Online learners sampled enrolled with the intention of achieving career benefits. Overall, 82 percent of respondents took the course(s) intending to achieve a specific career or academic benefit, while only 18 percent enrolled with the intention of learning more about the topic. Although 56 percent enrolled in the courses with the goal of achieving career benefits, just 3 percent were motivated by the goal of additional pay. However, 54 percent of learners received career benefits different from those they expected when they enrolled (Table 10.1).

Table 10.1   Motivations for enrolling versus benefits from completion

MOTIVATION FOR ENROLLING		BENEFITS FROM COMPLETION	
Learn something new about the topic	18%	Learned something new about the topic	48%
Wanted to improve job performance	23%	Improved job performance	15%
Wanted to get a promotion	5%	Got a new role	2%
Wanted a raise or bonus	2.7%	Received raise or bonus	0.8%
Wanted to start own business	13%	Started own business	5%
Wanted to improve application to degree program	8%	Improved application to degree program	6%
Wanted to supplement learning in formal degree program	11%	Supplemented learning in formal degree program	9%
Wanted to improve English language skills	4%	Improved English language skills	7%

MOOCs as a Funnel for Degree Programs

Eight percent of learners cited improving their application to a degree program as their primary motivation for taking the course (Table 10.1), yet 43 percent of learners reported that they planned to apply to a degree program after completing their business MOOC(s) (Table 10.2). This finding could indicate that learners feel a degree would be more beneficial than a MOOC credential,[14] which may not have produced the benefits they hoped for; on the other hand, learners could have been excited by the topics or empowered by their performance. Certainly, business schools could look at MOOC completers as a potential audience for degree programs, particularly in a time of declining applications to MBA programs in the United States.[15]

Table 10.2   Survey responses related to applying to or studying in degree programs

CURRENTLY STUDYING IN DEGREE PROGRAM		NOW PLANNING TO APPLY TO DEGREE PROGRAM	
Full time	16%	Yes	43%
Part time	7%	No	26%
No	77%	Undecided	31%

Learners Are Paying for Their Own Upskilling

Eighty-five percent of learners were responsible for their course fees, with 57 percent paying for the courses themselves, and 28 percent receiving financial aid from Coursera. Just 8 percent of learners reported that their employer paid for the courses. Coursera markets courses primarily directly to learners; additionally, Wharton Online has not participated in Coursera's business-to-business sales, so this data set of learners is less likely to include those whose employers paid for the courses, compared to many other courses.

Learners Are Interested Primarily in Quantitative Courses

Wharton Online courses cover a range of business topics, from more qualitative subjects—such as Business Strategies for Social Impact, Improving Communications Skills, and Corruption—to more traditional quantitative business topics—such as Introduction to Accounting or Introduction to Corporate Finance. Respondents to this survey overwhelming enrolled in those courses with a quantitative approach (Table 10.3). These course topics are more directly applicable to specific work tasks than are courses such as Influence or Management Fundamentals, for example; this finding could indicate that learners who are paying for their own upskilling find more value in courses with a more clearly defined application in the workplace.

Demographics

Almost twice as many men responded to the survey as women, which reflects the overall enrollment patterns in Wharton Online courses. In education and employment, women and men show some similarities in our sample, with a few key differences. Generally, the percentages of women and men who hold a bachelor's degree or higher are similar, with 88 percent of women and 87 percent of men; however, women are nearly twice as likely to hold a doctorate, compared to men (Table 10.4). Women are

Table 10.3   Enrollment in selected courses

COURSE TITLE	RESPONDENT ENROLLMENTS
Customer Analytics	810
Introduction to Marketing	746
Introduction to Financial Accounting	680
Operations Analytics	635
People Analytics	604
Introduction to Corporate Finance	535
Accounting Analytics	533
Fundamentals of Quantitative Modeling	490
Introduction to Operations Management	438
Introduction to Spreadsheets and Models	395

also more likely than men to work part time (Table 10.5). Men are more likely than women to take more than one course (Table 10.6).

Kizilcec and Halawa's study of twenty Coursera MOOCs showed a gender achievement gap in both performance and persistence.[16] Therefore, one might assume that men take more courses than women because the experience is more rewarding for men. Yet data show this is not the case for Wharton Online completers. In fact, women reported being more likely to experience career benefits from MOOCs than their male counterparts and were nearly twice as likely as men to have received a pay raise or a promotion as a result of taking the course (Table 10.7). Multiple explanations for this result exist, particularly the fact that all of Wharton Online's courses cover business topics and are highly relevant to the workforce; additionally, the brand name of Wharton may confer status in a business setting, especially for women. Certainly, this finding bears further research. However, it does support earlier research that MOOCs can be used to support employability[17] and also supports claims made by platform providers that MOOC certificates have value in the workplace.[18]

Forum Posting Behavior

Multiple studies show that contributing to forums in any way is associated with passing the course.[19] Additionally, more postings are correlated

Table 10.4   Education level of survey participants, by gender

	WOMEN (34%)	MEN (66%)
High school	5%	4%
Some college, no degree	5%	6.5%
Associate's degree	1.5%	1.8%
Bachelor's degree	43.2%	41.4%
Master's degree	34.1%	36.7%
Professional degree	4%	5.3%
Doctorate	6.7%	3.6%

Table 10.5   Employment status of survey participants, by gender

	WOMEN (34%)	MEN (66%)
Self-employed	13.4%	15.3%
Employed full-time	48.5%	50.9%
Employed, part-time	7.5%	4.4%
Unemployed, job seeking	10.9%	11%
Unemployed, not seeking work	1.6%	1.0%
On leave, retired, not able to work	2.2%	1.7%
Currently a student	15.9%	15.7%

Table 10.6   Number of courses taken, by gender

	WOMEN (34%)	MEN (66%)
One course	46.5%	35.6%
Two courses	15.8%	14.0%
Three courses	6.5%	10.0%
Four or more courses	12.1%	17.0%
Specialization	17.7%	20.7%
Two or more specializations	1.0%	2.4%
Currently a student	15.9%	15.7%

Table 10.7   Analysis of forum posting behavior

	WOMEN (33%)	MEN (67%)
Job promotion	1.1%	0.5%
New role	2.0%	2.2%
Pay raise	1.3%	0.7%
Improved performance	13.7%	15.9%
Improved English language skills	7.8%	6.9%
Learned something new about the topic	49.7%	46.4%
Courses helped me start my own business	4.3%	5.0%
Courses were helpful in getting my first job	1.7%	1.7%
Courses helped me get a new job	5.1%	4.5%

to higher rates of passing.[20] However, of the 2,808 learners who passed the course in this sample, only 980 (35 percent) posted in the forums. Of these posters, 531 were "core posters," posting three or more times.[21] This percentage is consistent with findings that forum usage in MOOCs has evolved over time and that learners are less likely to post in subsequent course offerings.[22] It is also consistent with the finding that learners who pass the course are more likely to "lurk" than post in the forums.[23]

Because forum posting data are taken across more than twenty courses, learners could have posted in one course and not another. A Mann-Whitney test was used to compare the forum posting behaviors of both completers and noncompleters and was corrected for outliers. The Mann-Whitney test showed that number of forum posts was greater for course completers than for non–course completers (Table 10.8).

Course Grades by Gender
Women both enroll in and complete MOOCs in lower numbers than men.[24] An earlier study found a gender achievement gap in MOOCs.[25] However, women and men who complete Wharton Online business MOOCs do so with comparable grades. A Mann-Whitney test showed that gender had no effect on course grades in the sample (Table 10.9). Additionally, a

Table 10.8   Analysis of forum posting behavior

COMPLETION STATUS	NUMBER OF FORUM POSTS (MEAN)
Completers	9.75
Noncompleters	4.86

Mann-Whitney $U = 54146009.5$ ($p = 3.203$)

Table 10.9   Analysis of course grades

GENDER	COURSE GRADE (MEAN)
Men	81.7
Women	81.0

Mann-Whitney $U = 5057820.5$ ($p = 0.118$)

chi-square test of independence was performed to examine the relationship between gender and passing the course in Wharton Online MOOCs ($N = 7{,}070$). The relationship between these variables was not significant ($x^2 (1) = 2.12, p = .14$).

Conclusion

MOOCs in business topics can provide value to both learners seeking career advancement and to the university that offers them. Particularly, MOOCs show potential for helping women advance in their careers. Rates of completion and performance are equal for men and women; however, women are more likely than men to report tangible career benefits (a raise or a promotion). While some employers are using MOOCs from Wharton Online to educate their workers, business MOOCs are most often used as a bottom-up credential, where learners are paying the cost ($80–$100 per course) to upskill themselves. More than a quarter of all learners (28 percent) use financial aid to take these courses for free, fulfilling the initial promise of MOOCs as a force for social impact. Still, those who report receiving career benefits from Wharton Online MOOCs are primarily college educated, employed, and male, which reflects the predominant demographic composition of learners who complete MOOCs.[26] On the basis of price, business MOOCs have the potential to reach underserved populations, but further work has to be done to deliver them to these populations.[27]

MOOCs on business topics also show potential as an effective recruitment tools for business schools. Upon completing a business MOOC, 43 percent of learners planned to apply to a degree program. Since 88 percent of respondents have a bachelor's degree or above, additional degrees would most likely be at the master's level. Fifty-four percent of respondents held a bachelor's degree or *below*, showing that a sizable proportion of learners are interested in more traditional degrees. If that is true, this finding could illuminate the market for master's degrees in a time of declining business school applications.[28]

Ultimately, the main conclusion from this research is that more research is needed. The value of MOOC credentials to both employers and learners should be examined from multiple points of view, particularly from the perspective of hiring managers. Doing so could create motivation for learners in MOOCs to persist to completion, as well as expanding the demographic of MOOC completers to those without college degrees. Universities can capitalize on these findings to expand their learner base through offering MOOC certificates to learners who will never come to campus, use MOOC assets to expand their professional development and executive education programs directly to employers, and create a data set of potential master's degree students. We also need to explore other models of credentials that might be well-suited for the future of work—as Matthew Pittinsky, for example, explores in another chapter in this book.

Currently, MOOC providers are capitalizing on the steady drumbeat of panic about job disruption by artificial intelligence and automation by positioning their products as a hedge against unemployment and displacement. Venture capital has followed suit. This year, Coursera and FutureLearn received a combined total of more than $150 million in funding from SEEK, an Australian employment and recruitment site.[29] Coursera alone is now valued at more than $1 billion.[30] MOOC providers clearly have the potential to enrich their investors. Universities can also take advantage of this opportunity by offering to help address the needs of the present and future workforce for lifelong education to remain competitive, and to develop models of educational innovation as well as significant new revenue streams to ensure their relevance and survival.

11   BACK TO THE FUTURE

Fragile Workers, Higher Education,
and the Future Knowledge Economy

Earl Lewis, Alford Young, Jr.,
Justin Shaffner, and Julie Arbit

ABSTRACT

This chapter presents research from a longitudinal study of low-income, working African Americans in Ypsilanti, Michigan, a former "single-industry" city that was home to two automobile manufacturing plants throughout much of the mid- to late twentieth century. We elucidate how a "back to the future" approach to these historical transformations makes these workers not just expendable but already obsolete for meeting the demands and requirements of the future world of work. These queries enable us to begin making explicit some of the normative frameworks and questions posed about the future world of work, especially around issues pertaining to race, class, and gender, opening up new lines of inquiry for American higher education.

The objective of this chapter is to reorient contemporary framings of the future of work within higher education by placing fragile workers at the center of attention. Fragile workers are not typical college attendees. Therefore, their relationship to higher education is one that we propose must be rethought as part of a larger agenda about rethinking the role and place of higher education in the future of work.

To advance our claim, we briefly discuss research from a longitudinal study of low-income, working African Americans in Ypsilanti, Michigan, a former "single-industry" city home to two automobile manufacturing plants throughout much of the mid- to late twentieth century. We focus here because fragile workers in Ypsilanti and other such places are currently living through one possible version of the future. As such, they make for an interesting case study through which to think about not only the future of work but also the kinds of opportunities it affords the future of higher education. Ultimately, our effort provides critical contexts for exploring the following questions:

- What does the plight of contemporary fragile workers tell us about the kinds of social realities that future fragile workers might face?
- Will automation continue to leave fragile workers behind, or provide new opportunities? What kinds of economies emerge, if any, in the wake of automation? How might, if at all, "platform capitalism" and the emergent gig economy provide meaningful work opportunities, or else bar entry and participation, into the future world of work?
- What historical experiences and future imaginaries are eclipsed in contemporary framings and discussions of the role of higher education in the future world of work? How might we open both contemporary conversations and the futures imagined to be more inclusive and equitable?

Exploring these questions enables us to begin making explicit some of the normative frameworks posed about American higher education and the future world of work, especially around issues pertaining to race, class, and gender, and creates new lines of inquiry for that relationship.

Fragile Workers in Ypsilanti, Michigan

The study referenced in this chapter unearths the experiences, thoughts, and perspectives about work and work opportunity held by 103 low-income African Americans who reside in Ypsilanti, Michigan (population about 20,000). Located about 30 miles west of Detroit, Ypsilanti is a 4.5-square-mile town on the eastern doorstep of Ann Arbor, a city that is home to one of America's most highly regarded public universities, the University of Michigan, and a place considered to be one of the most livable small cities in America.[1]

As a site of automobile manufacturing, Ypsilanti bloomed during America's twentieth-century industrial boom (along with much of southeastern Michigan and its anchor city of Detroit). The recent flourishing of postindustrialism, exemplified by the rise of technology and the kinds of specialized knowledge propagated in many university and college towns, did not benefit Ypsilanti as much as it has places like Ann Arbor. Thus, many of Ypsilanti's residents, including many of its African Americans, live in a small city that both reflects the demise of industrialism *and* sits near a model of postindustrial success.

In essence, many of these residents are *fragile workers*. Fragile workers are individuals who are either chronically unemployed or who have, might, or continue to experience consistently precarious relationships to the formal economy of work. They have been affected by the movement of industries due to labor flow and policy change, both of which are manifestations of postindustrial society, or by an employment sphere where technology and automation have replaced manufacturing and other aspects of industrialism.

The research garnered insight into how these individuals experienced and thought about work and work opportunity. Specific attention was given to their visions of good jobs (including the kinds of work they felt best suited for and why), the means of acquiring good jobs, the challenges and obstacles perceived to be standing in the way of finding good work, and the resources of personal dispositions they possessed or need to acquire in order to secure good jobs.

In short, we found that these individuals were caught between two distinct and different local economies. One was a decaying industrial economy proliferated with retail shops and informal and underground economic opportunities. The other, located in the neighboring town of Ann Arbor, Michigan, was consistent with the kinds of research and technology opportunities common in small cities that house major research universities. Essentially, the African American residents of Ypsilanti stand between the industrialism that flourished in decades past and a contemporary postindustrialism that has left them little room to figure out how they fit in.

In interviews with those surveyed, most conversations about work, especially about employment that is perceived as good and desirable, pivoted in some way or another around a focus on the factory. The decline of the factory as a prominent place of employment punctuated narratives we often heard about the decline of good work prospects. Even those who expressed no interest in pursuing factory work took notice of how pivotal factories were in shaping the image of good work in their city. Joblessness was not a defining condition in their lives. Rather, respondents often noted the absence of the kinds of jobs that they believed could lead to economic stability and an affirming public identity. Those jobs, found mostly in manufacturing, were the kinds available during the boom of industrialism but are on the wane in a postindustrial order. Men, in particular, continued to embrace the kinds of work associated with traditional industrialism as most desirable. They felt an enduring sense of threat and insecurity about the increasing importance of technology in the workplace. The proliferation of technology resulted in their inability to imagine themselves as firmly and safely embedded in a postindustrial world of work.

Discussions of good jobs among the men we interviewed focused on work that garnered respect. The men spoke about good jobs in terms of what possessing them did for their self-identity and feelings of self-worth. The kinds of work upon which industrialism was founded—skilled labor and material construction—were what the men believed would enable them to cultivate a desired sense of self-worth and a valued public identity. Women were much more inclined to stress the value of serving others as foundational to good work (invoking jobs more commonly found in the service sector of the labor market). Women, therefore, seemed less susceptible to the tragic consequences of the end of industrialism (at least in how they imagined a future world of work for themselves). For the men, looking forward in regard to hopes and expectations for work typically resulted in little more than looking back to a past that was rewarding for their older relatives.

This back to the future approach makes these individuals not just expendable but already obsolete for meeting the demands and requirements of the future world of work. Instead of anticipating a place for themselves in an increasingly automated workplace, they remain nostalgic for the kinds of work that brought comfort and security to prior generations, namely, manual labor associated with the factory. Less familiar with how to relate to automation, they remain fixated on the physical capacity of their bodies for manual labor, which they believe to be their best resource for work. Looking back to a secure past takes precedence over a forward gaze into an uncertain future. Perhaps with some validity, many feel that there is no obvious place for them, or their capacity for manual labor, in the future world of work.

This back to the future orientation, especially when coupled with an inability to pursue and complete higher education (the latter case not uncommon for people invested in traditional industrialist employment sectors), leaves many of the individuals we spoke with as victims of postindustrialism. As technology and automation take precedence, employment will become more complex. Higher education will become an increasingly more critical arena for connecting these individuals to future opportunities. Therefore, it is imperative that new possibilities for higher educational attainment unfold for those who will become increasingly more fragile in the world of work.

The Future of Work

Estimates suggest that as many as 800 million jobs will disappear across the globe by 2030, and up to 54 million workers in the United States, which is one-third of its contemporary workforce, will require retraining in order to maintain employment, given the anticipated effects of automation on the world of work.[2] Some observers might surmise, for example, that working-class jobs in the transportation field might be the first to be transformed—the idea being that self-driving vehicles would rapidly erase the need for drivers in long-distance trucking and cab, livery, and limousine services, including those employed for the new gig-economy companies such as Lyft or Uber. While those jobs are vulnerable, white-collar jobs are also susceptible to being transformed by such forces as machine-reading, artificial intelligence, and automation.[3]

Today, advances in science, technology, engineering, and mathematics or medicine (STEM and STEMM) have spearheaded a call for more technical education. But where does that leave fragile workers? Some will need access to technical skills and pathways to continuous reskilling. Others may want to move from two-year to four-year institutions, knowing that—as Joseph Aoun argues in *Robot-Proof: Higher Education in the Age of Artificial Intelligence*[4]—the most successful workers in the future will have deep domain knowledge as well as a set of skills and experiences that enable them to work effectively in teams on complex problems not easily automated. That trend underscores the need for a new educational framework that links access to just-in-time training, perhaps leading to certificates and badges, and perhaps ultimately to undergraduate and graduate degrees. This in turn implies that institutions of higher learning need to rethink their relationship to their communities and what it means to educate and serve.

Opportunities for Higher Education

In our study, Ypsilanti residents often described their hesitation about approaching Ann Arbor and the University of Michigan. A few made mention of community colleges and their town's Eastern Michigan University. Universities were where they went for medical care or entry-level, low-wage jobs as orderlies, kitchen help, or custodians. Aside from these experiences, higher education seemed well beyond the purview of these fragile workers.

Assessing these findings, we envision a broader role for higher education to play in the transmission of skill sets necessary for the contemporary and future world of work. That is, there is capacity to bring more fragile workers into higher education. To do so, several pertinent questions must be addressed:

- How might higher education meet the needs of those currently, or soon to be, left out?
- What social distances exist between fragile workers and higher education, and how might those gaps be bridged?
- With the emergence of "platform education," might it be possible for universities to meet prospective students where they are, on their own turf, in order to meet the challenges of the future of work?
- How can barriers to participation be lowered (such as changing how prerequisites are conceived, or by rethinking how prior credits contribute to degrees)?
- How might costs be addressed (e.g., corporate tax, sponsorship, or philanthropy)?

As the United States continues to evolve toward a postindustrial economy, a new approach to higher education must shrink the social distance between colleges and universities and fragile workers. It requires a new emphasis on continuing education and learning. It requires a kind of whiteboard exercise that leverages the traditional disciplines and modes of analysis in a manner that fosters creativity as well as subject-matter expertise.

What is needed for fragile workers to become robot-proof and robot-ready in the world of future work is a renewed version of the liberal arts in the nation's service. That vision must be inclusive of fragile workers and nontraditional students across the social spectrum. Many institutions previously endorsed the Liberal Education and America's Promise (LEAP) framework developed by the Association of American Colleges and Universities, which called for educators and employers to engage in new partnerships that advance "the importance of liberal education in a global economy and in our diverse democracy."[5] The original framework could not have fully anticipated the rate, scale, and far-reaching impact of automation of the fourth industrial revolution. Many observers have tried to answer the question of why the liberal arts remain an effective educational option but are only beginning to address what is durable and adaptable about the liberal arts in the face of automation. Liberal arts education must be modular; emphasize horizontal learning; offer stackable credentials and options for part time, online, and nonresidential programs; and be more accessible to nontraditional students.

As discussed by Earl Lewis,[6] higher educational institutions will most certainly require a sharper articulation of purpose and value as we enter a period of accelerated change. No one knows for sure what new jobs are in the offing, but the McKinsey report cited earlier hints that a college education alone is not a sure protector.

As something of a counterpoint to such existential uncertainty, Aoun makes the case for a learning model that builds on the core elements of the liberal arts, integrating the arts, humanities, and branches of the sciences (social, physical, and biological) rather than what is learned from science, technology, engineering, and mathematics or medicine alone. Aoun argues for a learning model predicated on creative, critical, and systems thinking; entrepreneurship; cultural agility; and mastering of the new literacies of technology, data, and what he calls human literacy or the ability to discern and create space for creative problem-solving. Reminiscent in some ways of ideas advanced by Scott Page, who has found that complex problems benefit from being addressed by diverse teams, Aoun believes a degree becomes robot-proof when it equips its holders with the tools to think *horizontally* rather than vertically.[7] The vertical thinker can only marshal tools from his or her subject-matter tool box and apply those tools in a linear fashion. The horizontal or systems thinker looks across knowledge domains to assemble teams with diverse subject-matter expertise. Here the key is knowing which question or questions to ask and knowing what is needed to provide adequate answers.

Also looking to the future, scholar Cathy Davidson argues in *The New Education: How to Revolutionize the University to Prepare Students for a World in Flux* that education in the twentieth century shifted from a founding mission focused on training ministers "toward the selection, preparation, and credentialing of future leaders of new professions, new institutions, and new companies." She concludes that the new conceptualization of education means "refocusing away from the passive student to the whole person learning new ways of thinking through problems with no easy solutions. It shifts the goal of college from fulfilling course and graduation requirements to learning for success in the world after college."[8]

Other models can be found elsewhere in this book. Susan Lund and Bryan Hancock offer a vision of a future in which automation will help shape the transition to new jobs and workplace roles, and changes in existing higher education approaches may only need to be modest in order to serve the workforce of the future. Greg Robinson describes how one highly technical organization, NASA, has found a path forward through cultural change within the organization to support continuous learning.

What Aoun and Davidson advocate borrows from and moves beyond the LEAP formulation, which focused on essential learning outcomes, principles of excellence, high-impact educational practices, authentic assessments, and students' signature work. Lewis suggests several key elements of what liberal arts in the future of service to the nation should look like:[9]

- Schools know the value of exposing students to a world beyond the geography of the campus. Emphasizing study-abroad opportunities has been one way to address this pedagogically. For many low-income students, the hurdle begins earlier. Institutions should require that all students who are eligible will acquire a passport in their first year, with assistance from the college, if needed. Dreamers would get a pass until legislation makes it possible for them to participate.
- The liberal arts could approach learning differently. Instead of broad subject-matter exposure in the first two years, it would emphasize broad exposure in year 1, more tailoring and subject-matter focusing in years 2 and 3, followed by concrete problem-solving work in year 4 that is tied to a major or course of study. This pattern hinges on demonstrated abilities to work in teams, oftentimes with robotic helpers, across knowledge domain fields, in real time, on real problems.
- Shifting to a STEM plus the arts and/or humanities approach to learning would create an emphasis on the interplay among the humanities, engineering, arts, technology, and science (HEATS). As STEM education is important but perhaps not sufficient, a HEATS approach portends a new and perhaps important innovation, as a recent National Academy of Sciences study provisionally suggests.[10]

- Abandon the assumption that all students will be eighteen to twenty-two years old. Instead, recognize the reality that while some students may be in residence, others may come to classrooms virtually and that a hybrid learning experience (online plus in residence) may soon become the norm.

Automation is poised to alter the future of work. Dramatic reductions in known jobs are forecast, and while new jobs are anticipated, no one can say with certainty what they will be. This places higher education at the center of an emerging discussion of who will work, what preparation is needed, and how many will need to be trained or educated. Aoun and others have led the way in calling for colleges to imagine what it will mean to produce a so-called robot-proof education. A renewed liberal arts education in the nation's service is exactly the recipe for a thoroughly educated worker-citizen.

12 THE EVOLUTION OF THE LIBERAL ARTS

Christopher Mayer

ABSTRACT

The high cost of higher education and resulting student debt, along with employers' concerns about readiness for work, has fueled public skepticism about the value of higher education. Adding to this skepticism is that the nature of work is changing due to the impact of technological advances. The liberal arts have been one of the main targets of this criticism due to their perceived inability to prepare students for the future of work. What is interesting about this criticism is that studying the liberal arts provides many of the skills employers claim college graduates are lacking and that numerous reports identify as essential for the future of work. This chapter highlights different approaches taken by several higher education institutions—including West Point—that are designed to provide students the benefits of studying the liberal arts while also preparing them for the future of work. These approaches represent an evolution from the traditional liberal arts model.

The decade since the Great Recession has been hard on higher education. Many people who graduated from college during this time could not secure well-paying jobs, which made it difficult for them to pay off their student loans. Those who graduated with liberal arts degrees faced additional challenges because their degrees did not have the clear connections with job requirements that professional degrees had. Even as the economy improved, the number of students enrolled in liberal arts programs has declined.[1]

One reason for this decline has been the call for more graduates with STEM (science, technology, engineering, and mathematics) degrees.

Another reason is that the story of the English major from a selective (and expensive) college working as a barista has become a cautionary tale for anyone thinking about majoring in a liberal arts discipline, especially the humanities. Although there is evidence that graduates with liberal arts degrees do well in the job market, this view of the employment consequences of studying the liberal arts has been widely accepted.[2] Finally, what one studies in liberal arts programs can seem irrelevant when compared with the skills gained by those studying disciplines like engineering and computer science.

Although some of the criticism leveled against the liberal arts is warranted, studying the liberal arts can provide students with the skills they need to thrive in the future. To fulfill their potential of preparing students for the future of work, the liberal arts (both programs and general education offerings) must evolve in terms of their curricular and pedagogical design. There is a great deal of work to do in this area, but there are many examples of colleges and universities strengthening the connection between study in the liberal arts and the future of work.

Skills Needed for the Future of Work

The recognition that the liberal arts are valuable hinges on consensus about what skills employees need to thrive in the future. Numerous studies and reports have concluded that not only are STEM-related skills essential for the future but so are skills most typically associated with the liberal arts.[3] Another conclusion derived from this analysis is that although many tasks and possibly even jobs will become automated, tasks that require uniquely human skills are unlikely to be automated in the foreseeable future. One report, *Robot-Ready: Human + Skills for the Future of Work*, presents the following list of uniquely human skills: "creativity, critical thinking, communication, emotional intelligence, judgment, ethics, and cognitive flexibility."[4] Although the report suggests that there are other ways these skills can be developed, it goes on to assert that liberal arts programs are "clearly geared toward developing these human skills and remain a chief, though not exclusive, pathway through which millions of Americans learn these skills."[5] Scott Hartley, author of *The Fuzzy and the Techie: Why the Liberal Arts Will Rule the Digital World*, writes that "it's the liberal arts and their cultivation of distinctively human abilities—which machines can't even approximate—that are paving the way to the most reliable employment today and will continue to do so in the coming years."[6] Hartley provides evidence throughout his book that the types of skills developed through the study of the liberal arts are valuable, and he offers numerous examples of people with liberal arts backgrounds exceling at the highest levels of the tech industry.

Although these reports stress the value of human skills, they also emphasize the importance of technical skills. *Robot-Ready* states the following: "We say, 'both, and': It is the integration of human and technical skills that will provide the best preparation for the future of work."[7] Joseph Aoun, author of *Robot-Proof: Higher Education in the Age of Artificial Intelligence*, writes that education must focus on both digital literacy and human skills because "every learner now has to be able to interact with machines, learn how to grasp data, and do things that machines can't, such as be empathetic, creative and entrepreneurial."[8]

This dialogue on the skills needed for the future of work supports two conclusions. First, the liberal arts are valuable in terms of preparing students for the future of work; and, second, the development of tech skills should be an essential element of the college experience, especially for those with liberal arts degrees.

Providing Opportunities for Students to Apply Their Skills

Students studying the liberal arts have traditionally developed and exercised skills in the classroom and applied them on academic assignments. This approach will not prepare them for employment. Students must be given opportunities to apply what they learn to real-world problems in and out of the classroom. This occurs most often through experiential learning. Aoun discusses how experiential learning helps students master proficiencies by helping them first acquire skills (typically in the classroom), then practice "integrating them in a given context," and finally "apply what they have learned in different contexts."[9] Experiential learning opportunities, such as internships and real-world projects, provide students the opportunity to exercise their skills in a "novel context" and transfer what they have learned from one context (the classroom) to another.[10] Students are capable of far transfer when they are able "to apply skills and knowledge learned in one context to a dissimilar context," such as "when the critical thinking skills honed in a Restoration poetry seminar are used to create a public relations campaign for a marketing company."[11] Graduates must be capable of far transfer if they and their employers are to benefit from the skills developed through the study of the liberal arts.

Clark University, through an approach dubbed Liberal Education and Effective Practice, provides one example of intentionally connecting student development to work. Clark frames the student experience in terms of four actions: Orient, Explore, Act, and Launch. The Orient and Explore phases are typical for higher education, with students being welcomed (academically) to the institution, usually through first-year seminars, and then receiving the breadth (general education) and depth in a discipline (major) that is usually associated with undergraduate education.[12] Traditional liberal arts education concludes at the Explore phase.

With the Act phase, however, Clark University students are required to complete internship-like experiences that focus on practical problems that, along with capstones, provide opportunities to exercise skills outside of the classroom. This enables students to engage in the type of far transfer that Aoun discussed. In these experiences, for example, a student studying art history might be required to write for the public. A French major might work as a professional translator. A history major could create a document on the history of a local community that requires interviewing local families.[13] A secondary benefit to the Act phase is that students are given the opportunity to discover what they might want to do after graduation.

The final phase, Launch, is an intentional effort to enable employment success through traditional internships and connections to alumni and community leaders.[14] This provides additional preparation for the workforce.

While labs are typically associated with the sciences, Arizona State University started a Humanities Lab that "provides students with the opportunity to engage in hands-on research on compelling social challenges of interest to today's students while working with others who are also invested in making a difference."[15] Students work with interdisciplinary teams of faculty members, graduate students, and undergraduate students in an experimental, collaborative, lab-like environment to examine issues such as immigration, food systems, the future of cars, and rebuilding Puerto Rico.[16] This prepares humanities students to apply their skills to real-world problems and also provides them the benefit of working in teams, which is typically associated with science and engineering disciplines but is an important skill needed to thrive in the future of work.

Partnering with Bootcamps and Employers

The emergence of nontraditional educational providers has led to predictions of the disruption of higher education. Clay Christensen, Kim B. Clark Professor of Business Administration at the Harvard Business School, predicted in 2013 that "the scary thing is that in 15 years maybe half of universities will be in bankruptcy, including the state schools."[17] One type of educational provider in particular, bootcamps, was identified by the Christensen Institute as a potential disrupter.[18] In practice, though, what appears to be happening is that universities and colleges are partnering with bootcamps. These partnerships allow students to pursue liberal arts degrees to develop skills that prepare them for careers while also developing skills that make them marketable for their first job.

One example is the partnership between Dominican University of California and the Make School. Make School is helping Dominican create a computer science minor while Dominican is helping Make School transform to an accredited degree-granting institution through an accelerated bachelor's degree in applied computer science.[19] This allows students with liberal arts degrees to complete computer science minors, which makes them more marketable for their first job.

Trilogy Education, which provides programs in web development, data analytics, UX/UI design, and cybersecurity, partners with forty-seven universities, including Northwestern, Rutgers, and Georgia Tech.[20] Trilogy's partnerships provide students access to bootcamps that develop job-specific skills.

Another example is Davidson College's partnership with Adjacent, a startup developed by the Entangled Group, which runs a program called Liberal Arts in Silicon Valley. The program is six weeks long and offers students the opportunity to "blend your liberal arts education with tech skills to make a difference." Students also interact with speakers who have liberal arts backgrounds to learn how they secured employment.[21] Five other colleges and universities participate, including liberal arts institutions such as Denison University, Scripps College, and Mount Holyoke College.[22] Participating students attain a high-quality liberal arts education and then have the chance to apply these skills and develop new skills.

Finally, CodePath.org, a nonprofit bootcamp, has partnered with twenty-five universities to provide widespread access to skills helpful for attaining their first job, including providing students coding training, opportunities for internships, and career counseling for a significantly lower cost than for-profit bootcamps. CodePath.org's courses also count for credit at some of the institutions.[23]

Colleges and universities are also working with employers to help students succeed in the workforce. One example is in Hartford, Connecticut, where Trinity College has partnered with tech firm Infosys. Infosys is experimenting with a training curriculum for new employees with liberal arts backgrounds. Jeff Auker, who leads Infosys's Hartford hub, explains why Infosys is eager to hire college graduates with liberal arts backgrounds: "We need people that don't just break down problems into solvable bits. We need people that understand how you put those bits back together to create great experiences." A news story about the partnership suggested that Auker "loves to find liberal arts majors who 'can speak tech,' and skilled data scientists who can think in the abstract." Participants in the training program study business analytics, design thinking, and business software, and learn how to apply the skills they developed through the study of the liberal arts to working with clients.[24]

As these examples demonstrate, partnerships between traditional higher education and alternative postsecondary providers like bootcamps and even employers are very promising. Although the rise of alternative education providers may have a negative impact on some colleges and universities, partnerships have the potential to provide students the best of both worlds by allowing them to benefit from studying the liberal arts and developing skills needed to make them more likely to secure and be successful in their first job.

Incorporating Tech into the Curriculum

The liberal arts, by definition, include math and science, and liberal arts curricula typically offer courses in algebra, calculus, chemistry, physics, and other sciences. While such courses provide a foundation in science and math, they do not necessarily prepare students for the type of work they will perform in the workforce. They may also not prepare students to use the technology they will work with once they graduate. But that is beginning to change.

Sweet Briar College, a liberal arts college in Virginia, recently restructured its core curriculum. The curriculum's focus, "women's leadership in the 21st century," includes ten core curriculum courses that all students are required to take.[25] Instead of the math and science courses traditionally offered by liberal arts colleges, Sweet Briar College students are required to complete courses like Design Thinking, STEM in Society, and Decisions in a Data-Driven World. The Design Thinking course is taught by faculty members from multiple disciplines and introduces students to the design thinking process, which is used by many businesses.[26] The STEM in Society course is designed to "empower students to develop evidence-based opinions, and make informed decisions, about societal issues related to science and technology."[27] Decisions in a Data-Driven World helps students develop data literacy by focusing on "data-rich topics drawn from the fields of economics, personal finance, science and technology, health, and political science to develop the ability to reason and work with data, as well as understand and present arguments supported by quantitative evidence."[28] These three courses reflect a new approach to the liberal arts that is more closely aligned with the skills students will need as employees in the workforce of the future.

The United States Military Academy's (West Point) core curriculum reflects the need for West Point to develop future Army officers who have a solid liberal arts foundation but who also are comfortable with and can employ technology. To achieve this, all cadets complete a core curriculum of thirteen STEM courses and seventeen humanities/social science courses. The curriculum's STEM focus includes two information technology courses (Introduction to Computing and Information Technology, and Cyber Foundations), multiple math and science courses, as well as a three-course engineering sequence for those not pursuing an engineering major. What this means is that cadets who major in traditional liberal arts disciplines like philosophy or literature are required to complete coursework in engineering, cyber, math, and science, while those who major in engineering complete course work in subjects like philosophy, literature, foreign language, and psychology.[29] This broad core curriculum ensures that all graduates, regardless of major, develop skills needed to thrive in environments that require them to lead humans and employ technology.

In addition to the curriculum, the evolution of the liberal arts is apparent in educational goals and pedagogy. In reshaping its curriculum in what it calls the New Liberal Arts, Hiram College, a liberal arts institution in Ohio, revised its educational goals to ensure that its graduates "demonstrate competency in a twenty-first century skill set and mind-set."[30] New goals call for students to learn "mindful technology," "systems thinking," and "design thinking." The word *digital* was also added to Hiram's written and oral communication goal to reflect technological changes to the workplace.[31] In addition to focusing on technology in the curriculum, Hiram has focused on infusing technology into the delivery of its curriculum. From facilitating learner-to-learner and learner-to-instructor collaboration using apps, to web conferencing and employing simulations to creating multimedia journals, technology is integrated throughout the student learning experience so that students are prepared to use this type of technology when they graduate.[32] Additionally, Hiram College has made a significant investment through its Tech and Trek program, which issues iPad Pros to all of its students and most of its faculty and staff so that students are comfortable with and capable of using such technology, and faculty and staff understand how to help students use it.[33]

Although the study of the liberal arts develops the human skills that students will need to thrive in the future of work, that is not enough. Those studying the liberal arts must be prepared for a workplace where technology will be ubiquitous. Partnerships with bootcamps is one way to do this, but it is also important for institutional curricula and pedagogy to reflect the importance of developing competence with technology. Elsewhere in this book, for example, Lance Braunstein argues that technological literacy ought to be taught as a foundational skill in all life-long learning. Kelly Otter addresses the need for higher education to apply more interdisciplinary thinking and to break down the artificial boundaries that tend to separate liberal education and workforce preparation.

Conclusion

The study of the liberal arts has benefits beyond preparing students for work. These include learning for its own sake and preparing students to live good lives as citizens and people. As worthy as these goals are, the liberal arts must also prepare people for the future of work. The cost of higher education, the need for graduating students to find meaningful work, and the requirements of employers all highlight the importance of a stronger connection between the liberal arts and the future of work. An evolved liberal arts can provide this connection and can help people thrive during the fourth industrial revolution.

13 THE EVOLUTION OF LIBERAL EDUCATION IN A TECHNOLOGY-MEDIATED, GLOBAL SOCIETY

Kelly J. Otter

ABSTRACT

This chapter articulates and reimagines the ideals and practices of liberal arts education for a rapidly evolving, interconnected, and yet unpredictable world. The current model of liberal education is organized around discrete, siloed disciplines. The next wave of liberal education will encourage an increasingly diverse (age, race, nationality, gender) population of citizens who are self-critical, ethically aware, and open to other cultures, not by imposing a Western or American model, but through dialogue within and across the globalized world. The evolving liberal education will develop a reflective perspective that is adaptable and in synergy with other cultures, histories, literacies, and technologies. This chapter explores the need for increasing interdisciplinary curricular approaches to prepare students for a globalized, interconnected world, and will provide examples of curriculum design from Georgetown University that illustrate how to implement them. It includes references to interdisciplinary models of liberal education at the baccalaureate and graduate levels, a method of blending liberal and professionally oriented education, and the incorporation of social justice values through Ignatian pedagogy that stems from the Jesuit tradition.

THE GROWTH OF THE INTERNET ECONOMY, artificial intelligence, and the extent to which data are becoming accessible and used in decision making are quickly and dramatically changing the nature of work, and are giving rise to new areas of academic study focused on technology.

This evolution has accelerated the debate about the value of a liberal education. At the same time, it also creates opportunities for long over-due examinations and revisions of curriculum design and pedagogical approaches. The underlying skills and competencies gained through interdisciplinary study, which must be thoughtfully crafted in curricula and made explicit in the learning process, are the core attributes on which the future workforce depends.

The Liberal Arts

The liberal arts fields are traditionally structured—and have thrived—in silos. A traditional liberal arts education incorporates subject-matter and cocurricular experiences from a variety of disciplines in the arts and sciences, guiding learners to think with broad, increasingly global perspectives. While students intuitively apply concepts and knowledge across disciplines to the social, economic, and ethical issues around them, the evolving approach to liberal education will be to make the underlying competencies explicit and to construct learning environments and projects around complex, contemporary issues.

The structures of our institutions, siloed departments and disciplines, were largely established in the nineteenth century. The natural formation of those research and teaching communities around specialized subject areas produced environments in which teaching and learning could be nourished and flourish, and in which inquiry and the pursuit of new knowledge could be supported. However, critics of those environments argue that in some cases they exist to replicate themselves rather than to meet the needs of the external environment. This organization around specific, discrete disciplines serves, at times, to produce and disseminate knowledge more deeply than broadly. Thus, the practicality and professional application of many social science– and humanities-based areas of study have always been challenged. The focus on content, as opposed to the underlying process of knowledge and skill formation, has blinded us to some of the most valuable components of a liberal education.

Engineering Learning

We can identify the cultivation of high-order competencies in standard curricula through various assessment tools, but the challenge before us is to take new approaches to curriculum development to make the learning explicit. Students must develop the capacity to identify and demonstrate their abilities as they grow from novice to master. For example, the process of learning to write is too often one in which instructors or tutors in writing centers edit and comment on student essays, as opposed to teaching them the process of editing so that they recognize such qualities as structure, logic, and syntax.

Two illuminating projects that offer tools to discover these components are the Liberal Education and America's Promise (LEAP) project,[1] and the Lumina Foundation's Degree Qualifications Profile (DQP).[2] These resources identify the intellectual and practical skills that are developed through a liberal education and display levels of mental development from foundational (or simple) through high order (and complex). Research by Herbert A. Simon contributed greatly to learning science and learning engineering, and identified how professional competencies could be woven into pedagogical approaches.[3]

The DQP model guides faculty in the construction of learning outcomes and maps intellectual skills with high-level competencies—for example, identifying how analytical inquiry is deployed to demonstrate specialized knowledge in a particular course. The LEAP project, more broadly, identifies skills and competencies needed to meet twenty-first-century challenges.

The establishment of interdisciplinary research and teaching centers—on issues of environmentalism and sustainability, for example, or on the study of aging, race, and gender equity—presents another shift in institutional structures that lead to curricula that are designed around complex issues requiring multiple disciplinary approaches and lenses of inquiry. The ability to work in interdisciplinary teams and to apply historical, qualitative, and numerical tools to complex issues are high-order skills in great demand by employers across sectors.

Evolving Educational Model

The evolving educational model will blend the cultivation of essential skills, technological literacies and abilities, and the application of all of these competencies to a variety of complex projects and problems across sectors in the world of work. Looking holistically at the educational life cycle, the Organisation for Economic Co-operation and Development *Education 2030* report sums it up well:

Epistemic knowledge, or knowledge about the disciplines, such as knowing how to think like a mathematician, historian, or scientist, will also be significant, enabling students to extend their disciplinary knowledge. Procedural knowledge is acquired by understanding how something is done or made—the series of steps or actions taken to accomplish a goal. Some procedural knowledge is domain-specific, some transferable across domains. It typically develops through practical problem-solving, such as through design thinking and systems thinking. Students will need to apply their knowledge in unknown and evolving circumstances. For this, they will need a broad range of skills, including cognitive and meta-cognitive skills (e.g., critical thinking, creative thinking, learning to learn, and self-regulation); social and emotional skills (e.g., empathy, self-efficacy, and collaboration); and practical and physical skills (e.g., using new information and communication technology devices).[4]

Professionally oriented and vocational education that reflects the growing bodies of specialized technical knowledge is also giving rise to new curricula emphasizing data analysis and technology management, for example, and is pushing the need for closer ties between industry competencies and curriculum development. Jobs are changing, skills to do them are evolving, tools we need to identify and prepare to do them need to be crafted, and the stakes are getting higher each day. Tasks are being performed by machines, and new roles and jobs are emerging that require not only technical knowledge but also higher order cognitive skills as well as "soft skills" such as leadership, empathy, and creativity. This need for tech-focused, vocationally oriented academic credentials increases the imperative for thoughtfully constructed curricula that lead to high-order intellectual skills such as analysis, evaluation, and prediction.

The success of any industrial sector, in all economies and civil societies, is built on a foundation of leadership, empathy, and creativity. In that regard, for example, Anthony Carnevale, director of the Center on Education and the Workforce at Georgetown University, has noted that "as the world got richer the value of standardized commodities declined [and] competition shifted to new kinds of value added. The increasing competition and the demand for new kinds of value added have created more intense and complex competitive requirements."[5]

Carnevale notes that because technology manages repetitive or computational tasks, humans need skills to manage the high-tech tools and to interact with each other:

> Most employers today cannot compete successfully without a workforce that can use solid academic skills in applied settings. Increased interaction with sophisticated computerized machinery requires good technical reading skills, and writing is frequently the first step in communicating with customers, documenting competitive transactions, or successfully moving new ideas into the workplace. Employers need workers who have mastered reading processes that allow them to locate information and use higher-level thinking strategies to solve problems. Similarly, writing on the job often requires analysis, conceptualization, syntheses and distillation of information, and clear articulation of points and proposals.[6]

Evolving Liberal Education

The next wave of liberal education, engaging a population of learners that will be increasingly diverse in terms of age, race, nationality, and gender, requires formation of citizens who are self-critical, ethically aware, and open to other cultures, not by imposing a Western or American model, but through dialogue within and across the globalized world. The evolving liberal education will develop a reflective perspective that is adaptable and in synergy with other cultures, histories, literacies, and technologies. Willard Dix helped put this in context:

> A liberal arts education can be very frustrating. It forces students to see multiple viewpoints and continually challenge their own. It removes the comfort of assuming there are "right" answers to big questions, that civilization moves in a linear fashion, or that facts are facts no matter who looks at them. But it also introduces students to the pleasures of debate and the ever-expanding world of ideas. It opens doors, enabling the mind to go wherever it wants in the pursuit of knowledge and understanding. It bends toward openness instead of containment.[7]

While we grapple with the external pressures on higher education to address workforce and economic development issues in the United States, it behooves us to take note of trends in countries that have taken very different routes over the past decades and are now adapting to current challenges from a completely different vantage point. For example, why is India introducing liberal arts schools and emphasizing liberal education? Why did the National University of Singapore (NUS) partner with Yale University to offer an undergraduate degree in liberal education?

In this country, too, other approaches are also evolving. In another chapter in this book, for example, Lance Braunstein argues that technological literacy ought to be taught as a foundational skill in all life-long learning. In other chapter, Christopher Mayer describes how some educational institutions are successfully integrating curricula that deftly blend the liberal arts and workforce preparation skills.

Eastern Perspectives

An informative lens through which we might examine the Western approach to liberal education is consideration of models emerging in the East. Mimi Roy, associate professor at the Jindal School of Arts and Humanities in India, explained that the liberal arts were diminished in the Indian education system due to the introduction of the "fixed curriculum" model of the British system, as well as the growing desire for professional degrees. The result over time was an emphasis on vocational training and an increase in graduates with technical degrees "with a very unidirectional and focused mindset," in an era when there was an increasing need for people with imagination who were prepared to join a global workforce. Roy observed,

> Recently, Liberal Arts education has started gaining recognition in various parts of our continent. Various Liberal Arts colleges have opened up in Singapore, Japan, China, Hong Kong, and India. . . . The Liberal Arts curriculum incorporates the best of content, course and knowledge in terms of interdisciplinary and experiential learning, use of technology, and mentorship. All of this is inspired to attract young minds towards the best educational experience and to prepare them to be global citizens.[8]

Roy added,

> A solid, well-grounded Liberal Arts education system in India is the need of the hour and is central to a twenty first century global imagination. From the last century, the United States education system has pioneered and sustained institutions with a focus on Liberal Arts education to create global leaders capable of solving intricate problems through rational and

critical thinking. This has quite obviously resulted in American institutions on the top spots of World University listing while Indian institutions fail to grab a spot even in the top one hundred. The Indian higher education system has often been described as a "sea of mediocrity with a few islands of excellence."[9]

Another example, the 2014 launch of a liberal education enterprise in Asia, Ashoka University in India, is a compelling case study. Ashoka is a private, nonprofit university supported through collective public philanthropy in India. It offers a multidisciplinary liberal education, blurring the lines between the arts and sciences. In India, universities are a conglomeration of independent colleges and typically offer little in the way of liberal arts. In contrast to the standard American model of shared governance, Ashoka employs high-quality visiting faculty from around the world. Out of concern for the narrow focus on STEM (science, technology, engineering, and mathematics) fields in India, and the stigma of having few high-quality institutions, Ashoka was established to produce graduates who could think critically and communicate well, and who could work collaboratively and be sympathetic and empathetic.

Ashoka used the liberal arts model in the United States as a guide. The curriculum is not a copy of those in the West, however, but rather moves the needle on the American model. The curriculum is infused with India, including Gandhi and the Indian election system, philosophy from Western and Indian perspectives, and Shakespeare. There is a strong emphasis on writing and experiential learning. This curriculum design approach offers insights to Western educators about assumptions about cultural perspectives in teaching and what it means to globalize the liberal arts.

The 2011 Yale-NUS partnership represents the first liberal arts college in Singapore, and one of very few in Asia, though there was no paucity of high-quality educational institutions in Singapore, nor were there concerns about student success on test scores. In his book *In Defense of a Liberal Education*, Fareed Zakaria offered some relevant perspective:

> When compared internationally, America's test scores are disappointing, but what explains its history and fast trajectory of economic growth? Quoting a former minister of education from Singapore who acknowledged that while his country was among the top performing nations on international tests, it was seeking to boost innovation and entrepreneurship among

students producing those top scores. "There are some parts of the intellect that we are not able to test well—like creativity, curiosity, a sense of adventure, ambition. Most of all, America has a culture of learning that challenges conventional wisdom, even if it means challenging authority. These are the areas where Singapore must learn from America."[10]

Tan Chorh Chuan, president of NUS at the time, said that "the Yale-NUS College is a bold and exciting initiative which provides an extraordinary opportunity to nurture talented young minds with the intellectual breadth and depth needed to address the complex issues of the future."[11]

Collaboration Is Essential

Employers consistently affirm these arguments, underscoring the need for workers with increasing technology knowledge and abilities but also those skills cultivated through liberal learning. The college learning outcomes that both universities and employers rate as most important include oral communication, critical thinking, ethical judgment, working effectively in teams, written communication, and the real-world application of skills and knowledge.[12] Further, partnerships between employers and higher education through co-ops, apprenticeships, internships, and service learning demonstrate the value executives place on real-world problem-solving and skills-building during the formal education process. Collaboration between educators and employers is instrumental to meet this challenge. There exists a close connection among education, the workforce, and the economy. The techniques used in curriculum design, as well as course and program learning outcomes, should cultivate the skills and competencies to prepare graduates to function at a high level across sectors.

It is of widespread concern that algorithms, especially machine-learning, can be susceptible to bias and that racial, sexual, and other discriminatory ideas will be coded into machines, despite the fact that we have progressed as a society to identify, address, and eradicate these issues in our language, culture, and institutions. Herein lies the ongoing and pressing need for the tenets of liberal learning: the cultivation of rational habits of mind and exposure and experiences across subjects. Studying literature and the arts across time and cultures, examining language through social and cultural lenses, and reading and discussing issues related to race and gender studies are just some examples of knowledge and awareness people must have when producing, managing, and making decisions with products in a machine-learning environment. The people behind the analytics are designers and interpreters.

Writing in the *Harvard Business Review*, Tony Golsby-Smith argued that

> there are plenty of MBAs and even PhDs in economics, chemistry, or computer science, in the corporate ranks. Intellectual wattage is not lacking. It's the right intellectual wattage that's hard to find. They simply don't have enough people with the right backgrounds. This is because our educational systems focus on teaching science and business students to control, predict, verify, guarantee, and test data. It doesn't teach how to navigate "what if" questions or unknown futures.[13]

There must reside a place in all institutions in which we demonstrate the relationship between the educational experiences we provide and how they align with the world of work. We must recognize that we need to take inter- and cross-disciplinary views of this relationship. If students can identify, articulate, and demonstrate the skills they have developed in the education process, they can align them with the skills demanded by employers. To accomplish this, faculty will need to acquire new skills in curriculum development and assessment, which will depend on institutional support and on revisions to curricula that prepare faculty for teaching careers. Faculty must construct and guide students through project- and problem-oriented approaches that merge disciplines in the analysis of complex issues to design solutions. Finally, we must take a global view of educational trends and of the cultural and economic impact of liberal and technical education systems. By doing so, we learn that by segregating these systems we isolate and bind the skills cultivated in the classroom, and those applied within the workforce, to disintegrated spaces and experiences. An integrative approach, moving beyond a division between the spaces of learning and work, will revolutionize and inspire creative, engaged teaching and more inspiring, innovative, and entrepreneurial work cultures.

14 THE CORE AND THE ADULT STUDENT

David Schejbal

ABSTRACT

The liberal arts or general education core is an essential part of under-graduate curricula. However, its value and utility are poorly understood both inside and outside the walls of academe. This becomes particularly problematic for institutions that want to attract adult and nontraditional students, because that demographic is far less tolerant of curricular ambiguity than is its traditional-age counterpart. Adult students want to know what they have to do to reach their academic goals, why what they are learning is important and valuable, and how it will help them throughout their lives. These are reasonable demands, and institutions will be well served to address them early, clearly, and often.

THE PREDICTIONS OF DISRUPTION and nationwide enrollment short-ages in higher education are beginning to be felt. Since 2016, a number of small liberal arts colleges have closed,[1] and more closures are likely soon.[2] Public institutions have so far turned to restructuring and merging cam-puses rather than closing campuses outright,[3] but administrators privately admit that campus closures are only a matter of time. In *Demographics and the Demand for Higher Education*, Nathan Grawe predicts a bleak future for colleges and universities, especially in the northeastern and midwest-ern parts of the country, due to demographic shifts and low birth rates exacerbated by the 2007–2009 recession.[4] In some regions, Grawe fore-casts, college enrollments might drop 25 percent or more due to a lack of college-goers aged eighteen to twenty-two.

What Grawe does not address but what Daniel Yankelovich[5], Anthony Carnevale,[6] and others have been discussing for many years is the growing need for higher education among adult and nontraditional students. In 2005, for example, Yankelovich wrote,

> The old pattern of attending college from 18 to 22 and then going directly to a job, career, marriage, child rearing, and "settling down" is evaporating before our eyes. Students are stretching out their higher education. Three-quarters of today's college students are nontraditional in some way—they delay enrollment after high school, attend college part-time, or are considered financially independent. Many are already working, and more than a quarter are parents.[7]

In 2019, the data reflect the changing demographics. Of the 19.9 million students enrolled in US colleges and universities, 38 percent are twenty-five years old or older.[8] Yet, even though the profile of college students is increasingly nontraditional, most institutions continue to serve primarily traditional students. For example, 92 percent of undergraduates at the University of California, Berkeley are under age twenty-five,[9] and at the University of Central Florida, 78 percent of undergraduates are in the same age bracket.[10] Private institutions focus even more on traditional-age undergraduates. For instance, at Tulane University, all but 15 undergraduates out of 7,501 are studying full time,[11] and at Northwestern University, 99.95 percent of freshmen live in university-owned or -operated housing.[12]

A significant portion of nontraditional students are served by community colleges and four-year schools that have built their business models on educating adult students. Southern New Hampshire University, Grand Canyon University, and University of Maryland University College are marquee examples. Online programs have been key to enrollment growth for these institutions, and those schools have become some of the largest universities in the country.

Faced with the specter of declining enrollments, many schools have and continue to develop online programs to try to capture a part of the adult and nontraditional student market. Yet for schools for which the under-twenty-five demographic is the primary market, attracting older students often proves to be difficult and frustrating.

One especially difficult obstacle to overcome is institutional culture. Culture is central to changing market focus, but changing institutional culture is difficult and slow. University faculty and staff like to see themselves as participants in the historic higher education ethos, steeped in the liberal arts, framed by the agrarian calendar, and energized by fall football games. The students who best fit that model are the ones who have time to engage in it: recent high school graduates, eager to learn, green enough to mold, and unencumbered by the weight of later life. Thus, there is a growing gap between the demands of the changing higher education market and the market that most colleges and universities want to serve.

Offering courses and programs in online formats is an important step in addressing the challenges of adult and nontraditional students. Online modalities can overcome barriers of time and place and make it possible for students who work and have family and other responsibilities to engage in postsecondary education. However, changing modality is only one step in addressing the needs of the adult-student market. A far more substantive and difficult change is to augment the curriculum to meet the needs of nontraditional students.

Many professionally oriented graduate programs have overcome curricular biases toward pure research and evolved to include application of knowledge as an essential element of successful program design. Undergraduate programs, however, are slow to make this adaptation.

The challenge begins with the undergraduate general education or liberal arts core.

The Liberal Arts Ideal

The 1998 Association of American Colleges and Universities (AAC&U) "Statement on Liberal Education" summarizes what a liberal education should be:

> A truly liberal education is one that prepares us to live responsible, productive, and creative lives in a dramatically changing world. It is an education that fosters a well-grounded intellectual resilience, a disposition toward lifelong learning, and an acceptance of responsibility for the ethical consequences of our ideas and actions. Liberal education requires that we understand the foundations of knowledge and inquiry about nature, culture, and society; that we master core skills of perception, analysis, and expression; that we cultivate a respect for truth; that we recognize the importance of historical and cultural context; and that we explore connections among formal learning, citizenship, and service to our communities.[13]

Champions of the liberal arts view the depth and breadth of knowledge that the liberal arts provide as fundamental to democratic citizenship and thoughtful human life. Critical thinking and appreciation of knowledge that the liberal arts engender are critical counterweights to the instrumentalist uses of information that drive modern culture. The task of a liberal education, Martha Nussbaum writes, "is to cultivate the humanity of students so that they are capable of relating to other human beings not through economic connections alone, but through a deeper and wider set of human understandings."[14] Hence, incorporating the liberal arts into university curricula elevates the educational experience beyond vocational training and prepares students for wide-ranging life experiences.

"The whole design of the liberal arts system is that courses in the humanities are required of all students, no matter what their major," Nussbuam told *Inside Higher Education.* "Students can major in computer science or engineering, but in such a system they are also required to take general liberal arts courses in history, philosophy and literature. This system has striking advantages, preparing students for their multiple future roles in [a] much more adequate way than a narrow single-subject system."[15]

The Core Curriculum

Nearly all undergraduate curricula include a general education core. For example, at the University of Wisconsin-Madison, students are required to take courses in the natural sciences, humanities, social sciences, communication, ethnic studies, and quantitative reasoning. As defined in Wisconsin's guide for undergraduate students, "[T]his core is intended to provide students with intellectual and practical skills, basic knowledge of human cultures and the physical world, strategies for understanding these topics, and tools intended to contribute to their sense of personal and social responsibility."[16] At Stanford University, the process is similar. Students must take one or more courses in four categories, and the outcome is that students "develop a broad set of essential intellectual and social competencies that will be of enduring value no matter what field [they] eventually pursue."[17] Central Michigan University offers yet another perspective:

> Graduates . . . demonstrate an understanding of the basic forces, ideas, and values that shape the world. They are aware of the structure of

organized human knowledge—the arts and humanities, natural and social sciences. They can organize and access a broad knowledge base relevant to the modern world. They are skilled in working with others, including those of diverse ethnic and cultural backgrounds, and in thinking reflectively about themselves as individuals and as members of society. Graduates value rational inquiry, honesty in scholarship, and life-long learning.[18]

The core is intended to provide students with disciplinary breadth, as well as to support depth in key cognitive skills including critical reasoning and effective communication. Faculty are strongly supportive of these learning outcomes. According to a national survey of college and university faculty, 99.5 percent rate the ability to think critically as either essential or very important, 91.3 percent believe it critical or very important that students be able to write effectively, and 95.7 percent rate the ability to evaluate the quality and reliability of information as essential or very important.[19] Yet few institutions have processes in place to ensure that institutions are really helping students acquire these cognitive skills, and fewer still have ways to evaluate the extent to which students achieve these outcomes.

Part of the problem is that general education or the liberal arts is not a discipline. It is a collection of disciplinary knowledge that in the ideal intersects and dovetails to provide students with multiple ways to learn and apply core cognitive skills. According to Ratcliff, Johnson, and Gaff, however, in practice:

> General education frequently is governed by a revolving cadre of faculty drawn from the various disciplines contributing courses to its requirements. The faculty committee that oversees the general education curriculum, if the institution has one, tends to draw those interested in internal institutional service and those committed to preserving the resources accruing to their department from the general education program. An associate provost, dean, or director frequently administers a program taught by borrowed faculty who seldom, if ever, convene to discuss the aims, organization, and outcomes of general education.[20]

Consequently, many students who go through the liberal arts core do not develop liberal arts competencies.

Frustrations

The disjointedness of the undergraduate core is frustrating to students, parents, and employers because they do not understand the structure or point of the curriculum. At the University of Kentucky, for example, the core curriculum is "based on a comprehensive set of student learning outcomes that all students are expected to be able to demonstrate upon completion of a baccalaureate degree."[21] Kentucky identifies four learning outcomes that define the core:

- Understanding of and ability to employ the processes of intellectual inquiry
- Written, oral, and visual communication skills both as producers and consumers of information
- Understanding of and ability to employ methods of quantitative reasoning
- Understanding of the complexities of citizenship and the process for making informed choices as engaged citizens in a diverse, multilingual world[22]

To master these learning outcomes, students must take one course from ten course areas for a total of thirty credits. The ten course areas are grouped into four sets relating to the learning outcomes above. The first course area under the first learning outcome—understanding of and ability to employ the processes of intellectual inquiry—is the Nature of Inquiry in Arts and Creativity. Courses available in fall 2019 that satisfy this course area include twenty-three courses. Topics range from drawing to engineering to philosophy to science fiction. The course descriptions highlight the tremendous differences among the courses. For example, Arts and Creativity 285, Lens Art, is described as follows:

> An introductory course in digital image making that focuses on the still and moving image as an art practice. Students will learn the fundamentals of camera operation and still and moving image editing software in order to build an individualized portfolio. Students will be introduced to contemporary lens arts practice through research and assignments.[23]

Another course satisfying the same course area in the same learning outcome is Chemical Engineering 455, Chemical Engineering Product and Process Design I. The course description reads as follows:

A lecture and problem-solving course emphasizing process economic evaluation, product design, and process synthesis as they apply to chemical units and systems. Appropriate use of software for simulation and design of chemical systems will also be emphasized.[24]

Courses in some of the remaining ten course areas appear to be more similar—in Composition and Communication, for example—but in others, such as Community, Culture, and Citizenship, the variation is extensive.

It is difficult to see how students master the four learning outcomes listed earlier simply by taking one course in each of the ten course areas. There appears to be no knowledge map, curricular tuning, or other process that would provide students a means to synthesize what they learn in ways that demonstrate applicable mastery of the learning outcomes. In addition, there do not seem to be any connections or intentional transitions among the courses and from course area to course area. Hence, students are left on their own to make meaning from the courses that they take and are likely left wondering about the value of the courses beyond just satisfying requirements for graduation. For adult students who juggle myriad responsibilities beyond school, this lack of coherence and utility would likely be particularly frustrating.

The core curriculum at the University of Kentucky is by no means unique. Core curricula at most universities are structured similarly, with little cohesion or connection among courses.

A Systemic Problem

Higher education is a highly individualist enterprise. Faculty sovereignty over their disciplines is sacrosanct, and each faculty member is considered an expert in his or her own right. Curricular collaboration is rare, especially in the humanities, and university reward models do not prize collaboration. Instead, publishing and research are what motivate most faculty—or, more precisely, how most institutions motivate faculty. As James Ratcliff writes, "It remains true that faculty from all forms of baccalaureate-granting institutions are rewarded more today for research than for teaching; research shows that faculty who publish more receive higher salaries. The research university leads the academic procession, and with it we have the celebration of research."[25]

The humanities have been inculcated into the research paradigm just like all other disciplinary areas. However, depending on how one views the purpose of a university, the research paradigm, especially in the humanities, can be seen as particularly insidious and destructive of the true goals of a liberal education. As Anthony Kronman explains, the goal of the university should be to help students understand their humanness, and the academic leadership and refuge for this goal should be the humanities. This specifically means helping students find and understand the meaning in and of life. Kronman calls this goal secular humanism once it is removed from a religious foundation. Unfortunately, the research ethos of the modern university abandons this holistic and cross-disciplinary quest and replaces it with specialized and segmented, discipline-based inquiry. As Kronman observes:

> The humanities destroyed themselves by abandoning secular humanism in favor of the research ideal. . . . The humanities' embrace of the research ideal compromised their sense of purpose and self-esteem by cutting them off from their connection to the question of what living is for. . . . This damage was not the result of an attack from without. . . . It was a self-destructive response to the crisis of authority that teachers of the humanities brought down on their own heads when they embraced the research ideal and the values associated with it. These values are the real enemy of secular humanism and the cause of its demise. They are the real source of the humanities' crisis of authority.[26]

The Dangers of Specialization

Disciplinary specialization is the hallmark of the research university. Most faculty spend their entire careers striving for greater depth and understanding of their areas of expertise. However, the quest for depth rather than breadth can undermine learning outcomes and the broader goals of a liberal arts education because there is no one to weave the silos of information together into a coherent whole. As a result, many students do not understand the value or usefulness of what they learn and are often unable to assemble the bits and pieces of knowledge they acquire into a comprehensive and applicable worldview.

Although specialization and differentiation of work is a fundamental part of large organizations, it poses risks and challenges that most organizations are ill prepared to address. The downside of job specialization tends to be that people can do only one task. They aren't trained to multitask or handle multiple areas of a workplace. The deeper the specialized knowledge of some members of an organization, the more likely it is that the other members of the organization will not possess the expertise or knowledge necessary to understand their fellow members.[27]

The risk of specialization is that the organization loses sight of its overall interests as the different entities within the organization pursue their own interests or specific tasks. A certain level of specialization is necessary in any organization that requires specific tasks to be performed. However, such specialization becomes an obstacle when specialized knowledge and experience that one person has interferes with understanding matters outside one's own job description. Such specialization narrows one's worldview, creating rigidity and resistance to change.[28]

There is an array of case studies, books, and articles pertaining to the challenges and unintended consequences of specialization.[29] Many case studies focus on disasters in top organizations because disasters are particularly jarring examples of failure.[30] In key cases, disasters occur not because of a lack of skill or knowledge on the part of experts, but because of organizational cultures that do not support holistic approaches to problem solving. As a result, communication breaks down and leadership either loses sight of the big picture or focuses on the wrong things.

Specialization in higher education seldom results in disaster, but it can lead to system failures that are like system failures in other organizations. Scott Snook and Jeffrey Connor reviewed three very difference cases that resulted in systemic failure. In each case, the authors concluded that

> [h]igh levels of differentiation can combine with unanticipated events to create a condition where no one sees the big picture, let alone feels ownership for it. As specialization increases, knowledge and interests become increasingly fragmented, often to the point where multiple organizational actors only see a small piece of the proverbial elephant. And when no one expects one, even an elephant can be difficult to see for what it really is.[31]

In higher education, the proverbial elephant is the undergraduate curriculum, with the greatest obscurity in the liberal arts or general education core. Because the building blocks of the core are courses designed and owned by individual faculty coming from discipline-based structures, the connections across disciplines and between courses and program-level learning outcomes are tenuous and fragmented. Few if any faculty understand the entire core or work to structure it holistically. Instead, they understand their individual parts very well and are reticent to engage in conversations about the curriculum outside of their areas of expertise. University leadership is loath to challenge institutional culture or to act in ways that might be interpreted as violating faculty governance and sovereignty. As a result, students are left on their own to formulate a holistic understanding of what they learn and to master program-level learning outcomes. This is seldom a strategy for student learning success.

The Process of Solving the Problem

Unfortunately, there is no simple solution to the problem. Curricular coherence in the liberal arts core requires joint ownership of the entire curriculum and a willingness to compromise individual academic interests for the larger goal of student learning. Most of the work must fall on the faculty because they are the content experts and the knowledge trust. However, they cannot behave as individual experts confined by the borders of their disciplines. Rather, they must take ownership of their full area of responsibility, the entire core curriculum, and address it jointly and holistically.

There are very good resources to help universities get started. For example, in its Degree Qualifications Profile, Lumina Foundation advocates for curricular tuning based on the European model of degree tuning.[32] A few institutions have embarked on a campus-wide tuning process, so there are examples of the process in practice.[33] Also, the AAC&U, through its Liberal Education and America's Promise (LEAP) initiative, advocates for specific liberal arts learning outcomes and assessments that measure student mastery of those outcomes, and makes available relevant resources and information.[34]

Mapping content and assessments to scaffolded and integrated learning outcomes is difficult and tedious. Changing institutional culture is even harder. Institutions would be well served to engage in a facilitated and sometimes arbitrated process to address core curricular coherence. Most institutions would not have to start from scratch because they have already articulated the learning outcomes for their general education core requirements. The challenge, then, is to embark on a reverse design process in which faculty take program-level learning outcomes and deconstruct them to find their constituent parts. From there, they develop clear and transparent curricular maps that include scaffolded learning outcomes leading directly to the program outcomes specified by the institution. Curricular maps should include lessons, projects, and assessments in all courses within the core curriculum, showing how they lead students to master learning outcomes with clear evidence (authentic assessments) of that mastery.

Rubrics that use courses as the primary curricular building blocks are seldom enough to achieve the level of detail required. Instead, courses should be deconstructed into lessons or modules with assessment-verified outcomes clearly mapped. Those outcomes should then be combined or scaffolded in line with Bloom's taxonomy, with increasing levels of complexity until they reach the program-level outcomes stipulated by the institution. Along every step, learning outcomes should be verifiable and measurable so that it is clear when students master them. This is also the critical step in conveying value. When students ask what this knowledge is good for, institutions should have good answers. Furthermore, when employers ask why they should believe that an institution does a good job at educating, the institution should have a well-constructed, evidence-based response.

The Adult Student Dilemma

Undergraduate curricula are designed for students who fit the traditional college profile: young, recently out of high school, and in need of formative learning experiences. However, most nontraditional undergraduate students, especially those studying online, have prior college experience and are well past the formative stages of their intellectual development. According to *U.S. News & World Report*, the average age of students in online bachelor's programs is thirty-two, and 84 percent are employed.[35] While many adult students need to acquire disciplinary knowledge and liberal arts competencies, their needs are more outcomes oriented and summative than their traditional-age counterparts. That may be one reason why Chris Dede argues, in another chapter in this book, for the need for higher education to show adult learners how to "unlearn" entrenched practices as a fundamental part of life-long learning. In another chapter, Yakut Gazi and Nelson Baker also discuss the need for "unlearning" and "relearning" in the context of ongoing professional development.

Institutions interested in attracting and retaining adult students in undergraduate programs should review their undergraduate curricula and the role of the liberal arts core therein to ensure that students understand the logic, structure, and relevance of what they are being asked to learn. Institutions should also find ways to incorporate students' prior knowledge into the curriculum when that prior learning demonstrates mastery of learning outcomes. That is not to say that the liberal arts core should be reduced or diluted for adult students. However, adult students who have already gone through many of the formative experiences needed to demonstrate mastery of core outcomes should be able to incorporate those into their summative assessments without having to undergo the formative process anew. Furthermore, because adult students are highly conscious of time constraints and costs, the structure, outcomes, and value of the curriculum should be clear, evident, and well communicated. After all, the contract between a student and a college is one that exchanges time and money for knowledge, and adult students are hyperaware of the value of all three.

Undergraduate curricula for adult students should address the differences between traditional and nontraditional students from the beginning. Most adult students say their primary motivation for pursuing a degree is to improve their career prospects.[36] That does not mean that universities should convert their undergraduate programs to vocational training, but it does mean that universities should make concerted efforts to connect curricular knowledge to applications beyond academe. For example, students should not have to wonder why they must satisfy general education requirements. Instead, the value of the general education or liberal arts core should be clearly explained to students upfront, including how the knowledge gained is useful in everyday life. A particularly effective means to achieve this end is to have clear curriculum maps, highlighting competencies, and delineating how assessments verify student mastery of requisite knowledge.

The Bottom Line

The liberal arts or general education core is an essential part of undergraduate curricula. However, its value and utility are poorly understood both inside and outside the walls of academe. This becomes particularly problematic for institutions that want to attract adult and nontraditional students, because that demographic is far less tolerant of curricular ambiguity than is its traditional-age counterpart. Adult students want to know what they have to do to reach their academic goals, why what they are learning is important and valuable, and how it will help them throughout their lives. These are reasonable demands, and institutions will be well served to address them early, clearly, and often.

15 PERPETUAL LEARNING AS ALUMNI ENGAGEMENT

Renewing the Social Contract

Matthew Rascoff and James DeVaney

ABSTRACT

Institutions like Duke University and the University of Michigan are rethinking their alumni learning strategies. New models are emerging to engage learners throughout their lives and to support learning communities to address the problems that matter most to individuals and society. What opportunities should institutions consider for this century, given our changing economy and the affordances of rapidly accelerating technology? This chapter explores the strategic considerations of supporting learners in the twenty-first century and the unique role of colleges and universities—as distinct from those played by employers, government agencies, and individuals. Universities have the capacity to invest in the lifelong success of their alumni, regardless of their particular pursuits. They have long provided access to expertise and trusted alumni networks, which can now be married with learning platforms that scale. The result is a new set of opportunities to reconfigure alumni networks for the benefit of universities and the societies they serve.

A NEW WORLD OF WORK has arrived and with it challenges and opportunities to rethink how learning works for individuals and communities. Universities have an opportunity to craft a new social contract with alumni that includes a clause for perpetual learning. A modern system of perpetual learning will engage alumni in the development of learning experiences at every stage of life and career.

Engaging alumni as learners through digital platforms is an innovative development in higher education. At institutions like Duke University and the University of Michigan it is part of a broader rethinking of the university's relationship with alumni—how the institution engages them, invests in their lifelong success, and empowers them to make change for the better.

Higher education institutions must avoid simply providing more educational opportunities to those who already have them. At our institutions, we are asking: In the twenty-first century, how can we empower alumni to make a positive impact?

We must activate alumni as partners in expanding the global classroom to benefit the academic and alumni communities—and our broader society. We must call upon purpose-driven alumni to contribute to a learning commons that begins with the university but extends beyond it. To achieve this, universities should build networks that provide multiple ways for alumni to contribute as creators, curators, and community builders.

Universities have long provided alumni with access to expertise and networks. With new digital platforms we can now help alumni access and contribute to learning throughout their lives and careers. Universities that invest in the long arc of knowledge creation, dissemination, and human development will position themselves as essential institutions to meet the evolving needs of society.

Framing the Need

Academic institutions rely on philanthropy to complement tuition and government funding. Alumni giving makes up approximately one quarter of the philanthropic support for US higher education.[1] But recent trends show a decline in the participation of alumni in higher education philanthropy. A recent analysis by the Council for Aid to Education showed that "in 1990, 18 percent of college and university alumni gave to their alma mater. . . . By 2013, that number had been cut in half to less than 9 percent—a record low and a culmination of a trend that has persisted for more than two decades."[2] While absolute dollars given are still rising, lower participation rates are a worrying indicator of the declining health of the relationship between institutions and their alumni communities.

To reverse this trend, universities must provide a recurring source of value beyond athletics, reunions, and legacy admissions. Alumni engagement needs to shift to a source of renewable intellectual energy: a system of perpetual learning.

The need for such a system is clear:

- Even the most valuable STEM skills have short half-lives. Recent research has shown that "the initially high economic return to applied STEM degrees declines by more than 50 percent in the first decade of working life." As skills grow stale more quickly, graduates will need to develop new ones more frequently.[3]
- At the macro level, the globalization and automation that have disrupted many legacy industries will likely affect more in the future—including professions that have previously been insulated from significant transformations.
- At the micro level, increasing entrepreneurial disruptions of established firms and sectors will lead to more instability and insecurity. There is a growing need for human adaptation in response to change.

It is by now a truism that graduates will switch jobs and careers more frequently. People already need resilience and nimbleness to pivot professionally and personally at multiple stages of life. To be successful in those pivots, alumni need new kinds of support and learning opportunities.

Too often, graduates view their relationship with their alma mater as shaped around a single, albeit foundational, exchange. Institutions can exacerbate this backward-looking perspective through excessive nostalgia and emphasis on fond memories of the alma mater. But we are currently facing an opportunity to better understand and meet the lifelong and "lifewide" needs of alumni through a relational and communal approach to learning. This moves beyond the transactional and shifts the emphasis to the future.

The Limits of Learning at Work

Industry brings a set of constraints on its ability to build a system of perpetual learning. Given the short-term expectations that often drive corporate decision-making and management practices, employers' interests in supporting professional development often emphasize immediate productivity and current demands for skills. Firms are not generally able to invest in human capital with the long horizons of mission-driven providers. In other chapters in this book, Chris Dede and coauthors Yakut Gazi and Nelson Baker discuss another challenge common to ongoing professional development of adults in the workforce: the need to help adult learners how to "unlearn" entrenched practices.

Similarly, regional workforce development strategies are tied to a particular geography and measure success based on their ability to grow regional skills. Without question, those motivations are important and such approaches have their merits. These approaches are appropriate for programs that are funded with local and state taxes. But they are nonetheless conditioned on—and limited by—where a learner works and lives.

Still another consideration is the rise of the gig economy. As freelancers make up more of the professional workforce, many do not have access to corporate training. Freelancers' professional development is largely in their own hands.

Within those contexts, key questions emerge for academic leaders. What role should colleges and universities play in building and providing this system of learning? How are universities positioned, relative to other educational providers, to offer something differentiated to alumni and the wider community? What is their comparative advantage relative to corporate learning and development departments, bootcamps, and other alternative providers?

The Role of Higher Education

At one level, engaging alumni through learning seems straightforward. Alumni already associate academic institutions with education. There is a continuity with the existing way alumni think about the academy. But that belies a deeper reason why universities are well positioned to invest in alumni learning.

Universities are invested in the lifelong success of alumni in ways that are different from other learning providers. Universities take a long view of professional and personal success and lead with ethical frameworks and human skills that stand the test of time while weaving in opportunities to acquire important just-in-time skills. The college president's calculation is different from the CEO's or mayor's: *We invested in you as a student. We now hope to engage you in a mutual value exchange where you provide intellectual energy to fuel a dynamic network and we continue to provide flexible, affordable, and relevant learning experiences to position you for long-term flexibility and success.*

Many corporate tuition reimbursement and professional development programs require employees to demonstrate how the choices they've made, and the lessons they've learned, apply to their current job. But how do you support the employee learner looking for a change? How can employee learners benefit from learning opportunities that stretch beyond competencies and skills tied explicitly to their current position? That gap can be filled with a higher education–led system of perpetual learning that harmonizes opportunities to obtain and apply human and technical skills.

Colleges and universities have a unique relationship with alumni that is different from the relationships they have with their employers or other learning providers. They already have distributed alumni networks and are not regionally bound in the way that local government agencies or community-based organizations might be. Municipalities are not able to invest in human capital with the geographic agnosticism of national and global institutions.

What makes higher education different is not just the relationship that institutions have with their communities, including alumni. It is also about their values and approaches. Relative to other educational providers, universities have comparative expertise when it comes to designing evidence-based learning experiences. University curricula invest in combinations of breadth and depth of options to meet learner needs at multiple levels. And they are motivated to support diverse, equitable, and inclusive learning communities that provide unequaled opportunities to understand a relevant set of problems and acquire new skills. Universities are uniquely positioned to support perpetual learning.

New Models

We are proposing to build on the past work that universities have done to engage alumni in learning and to ally with alumni associations and support their efforts.

Certain kinds of learning lend themselves to the system of perpetual learning we envision. It is not necessarily appropriate for all topics and all knowledge areas. The highest value learning experiences that institutions can offer their alumni are those that support life and career pivots.

Examples of such pivots include transitioning back to the workforce after having children, managing professional burnout and personal well-being, shifting employment from one industry to another, and managing retirement. What these themes have in common is that they are moments when alumni can benefit from the unique advantages that universities have as providers of perpetual learning—specifically, *expertise* and *networks*.

Expertise means universities can help alumni understand the frameworks of a new field. It means helping alumni identify their personal blind spots and learn the things they didn't know they needed to learn. That cannot happen in a purely consumer model, where people learn precisely the things that they search and click on. There is a level of ignorance that everyone has as a novice in a field that requires expert guidance in order to understand the contours of that field. That expertise can come from the faculty or combinations of faculty and practitioners.

The University of Michigan's Center for Academic Innovation developed a just-in-time approach to sharing expert frameworks from faculty in response to current events. The Teach-Out Series brings together people from around the world to learn about, discuss, and address important topics in society. Teach-Outs are global community learning events designed in response to a growing need for new modes of teaching, learning, and connecting in an increasingly digital society. They represent an important effort to reimagine how universities can engage with the global public and create engaged learning experiences with diverse learners.

Teach-Outs connect scholars with engaged citizens and bridge the gap between digital and physical communities. For alumni learners, Teach Outs provide an opportunity to engage with a geographically distributed network of University of Michigan learners at any time. They offer scale and multidirectional interaction around topics of widespread interest. Alumni can access expert frameworks through live events and archived content made available through Michigan Online. They can also leverage the flexible learning design of Teach-Outs to share their own expertise with other Teach-Out participants.

Michigan is building these learning experiences organically, for diverse communities to engage, level-up their understanding, and help each other to see new opportunities for positive impact. Recent examples include Teach-Outs on the opioid crisis, gun violence, free speech, self-driving cars, hurricanes, gerrymandering, and many more topics.

Through the Teach-Out model, a digital era response to the Teach-Ins that originated at the University of Michigan in the 1960s, global problem-solving communities form quickly. They are interdisciplinary, intergenerational, and interprofessional. The result is multidirectional engagement, communities forming and learning from each other, and elevated public discourse. Alumni and other learners can access these free learning experiences as live events and also utilize the content and resources to facilitate further learning in their own personal and professional communities.

After launching the new model in 2017, the University of Michigan created a Teach-Out Academy and invited other institutions to adopt and improve upon the Teach-Out approach. Notre Dame University, the University of Leiden, and Emory University have already launched Teach-Outs of their own; and many other institutions are exploring Teach-Outs to provide perpetual learning opportunities to their communities. Participants are learning with and from each other, counteracting digital polarization, and engaging around topics of societal significance.

Networks complement the kind of expertise that faculty can offer. They allow people initiating a life pivot to recognize that they are not on their own and that others have made similar changes. Well-managed networks inform choices with data and connect people with others who are willing to help. Online tools have made global networking more manageable. Universities need not be confined to place-based events to build and strengthen alumni networks. We can support alumni networking needs globally with tools like PeopleGrove, Slack, LinkedIn, Zoom, and other resources.

Duke University recently developed an alumni-learning experience that demonstrates the potential of this paradigm. Launched in fall 2019, Intentional Life Design for Physicians: Tools to Recover Your Calling is a five-week course for working physicians and physician leaders to empower them to improve how they experience their work. The course is based on an evidence-based cognitive-behavior-therapy approach that has been shown in peer-reviewed research to reduce burnout and increase work satisfaction.

Although there are many classes and resources about managing burnout through strategies like relaxation techniques, this course takes a different approach. Using a coaching framework as a guide, physicians examine the gap between where they are and where they want to be in life. Through on-demand short lectures, case studies, live video discussions on Zoom, and exercises (created with physicians' schedules and needs in mind), participants develop skills for responding differently to the challenges of practicing modern medicine. They use proven tools to candidly assess how they currently experience their work, learn response skills for managing stressors and road blocks on the job, reconnect with what makes practicing medicine meaningful, identify specific steps to make meaningful change, and create a personalized action plan that aligns with their values.

A 2019 pilot of the course with the alumni community served as a springboard to a wider rollout beyond Duke alumni to other physicians. Our hope is that initial alumni participants can become discussion leaders to help extend the impact of the course to the wider medical community.

Imagining a New Social Contract with Alumni

Colleges and universities now have the chance to support alumni through life and career pivots by combining infusions of expert frameworks with trusted communities of learners. Reinvigorated by a new social contract, alumni are activated and, when networked, provide a powerful source of renewable intellectual energy. There is an opportunity to scale the best forms of alumni learning and engagement to be more global, accessible, and inclusive. As campus communities become more diverse across all dimensions, colleges and universities must anticipate and adapt to the needs of these individuals and communities as alumni.

In consideration of the unique missions and strengths of higher education institutions, and the evolving needs of alumni learners, a new social contract should include the following:

- A commitment to research and development to anticipate the evolving needs of alumni learners
- Access to expert frameworks and applied learning experiences
- Access to a trusted community of learners and opportunities to activate those communities
- Opportunities to engage as creators, curators, community builders, and learners
- A commitment to flexibility, affordability, and relevance

Colleges and universities plan for the perpetual time horizon. They are able to build a system of perpetual learning that others cannot. From an institutional perspective, developing perpetual learning models requires new partnerships within and beyond campuses. Universities need to embrace new methods of instruction unbound from the credit-hour and connected more clearly to just-in-time, applied, and relevant learning opportunities. From a learner perspective, alumni learning opportunities are an invitation to remain part of the learning community beyond the degree and to treat graduation as a true commencement of a life of learning and sharing of knowledge.

Realizing the perpetual learning vision would be good for students. It would take the pressure off students to learn everything, and do everything, during their relatively compressed years on campus. That might reduce skills anxiety ("I need to major in CS") and "FOMO" (fear of missing out) by reassuring them that joining a college or university community is the beginning—not the end—of their learning journey. Indeed, some kinds of learning, such as courses in leadership, might best be offered just in time, later in life, when alumni step into leadership roles.

Everyone is going to need support from institutions as disruptions become more frequent and economic and social life become more volatile. Society needs strategies to help people build resilience and thrive. By providing access to expertise and networked learning communities, higher education is uniquely positioned to be the source of lifelong educational support.

PART III

BRIDGING THE GAP BETWEEN LEARNING AND LABOR

WHILE THE HIGHER EDUCATION SECTOR plays a significant role in preparing students for the workforce, there are persistent gaps in the training and preparation that employers would like their workers to have, which was addressed in Part I, and what higher education delivers, addressed in Part II. Part III explores an array of solutions to address this gap by presenting the insights of actors in the nonprofit, policy, and foundation spaces that actively work to bridge the gap between higher education and employers. Bell-Rose and Ollen of TIAA address the importance of a diverse talent pool and issue a call for higher education and employers to work collaboratively to achieve a diversity of people and skills. Wiener from the Aspen Institute argues that attention must be paid to secondary education to improve the alignment of skills and knowledge developed in high school so that students are fully prepared for the higher education experience. Zhu, Alonso, and Taylor present research by the Society for Human Resource Management that illuminates reasons for workers' resistance to technological change and deliver recommendations for how higher education and industry can work together to surmount the barriers in training workers for the ever-evolving workplace. The chapters by McCarthy at New America and Kuehn at the Urban Institute each examine the value of apprenticeships as a training model for the future workforce. McCarthy investigates the opportunities and challenges for higher education to engage in the apprenticeship model as a way to better meet the needs of students and employers. Kuehn dives specifically into STEM apprenticeships in his examination of a system of registered apprenticeships that prepare students for STEM careers typically requiring a bachelor's degree. Tyszko and Sheets discuss the need for improved information flows between businesses and higher education partners about the competencies needed in the workplace. They describe the US Chamber Foundation's Job Data Exchange system as a step toward improving the communication of standards for competencies and credentials across sectors. Similarly, the chapter by Fitzgerald, Cardenas-Navia, and Chen discusses the Business–Higher Education Forum's experiences developing cross-sector partnerships to equip students to enter the workforce with digital technology skills. Finally, the chapter by Srinivasan, Henson, and Asghar from the Carnegie Corporation of New York calls for collaboration that engages government, education, philanthropy, and the business sector in creating a coherent system that prepares students for life, work, and citizenship.

INTRODUCTION

Lauren Weber

IN THE FALL OF 2019, I came across an astounding number. There are an estimated 738,000 credentials offered to students and workers in the United States, a number that includes everything from coding bootcamp certificates to doctoral degrees from research universities to microbadges earned by taking a thirty-minute course about PowerPoint from LinkedIn Learning.

We're awash in learning opportunities. Yet how many of those credentials have educational or labor-market value? How many are recognized by hiring managers deciding on workers' professional and economic futures? We don't know.

That's the conclusion of Arne Duncan, secretary of education under President Barack Obama, and Jeb Bush, former governor of Florida. "What we still don't know is whether we have enough—or too many—credentialing programs for a country of our size or if we have the right mix of programs to meet employer needs across the country," they wrote in the foreword to a report from Credential Engine, the nonprofit organization that produced the above-mentioned estimate and is building a database to bring some transparency to the credential marketplace.

And here's the real puzzle: despite an explosion of learning opportunities, employers still report that they struggle to find qualified workers and that the candidates they see frequently lack technical skills, soft skills, or both. This is commonly known as the skills gap.

The good news is that there is lots of innovation. Some of it challenges the dominance of traditional educational institutions, by offering credentials that are job focused or that reject the paradigm of classroom-based learning defined by taking a fixed number of classes or spending a certain amount of time on a degree. Some efforts are focused on getting companies to look past degrees altogether and instead hire for competencies and skills that can be attained in a variety of ways.

Indeed, pushing more young people toward college cannot be the only solution. We're already seeing higher rates of college attendance and graduation than at any other time in history. Bureau of Labor Statistics data show that, in 2017, 45 percent of people between the ages of twenty-five and thirty-six had a bachelor's degree, compared with 35 percent for all workers over age thirty-seven. At the same time, the demand for college degrees is driving student debt to unsustainable levels. We can't keep pushing people to get bachelor's degrees when a diminishing share will earn the kind of income that makes it possible to establish a quality living standard and pay back five- or six-figure loans at the same time.

Fortunately, there are lots of examples of effective, employment-oriented training, often created as partnerships among employers, education providers, and, in some cases, nonprofit groups that act as intermediaries. In this part, you'll read about a number of these programs. In my reporting, I've come across others. Workforce Opportunity Services, begun by Columbia University professor Art Langer in 2005, provides training through universities, job placement, and social services to its students, many of whom are veterans or young people who might otherwise have fallen through the cracks of an education system that still sorts people according to class and race. Employers like Prudential and General Electric get access to workers trained in the specialized skills they require, often in hard-to-staff information technology jobs.

In San Antonio, Texas, a group called Project Quest offers intensive coaching and helps pay participants' tuition for community college classes leading to credentials that are in high demand. An independent analysis that examined nine years of data found that graduates earned an average of $5,000 more per year than people who didn't participate.

At the moment, these efforts are fragmented and difficult to scale, and they generally serve people with the luck to live near a major employer or organization that's investing in these opportunities. And although employer demand for such programs is high as I write this at the end of 2019, with unemployment at a historically low 3.6 percent, we don't know yet if employers will continue these efforts even when the economy falters and workers become more plentiful.

Skills don't just matter for people entering the workforce for the first time. If there's anything this fourth industrial revolution—the digital age—is teaching us, it is that skills get stale quickly, every occupation is evolving to incorporate technology, the technology itself is evolving fast, and the demands of jobs are changing. Marketing professionals once concerned themselves with ad design and distributing campaigns across a few media; today's marketers must understand data science, produce and read complex reports, and grasp algorithms that determine how many eyeballs see a particular ad or campaign across thousands of websites and other media.

Workers will need to reinvent themselves multiple times, and they'll need guidance and support from employers, government programs, and more. Lifelong learning has become a cliché, but it is an imperative. "You have to constantly upgrade your skills and find new ways of doing things," Barack Obama said back in 2011.

Which brings me back to the 738,000 credentials. Content isn't enough. Even content plus access isn't enough. What I fear we're missing amidst all the innovation is tools that will help individuals make sense of the many education options now available to them. "We're asking people to negotiate an increasingly complicated labor market on their own," says Andy Van Kleunen, the CEO of the National Skills Coalition, which advocates for better job training.

I think often about a former FedEx driver I once interviewed. He'd never made much money, in part because FedEx outsources ground delivery to small firms or independent contractors, which cuts costs to FedEx and transfers risk and costs to the drivers. He'd tried a few other professions too, including advertising sales; nothing stuck. While working for a delivery company in Austin, Texas, in the 2010s, he saw firsthand the growth in e-commerce as he delivered a growing load of packages from Amazon, Walmart, and Target, and others.

"I was reading the signals every day," he said. He decided to learn about digital marketing, hoping he could combine his background in customer service and delivery with tech-based marketing.

He did what policymakers want workers to do—think about technology and the demand for skills, and make informed choices about their careers. But here's what worries me: Jeremy, the driver, googled "digital marketing course," clicked on the first few results, and signed up for a $1,000 online class without gathering any objective information about the outcomes for people who had taken the same course.

Several months after completing it, he'd filled out multiple applications for marketing jobs and been on a couple of interviews, but hadn't yet found a position.

If workers are exhorted to take control of their careers and become lifelong learners, they need tools to help them figure out the investments of time and money that make the most sense for them.

"There are thousands of credentials and programs but very little in the way of pathway navigation," says Hamoon Ekhtiari, an entrepreneur who founded FutureFit.ai, a platform that uses data and artificial intelligence to help individuals and companies make smart choices about skills and career pathways.

Matt Sigelman, the chief executive of labor-market analytics firm Burning Glass Technologies, once said, "Why isn't there a Waze for your career?" He was referring to the navigation app that tells you how to get from Point A to Point B.

We need a system of career advising that's accessible, comprehensive, and, most likely, heavily reliant on technology. Where do people currently get advice on career and education decisions? From a patchwork of friends, family members, coworkers, high school guidance counselors, and maybe career counseling offices at colleges. None of those people will have the breadth of information to help a person who wants a career in cybersecurity decide between a three-month bootcamp, an associate degree, a master's degree, an apprenticeship, or teaching themselves hacking skills online in their spare time.

There is so much data available now—everything from LinkedIn profiles to occupational projections from the Bureau of Labor Statistics to consumer sentiment analysis that predicts economic demand. If we integrate that data, we can give people critical information to help them make good decisions about their lives and their livelihoods.

Individuals will have to be flexible and adaptable, too. Not long ago I spoke with the chief executive of a company that makes learning management software for employers. His firm had 500 engineers designing and coding products. But enterprise customers were demanding mobile versions of the software because their employees wanted to access content and services on the go.

This CEO's internal training team created a six-week class on mobile app design. They offered the class to all 500 engineers, telling them that the training was free and they'd be earning their regular salary while learning. And if they completed the course and demonstrated proficiency, they'd be hired into mobile-app jobs with a pay increase and more marketable skills, should they ever decide to take their talents elsewhere.

Twenty people accepted the offer.

We have more work to do in convincing people who have already invested in learning one set of skills that they have to remain relevant or risk falling behind. It's a mindset change. As Todd Tauber, an executive at online learning platform Degreed, once told me, "The idea that skills go obsolete is probably exaggerated but the idea that skills evolve is real." The shift from programming for computers to programming for mobile phones is an apt illustration.

That imperative is more challenging for the millions of Americans who freelance, temp, or work in the poorly understood gig economy and contingent workforce, and lack the institutional support that often goes along with a traditional job.

"If you're not in a regular office five days a week, it's a challenge to keep up as things change," Dean Case, a public relations consultant, told me in 2018. When he worked at Ford Motor Company earlier in his career, he said, employees were required to update their skills, and they did so on the company's time and dime. "It's really a challenge when you're freelance because, well, those are hours I can't bill anyone. It's not like Ford saying we're going to dedicate two weeks of your time a year to staying fresh."

Other countries understand this better than we in the United States do. Politicians spend a lot of time talking about training, but US workers receive relatively little career education. A White House report in 2018 showed that nearly all spending, public and private, on education and training occurs before a person turns twenty-five—essentially while they're in formal school. The United States ranked second-to-last among twenty-nine developed nations in terms of taxpayer-funded training investment, according to the Organisation for Economic Co-operation and Development, and has shown little interest in experimentation.

Other countries are more proactive: Singapore and France give workers an annual allowance for approved career training. Through a program called Second Career in Ontario, Canada, low-skilled workers displaced from their jobs receive grants of up to 28,000 Canadian dollars to cover training in growing occupations, along with costs such as child care and transportation.

We can learn from the experiments our global peers and neighbors are undertaking. With a combination of technology, ambition, and respect for the central role that work plays in people's lives and identities, we can create a talent pipeline that serves workers, employers, and the broader good.

16 HARNESSING THE POWER AND POTENTIAL OF DIVERSITY AND INCLUSION

Stephanie Bell-Rose and Anne Ollen

ABSTRACT

Employers and higher education institutions share concern for generating a pipeline of diverse talent with the skills and training necessary to have successful careers, participate in civic life, and contribute to business success and innovation. As the US population grows in diversity and our global interactions increase, developing diverse talent and cultural competence will become even more important in the future of work. Tomorrow's workers need to understand and be equipped to respond appropriately to the needs and interests expressed by racial minorities, women, different age cohorts, the disabled, veterans, religious groups, and other groups comprising an expanding gender and sexual orientation spectrum. Employers and institutions can and must help create environments that nurture and value an understanding and appreciation of differences, and in which all can achieve their potential.

BY 2044, the United States is expected to be a "majority minority nation," meaning no single ethnic or racial group will make up a majority of the population.[1] In the meantime, powerful social movements are raising the visibility and voices of minorities, women, the disabled, veterans, religious groups, and other cohorts comprising an expanding gender and sexual orientation spectrum. Age diversity, too, is more prominent in society today than in times past: in 2020, five generations are expected to be coexisting in the workplace.[2] Each generation has different traits, goals, life influences, and communication preferences. Today's student body, too, represents a vast array of backgrounds, values, and beliefs—and presents challenges for colleges and universities and employers striving to meet the changing needs of students and the next generation of workers.[3]

What does all this portend for the workforce of the future? And what does it mean for colleges and universities preparing today's students for tomorrow's workforce?

First, employers and institutions can help create environments that nurture and value an understanding and appreciation of differences, and in which all can achieve their potential. This chapter addresses the linkages among campus diversity and inclusion efforts, student workplace preparedness, and leadership's role in facilitating positive change.

Student Diversity and Academic Success

As the demand for highly educated and highly skilled workers increases, so too does the urgency to improve the degree-completion rates of marginalized student populations. Approximately 42 percent of US college students come from communities of color, 18 percent are nonnative English speakers, and 52 percent are the first in their families to attend college.[4] Those percentages are on the rise. However, increasing student diversity has exposed persistent disparities in higher education enrollment, degree attainment, hiring, and career advancement for communities of color.

Overall college enrollment among eighteen- to twenty-four-year-olds was 40 percent in 2017, but enrollment rates across groups vary widely (Figure 16.1). Enrollment rates for Asians, at 65 percent, are highest. Rates for Asians, Hispanics,[5] and individuals reporting being of two or more races have risen consistently over the time periods shown. In 2017, Hispanic and Black enrollment rates were even, at 36 percent, although that represents a decline for Blacks since 2010.

Figures 16.2 and 16.3 illustrate racial gaps in college enrollment rates by state, by comparing the number of Black (Figure 16.2) and Latino (Figure 16.3) high school graduates with the number who enroll in their state's flagship public university.[6]

The Education Trust recently released in-depth research about enrollment gaps for Latinos and notes emphatically in its report, *Broken Mirrors II: Latino Student Representation in Public State Colleges and Universities*, "If our public colleges and universities are to be true democratic engines of opportunity and upward mobility, then their student bodies and their graduates should mirror the state's demographics."[7]

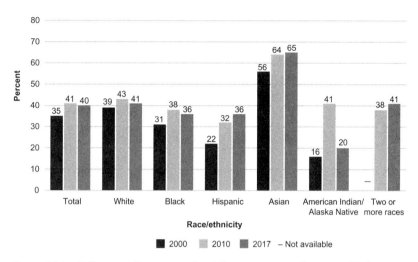

Figure 16.1   College enrollment rates for eighteen to twenty-four-year-olds by race and ethnicity

SOURCE: U.S. Department of Commerce Census Bureau, Current Population Survey (CPS), October Supplement, 2000, 2010, and 2017. See Digest of Education Statistics 2018, table 302.60.

NOTE: Data are based on sample surveys of the civilian noninstitutionalized population. Separate data for young adults who were of two or more races were not available in 2000; data for individual race categories in 2000 includes persons of two or more races.

Figure 16.4 shows the six-year outcomes for students who first entered college in fall 2012. Asian students had the highest completion rate, at 70 percent, followed by White students at 68 percent. Hispanic, American Indian/Alaskan Native, and Black students had far lower completion rates, at 50 percent, 44 percent, and 41 percent, respectively.[8]

Moving the Needle

To improve persistence and completion rates of diverse and underrepresented students, many colleges and universities are nurturing more equitable and inclusive student environments. Meaningful advances to this end have emerged, and numerous efforts have been undertaken to understand and address existing obstacles that thwart more rapid and significant progress.[9] In its 2017 report, the Commission on the Future of Undergraduate Education, cochaired by Michael McPherson, president emeritus of the Spencer Foundation, and Roger W. Ferguson, TIAA chairman and CEO, addressed several key issues in its recommendations focused on serving an increasingly diverse student body:

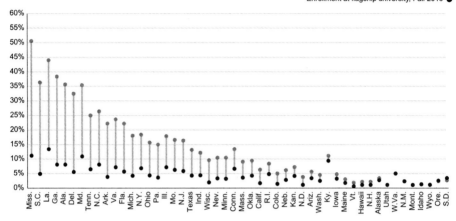

High school graduates in state, Spring 2016 ◐
Enrollment at flagship university, Fall 2016 ●

Figure 16.2 High school graduates and flagship university enrollment by state: Blacks

SOURCES: National Center for Education Statistics, ED Data Express. Analysis courtesy of The Hechinger Report, a nonprofit news outlet focused on inequality and innovation in education.

NOTE: Flagship enrollment rates include only first-time, degree-seeking undergraduate students.

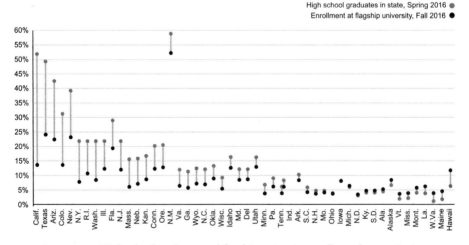

High school graduates in state, Spring 2016 ◐
Enrollment at flagship university, Fall 2016 ●

Figure 16.3 High school graduates and flagship university enrollment by state: Latinos

SOURCES: National Center for Education Statistics, ED Data Express. Analysis courtesy of The Hechinger Report, a nonprofit news outlet focused on inequality and innovation in education.

NOTE: Flagship enrollment rates include only first-time, degree-seeking undergraduate students.

- Faculty and staff need training and support to make possible campus cultures and classes that fully encourage and sustain active listening, discussion, and debate on critical issues of the day, informed by the rigors of reason and evidence. Colleges and universities collectively and individually comprise perhaps the most important sites where people from various backgrounds and perspectives interact, learn with and from one another, and gain healthy awareness of differences.
- Online courses and other technology-based teaching innovations may facilitate increased access, flexibility, and learning opportunities for students. But technology is only part of the answer. In general, and especially for lower-income and first-generation college students, there is evidence that existing technology and how it is being used cannot simply serve as a substitute for in-person instruction. Much more analysis is needed to create the best teaching models that combine "high-tech/high-touch" approaches.
- Faculty from a diversity of backgrounds should be equitably represented across higher education institutions and disciplines. There is growing evidence that when students see themselves reflected in the make-up of their university's faculty, they are motivated to reach for and actually do achieve higher standards of performance.[10]

Figure 16.5 shows the racial breakdown of the faculty who teach at US four-year colleges and universities, along with their gender, age, and contract status.

Nearly 70 percent of faculty are White, and more than half are men. Digging deeper reveals similar patterns. For example, 73 percent of faculty that are tenured or tenure-track are White, and 60 percent are men.

Clearly, colleges and universities must move beyond simply nurturing an inclusive environment to taking steps to actively uncover and address the needs of diverse students. Indeed, higher education institutions have become increasingly responsive to diverse students' needs, interests, and cultural backgrounds in their approaches to hiring and developing courses, curricula, pedagogies, assessment practices, and campus cultures that engage all students in high-quality learning experiences, and that ensure all members of the student population feel valued and respected. That said, there is more work to be done.

Higher education can fill a crucial role in advancing diversity, equity, and inclusion, not just on campus, but well beyond, as graduates participate in

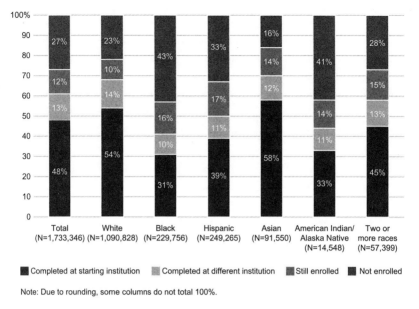

Figure 16.4 Six-year outcomes by race and ethnicity for students entering Fall 2012

SOURCE: Figure was created using the data from Shapiro, D. et al. (2018), *Completing College: A National View of Student Completion Rates* (Signature Report No. 16), Herndon, VA: National Student Clearinghouse Research Center.

the workforce. Patricia McGuire, president of Trinity Washington University and recipient of the 2016 TIAA Institute Theodore M. Hesburgh Award for Leadership Excellence in Higher Education, eloquently captured that in her Hesburgh Lecture, focusing on value derived from a college education in areas such as critical thinking, persuasive communication, insightful judgment, and cultural competence. It is these traits, she said, that liberate students from inchoate fear, prejudice, and the sense of powerlessness that often accompanies social change. McGuire elaborated:

> Economics in terms of the return on investment for a college degree may certainly be a legitimate part of the value proposition, but ROI [return on investment] stated only in monetary terms cannot be allowed to obscure the critical importance and vitality of other civic, social, and moral values, such as the development of deep cultural competence in our students, profound respect for human beings in all of our diverse glory, and enlargement of global perspectives as the best antidote to myopic nationalism that builds walls rather than opening opportunities for international solidarity

on the great issues of human civilization: peace building, relief of poverty, educational opportunities especially for girls and women who are so often denied essential literacy skills around the world, eradication of disease, solutions for climate change, and understanding that a commitment to peace and justice is not mere political correctness but truly essential for the future of the global village.[11]

Elsewhere in this book, several authors share other insights on how to achieve diversity. Amrit Ray and colleagues discuss diversity as a prerequisite for successful performance by global corporations. Similarly, Mike Ulica advocates for diversity in the context of understanding global cultures.

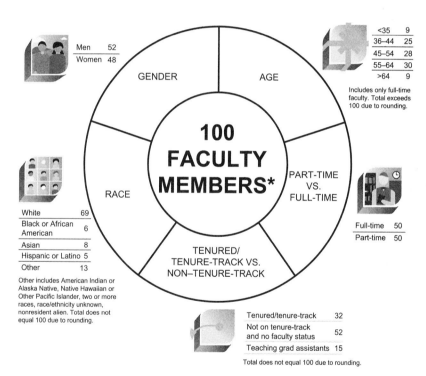

Figure 16.5   What would 100 faculty members look like at a US college?

SOURCE: TIAA Institute based on data from IPEDS (National Center for Education Statistics) and the Higher Education Research Institute.

*Faculty includes teachers with faculty status—tenured, tenure-track, and nontenure-track—as well as instructional staff and graduate assistants who teach at U.S. four-year colleges and universities.

Preparing for and Developing a Diverse Workforce

Today's college students need to be prepared to join a global workforce where they will be expected to work and collaborate with individuals from different countries, cultures, backgrounds, ethnicities, and more. Higher education can help students develop these skills by providing practical training and experiences related to cultural competencies. At the top, higher education leaders need to be culturally competent, both by demonstrating sensitivity to individual differences and by feeling comfortable engaging in purposeful conversations dealing with race, ethnicity, and ideological differences. Additional high-value actions include infusing concepts of equity and inclusion into interdisciplinary studies and curriculum; requiring incoming students to participate in diversity and inclusion orientation and training sessions; and convening courageous conversations about race, bias, and discrimination.

Yet colleges and universities are not consistently prioritizing initiatives along these lines. A survey conducted by the Association of American Colleges and Universities found, for example, that only 34 percent of its member institutions require students to participate in diversity studies and experiences, and just over half (53 percent) offer them on an optional basis.[12]

Students themselves are becoming more proactive in identifying and pursuing opportunities to enhance their cultural competencies. They are asking their institutions to provide professional development workshops that address topics such as implicit bias and inclusion, and to make available leadership roles within the campus community that reinforce the institution's diversity and inclusion values.[13] Students want to be able to hone their demonstrated skills in these areas and highlight them for potential employers. Intentional student-institution collaborations will enable students to more readily develop inclusive leadership skills and capabilities that graduates can take into the workplace.

Employers can help extend campus efforts through student internships and co-op experiences. TIAA, firmly established both in the corporate realm as a Fortune 100 company and in the higher education and broader nonprofit realm, presents one model for this approach. TIAA believes that by building a culture that allows all employees to contribute their unique talents and skills, it can provide its clients with fresh ideas and distinct perspectives to help them achieve their goals. At TIAA, student interns receive exposure to corporate diversity and inclusion initiatives, including an array of Employee Resource Groups that support and give visibility to specific population groups (e.g., African American, Hispanic, LGBT, and women, among others). Interns also participate in TIAA's Journey to Inclusion training program. Similar training programs are offered by companies across market sectors. Colleges and universities can benefit from exploring effective practices in the private sector, where resources traditionally have been applied more consistently to diversity and inclusion initiatives.

Another realm where employers can make an impact on advancing diversity and equity in the workforce is in their hiring practices. In her book *Pedigree: How Elite Students Get Elite Jobs*, Northwestern University sociologist Lauren A. Rivera documented the "persistence of privilege" beyond its many manifestations in higher education to the hiring practices of the nation's top investment banks, consulting firms, and law firms. Her extensive research shows that at each stage of the hiring process, "employers use an array of sorting criteria ('screens') and ways of measuring candidates' potential ('evaluative metrics') that are highly correlated with parental income and education."[14]

Understanding and Leveraging Generational Differences

Today, six distinct generations are currently defined in the United States, and up to five are working side-by-side in a single workplace,[15] as shown in Figure 16.6.

Generation Z, the youngest generation, is the most ethnically diverse group and is expected to be the last generation with a White majority. Table 16.1, which is based on extensive qualitative research, highlights characteristics and preferences of the five generations. TIAA uses it as a tool to encourage open-minded thinking about how intergenerational workplace relationships can be leveraged to produce positive outcomes.

As colleges and universities and employers strive to develop an effective future workforce, it is important to build respect for generational differences. Even as employers appropriately seek to create more welcoming work environments for Millennials and Gen Zers, for example, they should remain committed to ensuring that Baby Boomers feel valued and that their experience and wisdom are tapped.

The Role of Leadership

Committed leadership from the top of any organization—in the corporate world or at higher education institutions—is critical to making progress.

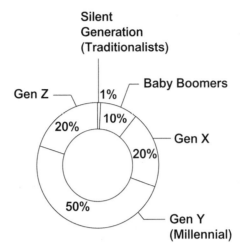

Figure 16.6 Workforce 2020: Five generations

SOURCES: Hudson (March 9, 2018). The Great Generational Shift. Retrieved July 2019, from https://be.hudson.com/en-gb/the-great-generational-shift; Workforce of Tomorrow. (n.d.). Retrieved from https://www.slideshare.net/mobile/ArkadinCollaboration/workforce-of-to-morrow; Bennett, M. (2017, February 07). A Breakdown of the Five Generations of Employees in the Workplace. Retrieved July 2019, from https://www.navexglobal.com/blog/article/for-mal-introduction-five-generations-employees-your-workforce/; Perry, J., Orrick (2019, May). Operating in the Age of Millennials: Strategies for Managing a Multigenerational Workforce.

Leaders can seize every opportunity to articulate expectations, suffuse their organizations with their values, and make their mark on the workplace of the future. At most colleges and universities, conversations about diversity, equity, and inclusion seem to call for action by university administrators, faculty, and students—but typically not by boards of trustees. Yet boards have a vital role to play and should work with institutional leaders to address the challenges at hand. Boards face many issues, including overall organizational performance, risk and compliance, financial well-being, and strategic focus and mission. The issue of diversity weaves through all of these matters. For example, the ability to recruit and retain a diverse student body that reflects our changing population is closely related to institutions' financial well-being; the ability to do so better than one's competitors is a strategic issue.

The fact that most boards themselves are not diverse presents a hurdle that must be overcome if boards are to successfully advance a campus diversity agenda. Working to diversify their own membership and to adopt inclusive practices and diversity policies are first-order tasks in addressing

Table 16.1 Workforce 2020: Characteristics and preferences of five generations

	TRAITS	GOALS	LIFE INFLUENCES	COMMUNICATION PREFERENCES	VALUES/ PRINCIPLES
SILENT GENERATION (TRADITIONALISTS)	• Hard working • Work is a privilege • Disciplined	• Tech challenged • Strict rules and directives	• Great depression • WWII	• Face-to-face • Written letters	**Self-worth**—Need actions to contribute to good of company
BABY BOOMERS	• Independent • Personally identify with their job	• Loyal to company • Respect authority	• Cold War • Women's liberation	• Face-to-face • Phone calls	**Achievement**—Need to have impact and for actions to make a difference
GEN X	• Individualistic • Loyal to occupation (not company)	• Value work-life balance	• Vietnam • War Civil rights	• Phone calls • Email	**Security**—Need to feel trusted and have flexibility to get job done on their schedule
GEN Y (MILLENNIAL)	• Lifelong learners • Value diversity	• Seek meaningful work and C-suite access • Collaborative, but only 16% anticipate 10 years with employer	• 9/11	• Text • Mobile calls • Email	**Greater good**—Need to see connection between responsibility and personal goals
GEN Z	• Social media-focused • Innovative	• Always connected	• #MeToo	• Text • Social media	**Determination**—Need to be creative and have entrepreneurial opportunities

SOURCES: Hudson (March 9, 2018). The Great Generational Shift. Retrieved July 2019, from https://be.hudson.com/en-gb/the-great-generational-shift; Workforce of Tomorrow. (n.d.). Retrieved from https://www.slideshare.net/mobile/ArkadinCollaboration/workforce-of-tomorrow; Bennett, M. (2017, February 07). A Breakdown of the Five Generations of Employees in the Workplace. Retrieved July 2019, from https://www.navexglobal.com/blog/article/formal-introduction-five-genera-tions-employees-your-workforce/; Perry, J., Orrick (2019, May). Operating in the Age of Millennials: Strategies for Managing a Multigenerational Workforce.

campus diversity and improving governance. Board-level strategies to advance campus diversity include taking ownership of the issue, defining success and setting goals, recognizing that conflict is inevitable, holding the president accountable and supporting that individual, and translating their own experiences from outside of higher education to the issues at hand.[16]

Conclusion

Research has demonstrated repeatedly that the innovative potential of an organization is unleashed when individuals from a diverse range of backgrounds, proficiencies, and voices are brought together. Companies in the top quartile for gender diversity, for example, are 15 percent more likely to have financial returns above the national median. Similarly, companies in the top quartile for ethnic diversity are 30 percent more likely to have financial returns above the national median.[17]

These realities, along with inexorably changing demographics, mean that those who thrive in the workforce of the future will be those who embrace diversity in all its manifestations. Such an outlook needn't be innate: indeed, as described earlier, colleges and universities, employers, students, and workers can all take action to create environments that foster such success.

17 PUBLIC EDUCATION AND THE FUTURE OF WORK

Ross Wiener

ABSTRACT

Young people will enter a workforce—and a world—buffeted by continuous innovation and disruption. Navigating change will be a constant. To thrive in the future of work will require lifelong, continuous learning. Jobs that pay a living wage will demand human interaction and social skills, including the ability to work well in teams and with dynamic configurations of partners and clients. Today, employers say they have the hardest time finding new workers with "soft skills" rather than technical skills. Finally, America is becoming even more diverse, which can be a powerful driver of economic progress—for those with cultural competence and the ability to create value out of diversity and pluralism. Within those contexts, this chapter examines the current state of secondary education and its ability to establish a foundation for students' advanced learning in postsecondary institutions and across the lifespan.

STUDENTS ENTERING SECOND GRADE in 2019 are the class of 2030; for K–12 education to meet the needs of a rapidly evolving economy, the future of work is *now*. As the knowledge- and technology-fueled economy continues to mature, young people will enter a workforce and a world buffeted by continuous innovation, disruption, and rapidly evolving expectations about the relationship between employers and employees. Navigating change will be a constant.

Automation and artificial intelligence (AI), in particular, will profoundly influence job availability and wages. Purely technical tasks increasingly will be automated; problems that have a single answer will be solved by software and algorithms.[1] Jobs that can command a living wage in the market will require human interaction and social skills—for example, working on teams and with dynamic configurations of partners and clients. To create value, workers will need to be able to make informed judgment calls and adapt routine practices based on evolving contexts.[2]

K–12 education can't prepare workers to confront these changes through a few tweaks in the system or by merely improving traditional outcome measures. Profound changes are required to enable young people to thrive in the workplace and navigate the increasingly complex challenges confronting our increasingly diverse society. The industrial model/basic skills/assimilationist education that fueled generations of progress must be replaced with approaches to education that cultivate lifelong learning, adaptability, and teamwork. This transformation *can* be designed but only if the nature and magnitude of the change is acknowledged and addressed proactively.

Three primary dynamics deserve urgent attention in updating public education for the future of work: teamwork and adaptability, social-emotional skills and social capital, and improved equity.

Teamwork and Adaptability

The United States has an individualistic society,[3] and its schools reflect this value. Students complete assignments on their own and are graded on individual achievement. Moreover, the test-based achievement paradigm prioritizes *knowing* over *doing*. Accrual and recitation of relatively discrete chunks of knowledge is rewarded, while training in completing longer-term projects or functioning on a team is generally reserved for affluent students or for students identified as gifted.[4]

In the workplace, however, the unit of performance is shifting from the individual to the team. Increasingly, employees need to navigate complex and diverse teams, and they need to see their work as one component of a larger value chain and be cognizant of how their contribution fits into the whole. Gone are the days when hard work on its own or routine tasks done with precision and fidelity will pay a living wage; employees will need constantly to learn new skills and to navigate dynamic teams, many of which will engage colleagues from different backgrounds and cultures, in person and virtually.[5]

Public education must create learning environments and experiences that prepare students for working on teams, adapting to change, and integrating new information to update processes that will become outdated before they can become routine. Many practices relevant to this mission are highly developed and already available but are too often relegated to progressive independent schools most likely to be preparing their students for an advanced liberal arts education. The public policy opportunity and challenge in front of us is to make this type of education the norm for all students rather than the exception.

Social-Emotional Skills and Social Capital

Employers are already asking for workers who have greater emotional intelligence and stronger social-emotional skills.[6] The future of work will place even higher premiums on these skills, making them table stakes for entry to the workplace, no longer reserved for executive leaders and managers.

Current K–12 practice tends to silo academics from social-emotional learning, with most schools primarily emphasizing the learning of book knowledge, with social-emotional competencies added on as a complement.[7] Social-emotional skills are most frequently taught in discrete interventions and programs—if they are taught at all. Building social capital—developing relationships and networks—is not prioritized or resourced in school, despite its significance for awareness of and access to opportunities.[8] The most positively impactful social-emotional development young people experience in school likely happens outside the classroom, in sports and other extracurricular activities. Significant social-emotional development inevitably happens in classrooms, too, but often unintentionally: students learn they are expected to comply, to regurgitate what they picked up from textbooks and lectures, and to subordinate their own identity and creativity to fit in the neat rows and boxes that have been created for them to succeed in the artificial environment of school.

K–12 practitioners need to develop new pedagogies and new learning experiences that recognize that learning inherently has social and emotional dimensions, and that these can be harnessed to prepare students to thrive in the world of work (and beyond).[9] Athletic coaches and after-school programs have proven strategies for building teamwork skills and developing mindsets and interpersonal practices that are valued in the future of work; K–12 educators can engage actively and productively with these communities. In the future of work, learning and development are no longer separate, opt-in sessions, but rather are constants and givens.[10] Schools would do well to model such training for students.

K–12 is experiencing a boom of interest and investment in updated career-technical education (CTE), which for too long had been seen as an alternative for students who weren't deemed "college material." The acute need for technical skills in the current labor market (and the availability of immediate returns for students who concentrate in a technical field) is fueling a renaissance for CTE. Too many of these efforts are geared toward the current reality of work, not the future, with an emphasis on "stackable credentials" and hard technical skills. Too few of these efforts are aimed at evergreen skills, such as learning to think, learning to communicate clearly orally and through writing, and learning to solve problems in a team setting. Technical skills will expire; thinking and interpersonal skills, the so-called soft skills, will only gain in currency as employees practice them in the workplace.

Equity and Political Implications

The "future of work" conversation is frequently couched with a cold, technocratic frame, but changes in the employment marketplace also have broad and significant equity and political implications. The future of work is not an inevitable, unfolding plan but is shaped by political decisions. Race and gender dimensions need focused attention to ensure that opportunities and risks are allocated fairly.

America is becoming ever-more diverse, which can be a powerful driver of economic progress—for those with cultural competence and the ability to create value out of diversity and pluralism.[11] But historical discrimination and current practices create large gaps in opportunity and employment outcomes, which will be exacerbated by the future of work. For example, Black and Hispanic workers are projected to be disproportionately displaced by automation and artificial intelligence. These groups are overrepresented in jobs that are at risk of elimination (e.g., food service, cashiers, customer service representatives). According to the Brookings Institution, 45 percent of jobs held by Hispanic workers and 44 percent of jobs by Black Americans are exposed to elimination through technology, compared to 40 percent of jobs held by White Americans.[12] Rather than disrupting these patterns of preparation for low-skill, low-growth jobs, public K–12 education has exposed students from these groups disproportionately to instruction and learning experiences that are aligned with limited career options—such as rote learning; inordinate emphasis on basic skills; and limited opportunity for creativity, teamwork, or advanced problem-solving.

There is a substantial gender challenge, too. Men are disproportionately slated to lose jobs in the future of work and are less well-positioned than women to navigate the changes. In terms of likely employment in the future, 53 percent of jobs that will be lost are projected to be those currently held by men, versus 47 percent for women.[13]

By dint of educational status and gender-role stereotypes, men are further disadvantaged in weathering the shifting expectations of work. Since 1980, women have earned most college degrees. For more than fifteen years, women have earned 57 percent of baccalaureate degrees compared to just 43 percent for men; in master's degree achievement, which contributes to both higher wages and job security, women outpace men 60 percent to 40 percent.[14] Men still outpace women in earning STEM (science, technology, engineering, and mathematics) degrees, but that gap is likely to shrink—as it should.[15] These trends portend tectonic social change in the traditional bread-winning role of men.

Men are further disadvantaged by the disjuncture between traditional gender-stereotyped roles and what is valued for employment in the future of work. For example, in the most recent technology and engineering test results from the National Assessment of Education Progress (NAEP, or "The Nation's Report Card"), women gained while men were stagnant, opening a significant performance gap. Girls outperform boys *most* in the "communicating and collaborating" category, which are critical skill sets in the future of work.[16]

Going forward, the competitive advantages of socially constructed roles that benefited men in the eras of manual labor and industrialization will likely erode. Men have been conditioned and celebrated for their individual skills and strengths, while collaboration, teamwork, and empathy, all of which are prized in the future of work, have been associated more closely with traditional female roles. One positive aspect of this trend is the possibility that society will begin to address the historic injustice and inequity that has devalued what was seen as women's work, and there is hope that women will be accorded more of the respect and remuneration they have always deserved but have been denied. As public schools adjust to meet the demands of future work, however, a concerted effort is also warranted to engage boys and young men in rigorous teamwork, collaborative problem-solving, and perspective-taking that will enable them to learn skills that will be valuable for gainful employment.

In the end, political decisions will be even more important than any technology in defining the future of work. Traditional relationships between employers and employees already have been indelibly changed by the gig economy and the ability to outsource instantly around the globe. K–12 plays a crucial role in the social contract, preparing young people not only to take jobs but also to actively engage in democratic decision-making that regulates working conditions, income levels (e.g., minimum wage and tax policy), and access to benefits like health care and retirement savings that historically have been provided by employers. Many aspects of the future of work are in the hands of scientists and engineers all over the world, but myriad political decisions will determine what it means for American workers. For instance, who should pay (individuals? government? employers?) for the retraining and upskilling that inevitably will be needed? K–12 needs to prepare young people with agency to shape the future and not merely to be objects of it, which requires reinvigorating the civic mission of schools.

K-12 Priorities to Prepare Young People for the Future of Work

Schools need to prepare students with the skills and mindsets that support adaptability, as well as practice that builds confidence in learning new things and applying acquired knowledge and skills in novel settings. Credentialing schools and students on a broader range of competencies and mindsets (e.g., collaboration and teamwork, problem solving, navigating diversity, and fitting tasks into a larger project) is an opportunity for K–12 educators and policymakers to act on the science of learning that we already have. Healthy relationships, strong personal identity, and the ability to persevere are not simply by-products of good schooling—they are the very essence of a rich educational experience and the traits of successful adults.

Schools need to replicate real-world work, displacing some of the current focus on test-based achievement scores with more meaningful projects and tasks that better reflect traits valued in the workplace, such as conscientiousness, creativity, teamwork, and medium- and long-term time management.

Drivers of opportunity in the future of work, such as adaptability, teamwork, and other social-emotional/soft skills, raise profound questions about the nature of assessment. Employers are building technologies that assess candidates' ability to thrive in the dynamic, complex, diverse situations that increasingly are needed to create value in the workplace. Public schools would do well to design their own systems, structures, and practices for meeting this imperative in the ways students complete their work in school and how their progress and achievements are assessed. New discipline needs to be created in assembling portfolios that illustrate and credential what students can do, not just what they know. School faculty need more exposure to the reality of changing work expectations so that school can model what comes next; stronger partnerships with the private sector and summer externships can be parts of the solution here.

Finally, K–12 has a critical role in preparing citizens who are actors and not objects when it comes to the future of work. Renewed interest in civics education needs to orient to the very real and daunting challenges our society must confront, including updating the fundamental rules that govern employer-employee relationships.

K–12 is of course not the only potential partner with higher education to advance lifelong learning. In another chapter in this book, for example, LaVerne Srinivasan and colleagues from the Carnegie Corporation of New York argue for multi-sector partnerships that might include education, government, and the business sector. In two other chapters, Jason Tyszko and Robert Sheets and Brian Fitzgerald and colleagues from the Business–Higher Education Forum describe models for how the private sector and higher education can partner to support future workforce training needs.

Conclusion

High school graduation was not even the norm until fairly recently. In 1940, fewer than 25 percent of American adults had a high school diploma; now that figure is more than 90 percent.[17] The remarkable progress we made as a country in making high school graduation a universal expectation is a good reminder that we know how to expand educational opportunity at scale. Now, we need for matriculation into some postsecondary education and/or formal training to become an expectation. This noteworthy new cultural shift has been embraced rhetorically but has not yet deeply affected the structure or culture of high schools, which still look a lot like industrial-era institutions that prepare only a small minority of graduates for future learning—and for the future of work.

American public education has always reflected the employment imperatives and values of its times, from assimilation and basic skills through expanding access to all, yet throughout it also has played a sorting function for vocations versus college. The demands of future work align equity aspirations with the interests of private enterprise. Every American needs the higher-order thinking, problem-solving, and social-emotional skills that historically have been reserved for the privileged. There are political obstacles to be addressed, especially relative to seeing the dignity and worth of every young person, and eradicating the impulse among the already privileged to hoard opportunity. But the needs of our democracy and our economy are converging, with the potential to reanimate the historic education reform coalition among business leaders and civil rights advocates that propelled the prior era of education reform.

The future of work calls on education leaders and policymakers to once again reenvision public schools as engines of opportunity. Learning science and research already have identified a lot of promising practices, and educators and students already clamor for the opportunity and space to do this kind of work. If we create enabling conditions through policy and resources, then children and educators can get us there—and will thus be well positioned to advance shared American prosperity through the future of work.

18 DEVELOPING WORKERS FOR THE WORKPLACE

How Businesses and Higher Education Can Alleviate Worker Barriers to Retraining or Upskilling

X. Susan Zhu, Alexander Alonso, and Johnny C. Taylor

ABSTRACT

Research shows that, by 2030, automation and technology may displace 400 million workers worldwide. In conjunction with the aging workforce, such that one in every five individuals will be over the age of sixty-five by 2030, a staggering proportion of workers will need to learn new skills and adapt to changing technologies. Businesses, educators, policymakers, and workers must work together to retrain and upskill to prepare for the jobs of the future. Some observers worry about the negative effects of learning and embracing innovation and technological changes, such as unemployment and inequality. The idea that people are threatened by the potential loss of jobs caused by technological change can be described as a fear of technological unemployment. This chapter presents current research on why individuals may be resistant to technological change, discusses best organizational practices for developing and managing talent, and provides recommendations to industry and higher education leaders on how they can prepare workers to obtain skills and competencies for the jobs of the future.

WE ARE IN THE MIDST of a fourth industrial revolution, where innovation and technological developments are taking place at record speed.[1] The rise of global expansion, workforce mobility, the gig economy, workplace automation, and a more diverse workforce are significantly impacting both traditional business models and higher education. Research shows that, by 2030, automation and technology may displace 400 million workers worldwide.[2] In conjunction with an aging workforce, in which one in every five individuals is projected to be older than sixty-five by 2030, a staggering proportion of workers will need to learn new skills and adapt to changing technologies.[3]

Businesses, educators, policymakers, and workers must work together to retrain and upskill to prepare for the jobs of the future. Whereas some people may see the future of employment as an opportunity to change the existing landscape of work, others may worry about the pressures inherent in an expanding need for more learning and innovation as well as the potential downsides of workers displaced by technology and the workplace inequality that displacement might engender.[4] The idea that people are threatened by the potential loss of jobs caused by technological change can be described as a fear of *technological unemployment*.[5] The concept of technological unemployment can be traced back to the early nineteenth century when British textile artisans protested their replacement by the introduction of textile machinery.[6]

Research suggests that workers are resistant to retraining and upskilling based on the impression that technology and automation will lessen the perceived value they provide to their employers.[7] That reaction might be well founded. Workers who wish to retrain and upskill, for example, may be stigmatized in the workplace.[8] At the same time, employee resistance to technological changes, training, and upskilling can drastically hinder the workforce's ability to grow as technology evolves quickly. Related challenges to reskilling are discussed in several other chapters in this book. Both Chris Dede and the coauthors Yakut Gazi and Nelson Baker, for example, reflect on the need for adult learners to "unlearn" entrenched practices before they can learn new skills. To drive inclusive growth and effect change in the workforce, workers need to be ready and motivated to retrain and upskill. We need to better understand this from the employees' perspective in order for industry and higher education to identify areas of interventions. For instance, how can organizations and higher education foster a culture of lifelong learning to motivate workers to embrace technological change? How can organizations reduce resistance to retraining or upskilling from their employees and better prepare their workforce to be adaptive to evolving technological change?

In this chapter, we present findings from a survey of perceptions on technology and training from employees and individuals looking for work. The survey results help us better understand how workers perceive technological change. Based on these findings, we discuss best organizational practices for developing and managing talent and provide recommendations to industry and higher education leaders on how they can prepare workers to obtain skills and competencies for the jobs of the future.

Survey Findings and Recommendations

A sample of 692 individuals who are either currently employed or actively seeking jobs responded to an AmeriSpeak omnibus survey, a monthly multiclient survey using NORC at the University of Chicago. It is a probability-based panel designed to be representative of the US population: 64 percent of respondents were White, 52 percent female, and the average age was forty-seven years old. The most prevalent work industries among the respondents were education and health services. We asked respondents to answer questions regarding retraining and upskilling in their profession as well as major barriers that would prevent them from engaging in those activities.

Although a quarter (24 percent) of the respondents were unwilling or unsure if they want to retrain or upskill, most (76 percent) said they are willing to retrain or upskill in their job. This is an optimistic sign for organizations that wish to upskill their workforce. For instance, Amazon is planning to retrain a third of its US workforce to gain new skills that will help workers transition to new positions. Similarly, Accenture decided recently to retrain a portion of its workforce instead of laying them off. Retraining has been shown to boost employee morale and can be an effective strategy to solve an organization's talent shortage.[9] The results suggest that American workers are willing to obtain new skill sets to compete in the workforce.

For individuals who responded that they were unwilling or unsure about retraining or upskilling, the worker's age played a potential role. On average, individuals who were unwilling to retrain or unsure about retraining were seven years older than individuals who were willing to retrain. Open-ended responses from the survey indicated individuals who were unwilling or unsure were often approaching retirement age or were more invested in spending time with family such that retraining or upskilling would require them to invest time outside of work.

Potential barriers may prevent workers from retraining or upskilling in the workplace. For workers, the number-one barrier was that they "do not have enough time outside of current job," followed by "don't know of any programs for retraining or reskilling in their own profession or industry," and, finally, "their organization would not provide the necessary resources (e.g., time off, cost support)." These reasons are to be expected since retraining would require additional time and resource commitment from employees. However, organizations can potentially do more to help their employees find opportunities to develop additional skill sets in order to be prepared for additional job responsibilities. Further, even if organizations are unable to reimburse or subsidize the cost of training, providing employees the time off they need can be a worthwhile investment.

For individuals looking for work, the number-one barrier was that they "don't have the financial resources to afford it," followed by "don't have enough time due to other responsibilities (e.g., family care, health issues)," and, finally, "don't know what skills are needed to be a competitive candidate on the job market." When it comes to retraining and upskilling, applicants looking for work face different barriers compared to workers who are currently employed at an organization. For applicants, the retraining and upskilling can be extremely beneficial and allow them to procure a job offer. However, it can also be risky because it requires a significant amount of resources, both financially and time-wise. There is no guarantee that if an applicant invests time and money in finishing a training program, he or she will be able to get a job.

Addressing these barriers or difficulties may require partnering between higher education and industry. For instance, higher education and industry can partner to create internship or apprenticeship programs that provide training but also allow individuals to work at the same time, which would alleviate some financial burdens on employees. Higher education is uniquely equipped to communicate the skill needs of industry to applicants and to design programs to provide the skills that employers are looking for. Additionally, higher education needs to be aware that individuals looking to retrain may be nontraditional students and have commitments that students of a traditional age might not have, such as family care. As such, offering training programs in the evenings or on weekends can be helpful for individuals who wish to retrain but have other time commitments. Other examples include new training models in professional services within organizations or organizational programs to ease worker transitions, and innovative partnerships between industry and higher education.

With technological unemployment, large-scale technology changes may differentially impact certain workplaces. We found that whereas 32 percent of American workers said large-scale technologies *will* impact their profession or workplace within the next five years, 27 percent said those technologies have *already* impacted their profession or workplace. As such, industry and higher education need to start focusing on retraining and upskilling efforts. However, workers themselves also need to be prepared and willing to retrain or upskill. Our findings suggest that although a majority of American workers are willing to do so, they are facing some big challenges. In particular, human resource departments in organizations need to consider themselves as part of a larger ecosystem of society and work, rather than existing in a specific organization.[10] For organizations and human resource departments, providing training and developing employees can better serve the workforce in a "rising tide lifts all boats" manner such that organizations will be able to reap the benefits of a more skilled workforce.

The time to act is now. For instance, the US Department of Commerce and the White House are currently working on an initiative to encourage employer-led training efforts as part of the American Workforce Policy Advisory Board to prepare for the future workforce. Industry, higher education, and employees need to work together to better communicate the needs from all three perspectives in order to prepare for what will likely be the proliferation of technology in the future of work.

19 PAST AS PROLOGUE

Apprenticeship and the Future of Work

Mary Alice McCarthy

ABSTRACT

Apprenticeship is a centuries-old model of teaching and learning that is finding a new home in leading-edge industries—from cybersecurity and software development to early education and health care. It is an education and employment strategy that addresses some of the key challenges facing job seekers and employers alike, including the rising cost of higher education and the need to develop systems of continuous and lifelong learning that are connected to work. But expanding apprenticeship into new sectors and for jobs that require more advanced knowledge and skills depends on close coordination with our higher education systems. A number of European countries are developing strategies for integrating their higher education and apprenticeship systems—for instance, degree apprenticeships in the United Kingdom, applied universities in Switzerland, and dual-study programs in Germany. In the United States, a growing number of colleges and universities are doing the same. This chapter explores opportunities and challenges for connecting higher education and apprenticeship in ways that address the needs of future students and employers.

SCENARIOS DESCRIBING the future of work run the gamut from the dystopian to the utopian. In some, automation eliminates many more jobs than it creates, leaving millions of workers idled. In others, robots take over routine manual work, freeing us up for more creative pursuits that require a uniquely human intelligence.[1] Although there is little agreement about the long-term impact of artificial intelligence and machine learning, there is one common element to all the various "futures of work": being better educated increases one's odds of ending up on the bright side of any future. And on this dimension, the future is much like the past: the transition from an industrial to a knowledge economy rewarded those with advanced education, as did the shift from agriculture to industry a few hundred years earlier. The benefits of technology flow disproportionately to those with more education.

It is no surprise that education, particularly higher education, is at the center of conversations around the future of work. College completion has already become a stark dividing line in American society, associated with distinct life trajectories.[2] College-educated Americans live longer, earn more, are less likely to become unemployed, and are more apt to marry and stay married than their counterparts with no degree.[3] And the educational goalposts for many jobs keep moving further out, extending the time Americans need to spend in school.[4] The up-and-out model, in which individuals finish schooling in their late teens or early twenties, is being replaced by the expectation that workers will continue their education throughout their lives. As a result, access to opportunities to acquire new skills and credentials throughout adulthood will likely further separate Americans into winners and losers from technology-driven change.

The challenge of educating a much larger share of Americans for a longer amount of time, even as they raise families and work full time, is forcing us to reevaluate how we design, deliver, and fund higher education and skills training. And although colleges and universities are notoriously resistant to change, the past two decades have been a period of significant innovation and experimentation, with the rise of competency-based education, fully online degrees, massive open online courses (MOOCs), coding bootcamps, and income-share agreements, to name just a few.

Many of these new approaches are broadening access to higher education, particularly for adult and working learners. But thus far none has moved the needle significantly on postsecondary attainment or disparities in degree attainment among socioeconomic, racial, and ethnic groups. Over the decade from 2007 to 2017, the share of Americans older than twenty-five with a bachelor's degree grew from 30 percent to just 33 percent, even as the educational requirements of good jobs increased.[5] Even these gains have not been shared evenly: the data reveal persistent gaps in completion rates across different racial and ethnic groups, with fewer than half of Hispanic students and just 39 percent of African American students completing a bachelor's degree in six years.[6] Graduation rates are even lower for part-time students, many of whom are working adults. Indeed, higher education is reinforcing social and economic inequalities as students from poor backgrounds increasingly attend low-quality institutions, acquire debt, and are more likely to drop out.[7]

Why have these new approaches fallen short? The reasons are complex and manifold, but one underappreciated limitation on their impact is that they are all built on the assumption that formal education is an activity that takes place outside of work, on the learner's own time, rather than as part of his or her job. Apprenticeship is an educational strategy that turns that assumption on its head.

Adding Apprenticeships

A centuries-old teaching and learning model that integrates formal academic instruction with structured, paid, on-the-job learning, apprenticeship has been used to develop generations of workers, from stonemasons and silversmiths, to plumbers and carpenters, to bankers and cybersecurity specialists. It can prepare individuals for entry-level jobs, like medical assistant, or higher-level occupations, like registered nurse. Most important, it is an educational model that addresses the three biggest challenges that keep adults from staying in or going back to school: cost, time, and relevance. Because apprentices are paid to learn, apprenticeship makes education more affordable. Because apprentices learn on the job, they do not have to squeeze learning into time outside work. And because the learning is tied directly to the occupation for which they are being trained, they don't have to worry about whether the program is teaching them relevant knowledge and skills. What's more, apprentices can use their program to build professional networks, because they are already working.

The future of work is still unclear, but much of it will depend on our capacity to develop a more educated workforce. Adding apprenticeships to our growing supply of postsecondary education and training options would enable more Americans to start their careers while accessing formal learning opportunities. It would also create opportunities for employers to engage more directly in the development of their workers, rather than simply providing tuition assistance benefits to employees to study outside of work. But making apprenticeship a viable postsecondary option will require a new policy infrastructure that connects work-based learning to college degree pathways and addresses the costs to employers and institutions of higher education of developing and sustaining apprenticeship programs.

American Apprenticeship: Small but Mighty

Apprenticeships have deep roots in the United States, dating back to the colonial days when professional training opportunities were scarce. Both Paul Revere and Benjamin Franklin were apprentices. While initially based on personal networks and handshake agreements, apprenticeship arrangements were eventually formalized under the Fitzgerald Act of 1937, as part of a raft of New Deal labor legislation designed to protect workers. The law established our current national system of registered apprenticeship, which rests on a regulatory structure that clarifies the rights and responsibilities of apprentices and their sponsors as well as required program elements. Those elements include the minimum amounts of time apprentices must spend learning on the job and in the classroom and a wage structure that builds in a series of raises as the apprentice advances in the program. The progressively higher wages ensure apprentices capture some of the productivity gains that come from their growing mastery.

Our national apprenticeship system is high performing: more than 90 percent of apprentices move directly into jobs in their field, they incur little or no educational debt, and they earn starting salaries of more than $55,000 a year, on average.[8] Surveys of apprentices and employers indicate high levels of satisfaction with the model. But our national apprenticeship system is also very small and narrowly focused.[9] In 2018, there were just 585,000 registered apprentices, and more than 85 percent of them were preparing for occupations in the building and construction trades.[10]

The small size of our apprenticeship system is no accident. In contrast to other countries, American apprenticeship developed separately from our formal education system. In Germany and Switzerland, vocational education and apprenticeship form part of an integrated "dual education" system, with public high schools and colleges providing the related classroom instruction for apprentices across a wide array of occupations. In both countries, young people transition out of high school into one of two tracks: apprenticeship or university. In another chapter in this book, Daniel Kuehn offers a wealth of relevant insights on the European model of apprenticeships.

By contrast, the national apprenticeship system in the United States emerged out of the trade union movement, which created its own schools, credentials, and career paths for apprentices, whereas our vocational education system was anchored in comprehensive high schools and colleges.[11] In fact, the Smith-Hughes Act of 1917, which established our national system of vocational education and was the country's first federal education law, was designed in part as an alternative for employers to apprenticeships, which were controlled by powerful trade unions and required significant commitments from employers.[12]

Over time, our school-based system of vocational education became increasingly marginalized, and our system of higher education became the primary locus of career preparation for the vast majority of professions, except in the building trades. As a result, apprenticeship never became widespread in the United States, and our vocational education system never developed formal work-based learning opportunities. Americans go to school before they start their careers, not while they are learning their profession. And although many will return to school to continue advancing in their careers, often with the support and encouragement of their employer, "continuing education" typically takes place on the learner's own time.

There are many drawbacks to relying so heavily on traditional higher education to prepare people for careers, particularly when thinking about the future. For one, higher education in the United States is expensive, often prohibitively so, leaving low-income students with no option other than financing their education with loans. For another, many students prefer to learn through experience and benefit from the mentoring and networks that come with work-based learning opportunities. But, too often, those opportunities—where they exist—come in the form of unpaid internships, which many low-income students cannot afford. Finally, our higher education system asks very little of employers, who simply hire graduates rather than engage directly in their preparation—an arrangement that not only puts too much of the cost (and risk) of career preparation on students and taxpayers but also results in mismatches between what employers need and what students are taught.

Growing American Apprenticeship

Apprenticeships can address inequities that are often exacerbated by our system of higher education, particularly in relation to affordability and access to mentors and work experience. But can apprenticeships teach people the knowledge and skills they will need for the jobs of the future, including programming and data analytic skills, systems thinking, diagnostic abilities, and new cultural competencies? The answer is yes. In fact, there are already many examples, in the United States and other countries, of apprenticeships in occupational sectors that are expected to grow in the future, including health care and information technology. For jobs that require strong teamwork, communication, and problem-solving skills, apprenticeship may even offer significant advantages over traditional, classroom-based approaches. And because apprenticeship includes instruction outside of work, it can also incorporate advanced academic coursework. In the United Kingdom, for example, apprenticeships are being used to prepare workers for jobs that require the equivalent of a master's degree.[13]

But for apprenticeships to truly be a high-quality option for students, they also need to result in college degrees, given that degrees are increasingly necessary to enter and advance in most careers. In fact, in many occupations—such as nursing, accounting, and teaching—individuals cannot even sit for the certification or licensure examinations necessary to enter the profession unless they have graduated from an accredited institution of higher education. Graduates of registered apprenticeship programs are awarded a national certificate from the US Department of Labor—also referred to as a "journey card"—which is of limited value outside the skilled trades. Enabling apprentices to earn college degrees—and college students to participate in apprenticeship—will require coordination between the two systems and the ability to jointly deliver a "degree apprenticeship" program.[14] But the policy infrastructure underlying our higher education and registered apprenticeship systems, particularly the financing and quality assurance models, are not designed for collaboration. In particular, neither system is built to support or recognize learning that occurs outside its domain.

Examples of Degree Apprenticeships

Connecting systems with distinct traditions, institutional models, credentials, and funding strategies is not easy, but some promising trends show it is possible. Over the past decade, a growing number of institutions of higher education have been delivering registered apprenticeship programs that culminate in a degree, usually an associate degree.[15] The programs span a diverse array of fields, from health care to applied engineering to public administration. A few examples illustrate the potential of apprenticeship to enrich traditional higher education offerings and help students overcome critical challenges to completing college and/or succeeding in the labor market:

Building Experience into Degree Programs in Cybersecurity

According to the US Bureau of Labor Statistics, job growth over the next decade in the cybersecurity sector will exceed 30 percent, above average for most sectors.[16] Although demand is strong, many companies will not hire cybersecurity specialists until they have several years of experience and have earned specific industry certifications, which often also require work experience to be able to sit for the exam.[17] The work experience requirements for cybersecurity jobs make the transition from college into jobs particularly challenging for recent graduates. Cybersecurity apprenticeship programs like the one delivered by Harper College of Illinois for Motorola Solutions solve that problem for students and employers alike by providing two years of structured, paid, on-the-job learning with coursework at the college.[18] Program graduates come out with experience detecting and responding to the threats that employers are looking for as well as foundational coursework in computer science.

Preparing Nurses for Real-World Settings

Attrition rates among first-year nurses are high, a fact widely attributed to their lack of preparation for the pressure of acute-care settings.[19] Norton Healthcare, a regional system that includes forty clinics and hospitals in northwestern Kentucky and southern Indiana, recently launched a registered apprenticeship program that allows local nursing students to spend a full year of their bachelor's degree program in a structured, paid, on-the-job clinical work experience.[20] Nursing students already have to complete clinicals to sit for their licensure exams, but those traditional experiences generally last a few weeks and are not paid. Students in the Norton Healthcare registered apprenticeship complete their clinicals as part of a year-long, paid work experience program while also taking courses toward their degree. By the time they graduate, these nurses will have ample experience working in a hospital or clinic along with the academic preparation necessary to pass their licensure exams.

Upskilling Incumbent Workers in the Field of Early Education

Apprenticeship can also offer an equity-based strategy for upskilling incumbent workers that leverages their experience while strengthening their understanding of underlying theories and background knowledge. The field of early education and care is undergoing rapid growth as the demand for high-quality pre-K education increases. A growing body of research also points to the importance of professional training for the early education workforce, which, in turn, has led many cities and states to require that early educators obtain an associate's degree to teach in publicly funded centers.[21] But the majority of current early education workers lack a college degree. What's more, wages in the sector are very low; the average early educator makes $13 an hour.[22] This combination of degree requirements with low wages and the rising cost of college has created a difficult equity challenge for the field. Apprenticeship can help address that challenge by providing incumbent workers the opportunity to earn a degree while working and receiving credit for both their previous work experience and additional on-the-job learning. The Community College of Philadelphia, in partnership with the 1199C Training & Upgrading Fund, has implemented a program for early education workers in the city that culminates in a transferable associate of arts degree in early education, is free for the student-apprentices, and includes a series of wage gains for participants as they progress through the year-long program.[23]

Policy Solutions

Adding degree apprenticeship programs to the mix of higher education options for students, workers, and employers can address some of the critical challenges of a future of work in which good jobs require more education. Although some institutions and their employer partners have succeeded in starting up individual programs, expanding the availability of degree apprenticeships will require federal and state policies that make it easier to build, finance, and sustain the programs. Discussed here are three concrete examples of policies that address barriers to the development and scaling of degree apprenticeships:

- *Ease financial burdens for colleges and universities.* Traditional apprenticeship programs do not require apprentices to pay for their learning, which is one of the great advantages of the model. Union-affiliated apprenticeship programs often have their own schools and finance instructional costs through the dues and fees they charge their members and employer partners. But when the education provider is an institution of higher education, tuition costs need to be covered. In most cases, the employer pays the tuition—or at least the lion's share of it—which can make apprenticeship a tough sell to employers since they are also already paying the apprentice to learn on the job. And without some way to cover the instructional costs, institutions of higher education have little incentive to build apprenticeship programs.

A number of states have developed policies to share the costs of apprenticeship with employers, covering the tuition costs of an apprentice. In North Carolina, for example, the state pays the community college tuition for a young person enrolled in a registered apprenticeship program.[24] In doing so, the state creates incentives for both employers and colleges to offer apprenticeship programs that build the state's workforce and local economies.

- *Facilitate recognition of on-the-job learning.* Another advantage of apprenticeship over more traditional higher education programs is structured on-the-job learning. But with few exceptions, apprentices do not receive college credit for what they learn on the job, even though it is clearly defined and assessed. As a result, apprentices have to earn all of their credits through coursework if they want to graduate with a degree, often prolonging the programs and adding to their cost.

  State policy can help colleges build fully integrated programs, in which on-the-job and classroom learning count for credit, by establishing credit awards for specific apprenticeship programs or for industry credentials apprentices can earn at the workplace. For example, Virginia requires that each community college develop policies and procedures for the award of academic credit to any student who has successfully completed a state-approved registered apprenticeship credential.[25] In Indiana, Ivy Technical Community College, the state's largest public postsecondary institution, awards associate of applied science degrees to individuals who have completed a registered apprenticeship in one of sixteen occupations.[26]

- *Expand program registration authority.* Another strategy for bringing more institutions of higher education to the apprenticeship table is to make it easier for them to serve as sponsors and to register programs. The registration process ensures that apprenticeship programs meet a set of requirements designed to ensure their quality. Under the current system, only state apprenticeship agencies and the federal Office of Apprenticeship are authorized to register programs.[27] Expanding the types of state agencies that can register programs to include state education agencies could facilitate the process for colleges and universities, since they are already accustomed to working with state agencies on program approval.

The Future We Need to Build

The future holds many uncertainties, but few experts doubt the central role that higher education will play in preparing Americans for it. Indeed, Americans who complete higher education today are already moving into a different—and more secure—future than Americans who only complete high school. But our system for delivering higher education is inadequate to the task of educating a much larger share of our population over a longer period of time. Among the reasons many Americans fail to graduate from college is its increasing cost, the difficulty of studying while also working to support oneself and/or one's family, and its perceived lack of relevance. Adding apprenticeship to the mix of higher education models could help more students earn a degree by making college more affordable, convenient, and relevant. But integrating apprenticeship into American higher education will require openness to new degree designs and assessment techniques along with supportive public policies that address financial and regulatory challenges.

Apprenticeship might seem like an odd fit for a future that will include augmented reality, autonomous vehicles, and smart machines, but the process of learning through practical experience, under the guidance of a skilled mentor, is likely to be as effective in the future as it has been for centuries. In fact, a future that includes many more high-quality apprenticeship opportunities across a wide array of careers is more likely to be one in which the benefits of technology are broadly shared—and that's the future we need to build.

20 BACHELOR'S-LEVEL REGISTERED APPRENTICESHIP FOR ENGINEERS

Possibilities and Challenges

Daniel Kuehn

ABSTRACT

Science, technology, engineering, and mathematics (STEM) skills are essential for the future of work, both to guarantee workers high-quality jobs and to ensure the stream of innovations that propel the modern economy. This chapter reimagines the delivery of high-quality STEM education through registered apprenticeship programs. Apprenticeship combines classroom training with structured on-the-job training for apprentices who are productive paid employees of a sponsoring employer. Registered apprenticeship is a proven strategy for teaching technical skills, raising wages, and increasing productivity and retention. Continued expansion of apprenticeship for sub-baccalaureate positions is essential for guaranteeing a skilled technical workforce, but this chapter explores more radical options for using apprenticeship to educate individuals for STEM jobs that typically require a bachelor's degree. This chapter focuses on engineers as the most logical place to begin reimagining STEM education in the United States, but it also considers other fields that are increasingly demanding bachelor's degrees, such as certain information technology and lab technician jobs.

SCIENCE, technology, engineering, and mathematics (STEM) skills are essential for the future of work, both to guarantee workers high-quality jobs and to produce the stream of innovations that propel the modern economy. This chapter reimagines the delivery of high-quality STEM education through registered apprenticeship. Apprenticeship combines classroom training with structured on-the-job training for workers who are productive paid employees of a participating employer. Registered apprenticeship is a proven strategy for teaching technical skills, raising wages, and increasing productivity and retention.[1] Almost all of the STEM apprenticeships that currently exist in the United States train for jobs that do not require a bachelor's degree.[2] This chapter explores more radical options for using apprenticeship to educate individuals for jobs that require a bachelor's degree, focusing on engineers as the most logical place to begin reimagining STEM education in the United States.

STEM Apprenticeship in the United States and United Kingdom

In the United States, registered apprenticeship combines structured on-the-job training and mentoring with related technical instruction (RTI) provided in a traditional classroom setting, online, or at the apprentice's place of employment. A registered apprenticeship program's on-the-job training and RTI plans (called apprenticeship standards) are regulated by the federal government and approved by either the US Department of Labor or a state apprenticeship agency. A sponsor is responsible for the daily operations of every apprenticeship program. Often, the employer acts as the program sponsor, although RTI providers or another intermediary organization can also sponsor the apprenticeship program. The sponsor role is often determined by the structure or particular circumstances of an apprenticeship program. For example, unionized apprenticeships in the building trades are often sponsored by a joint labor-management organization rather than by individual employers. In the case of a bachelor's-level engineering apprenticeship program, it may be most appropriate for the college or university providing the classroom training (i.e., the RTI) to sponsor the program, rather than an employer.

Employers are thirsty for increased work-based learning opportunities for their engineers. This point was emphasized by a community college administrator interviewed for Kuehn, Hecker, and Simon's report on STEM apprenticeship.[3] The community college provided RTI for a registered engineering technician apprenticeship program but found that the employer they worked with also sent their engineers through the technician's on-the-job training. The employer found that their new engineering hires did not have sufficient hands-on experience, and they wanted them to participate in certain elements of the technician apprenticeship program even though there was no engineering apprenticeship program.

Most STEM apprentices in the United States are technicians working in jobs that do not require a bachelor's degree. Between 1999 and 2016, in the thirty-three states reporting detailed administrative data to the federal government,[4] 9,201 individuals registered as apprentices in engineering technician occupations. Another 2,010 are registered in computer science and information technology occupations. In contrast, from 1999 to 2016, only 1,366 individuals registered as apprentices in an engineering occupation. The thirty-three states included in these administrative data represent about three-quarters of the national workforce, so it is plausible that as many as 1,821 engineering apprentices were registered during this period, or approximately 105 to 110 engineering apprentices per year.[5]

Most of the engineering apprentices registered in the United States are mine safety engineers registered with an apprenticeship program sponsored by the US Mine Safety and Health Administration (MSHA). Mine safety engineering is a subfield of engineering, but it is notable that apprenticeships in more common engineering fields, such as electrical or mechanical engineering, are nonexistent in the United States. Without the MSHA's decision to register its program, the number of engineering apprentices in the United States would be negligible. STEM employers share that they are most concerned about the costs of apprenticeship, the difficulties of the registration process, and the development of appropriate apprenticeship standards.[6]

Considerable recent attention in the English-speaking world has focused on the United Kingdom's experience with bachelor's-level apprenticeship. The United Kingdom instituted these "degree apprenticeships" in 2015 as a part of a broader effort to scale apprenticeship training. Since the policy environment in the United Kingdom is in many ways more comparable to the United States than to continental Europe, it is worth reviewing the nation's experiences with engineering degree apprenticeships. Table 20.1 provides the numbers of individuals who have started an apprenticeship in the United Kingdom by level of apprenticeship and subject area. In the United Kingdom, a level 6 is equivalent to a bachelor's degree in the United States and a level 7 is equivalent to a master's degree. Lower levels are equivalent to successively lower levels of educational attainment.

Table 20.1 Science and engineering apprenticeships in the United Kingdom, 2017–2018.

	SCIENCE AND ENGINEERING APPRENTICESHIP	TOTAL APPRENTICESHIP	SCIENCE AND ENGINEERING SHARE
Level 7 (master's equivalent)	130	9,000	1.4%
Level 6 (bachelor's equivalent)	260	12,730	2.0%
Level 5	0	40,960	0.0%
Level 4	190	33,620	0.6%
Level 3	13,170	332,500	4.0%
Level 2	5,060	322,790	1.6%
Total	18,810	751,600	2.5%

SOURCE: "Apprenticeship Framework/Standard and Sector Subject Area Table: Starts and Achievements 2017 to 2018 to Q3 2018 to 2019," https://www.gov.uk/government/statistical-data-sets/fe-data-library-apprenticeships.

As in the United States, science and engineering apprenticeships in the United Kingdom make up a small share of the total population of apprentices (18,810 out of 751,600 apprentices registered in the 2017–2018 program year), even allowing for inevitable differences in how certain occupations are classified across different national contexts. Even fewer apprentices study science and engineering at the bachelor's or master's degree level (260 bachelor's level and 130 master's level).

The large majority of British science and engineering apprentices are, as in the United States, at the sub-baccalaureate technician level rather than the bachelor's degree level. The United States is therefore not as far behind the United Kingdom in engineering apprenticeship as the total figures seem to indicate. The field of engineering typically implies the attainment of a bachelor's degree in the United States, so many of the workers classified as "engineering" apprentices in the United Kingdom would be considered engineering technicians in the United States. Although few bachelor's-level science and engineering apprenticeships currently exist in the United Kingdom, their number is growing. Data for apprenticeship starts for the 2018–2019 apprenticeship program year are available only for the first three quarters of the year, but the number of level 6 and 7 science and engineering apprenticeships in the United Kingdom already exceeds the full year total for 2017–2018, presented in Table 20.1.

Co-op Programs: The Raw Material for Engineering Apprenticeships

Extending the degree-level apprenticeship model to the United States in the form of bachelor's-level engineering apprenticeship requires satisfying the requirements of two different regulatory bodies: the Accreditation Board for Engineering and Technology (ABET), which accredits engineering programs in the United States, and the US Department of Labor, which regulates registered apprenticeship. Both ABET's requirements for accredited engineering programs and the Department of Labor's requirements for registered apprenticeship programs can be met by existing engineering programs with substantial co-op components, although this would result in an apprenticeship program that is weighted more heavily toward RTI than a standard program.

One reason for optimism on the prospects for bachelor's-level engineering apprenticeships is that the most celebrated engineering programs in the United States already rely heavily on work-based learning through internship programs and especially through co-op programs. These co-op programs can serve as a model for registered apprenticeship training that meets bachelor's-degree standards.

Building bachelor's-level engineering apprenticeships on the foundation of existing bachelor's degree programs is desirable because it would require navigation of only one approving body (the Department of Labor), rather than two (the Department of Labor and ABET). This would require the most compromise and adaptation from the Department of Labor, and the least compromise and adaptation from either ABET or the engineering programs themselves. Since the apprenticeship system is interested in broadening its reach into new occupations, this balance seems appropriate. The four-year-college system is not actively courting involvement with apprenticeship in the same way that the Department of Labor is trying to scale apprenticeship. It is hoped that a successful pilot of the model would encourage ABET and entrepreneurial four-year colleges to experiment with new instructional models that rely more heavily on work-based learning and apprenticeship.

Taking ABET requirements for an engineering program as given, the minimum requirements for a registered apprenticeship program are outlined in the Code of Federal Regulations, Title 29 §29.5. A traditional time-based apprenticeship "measures skill acquisition through the individual apprentice's completion of at least 2,000 hours of on-the-job learning as described in a work process schedule" (29 CFR §29.5(b)(2)(i)). Requirements for RTI hours are even less proscriptive, with a requirement only of "[p]rovision for organized, related instruction in technical subjects related to the occupation. A minimum of 144 hours for each year of apprenticeship is recommended" (29 CFR §29.5(b)(4)). Although 144 hours is only recommended by regulation, it is standard that all apprenticeship programs are expected to meet this 144-hour threshold, and programs with weaker provision for RTI may have greater difficulty getting successfully registered.

Clearly, any bachelor's degree program meeting ABET accreditation requirements easily meets the 29 CFR §29.5 requirements for RTI hours. Assuming a normal 120-credit-hour bachelor's degree and a fifteen-week semester, an engineering bachelor's degree would entail approximately 1,800 contact hours, far exceeding the RTI requirements of the Department of Labor. Some of these credit hours would be associated with engineering co-ops. Co-op hours would be counted as on-the-job training for the purposes of the registered apprenticeship system, not RTI, but even after removing co-op hours, any bachelor's degree program in the United States clearly satisfies RTI requirements many times over.

The more difficult question is whether engineering bachelor's degree programs with co-ops satisfy 29 CFR §29.5's on-the-job training requirements. To answer this question, I provide a rough estimate of the number of hours implied by co-op programs at Purdue University and Drexel University (Figure 20.1). Both Purdue and Drexel are celebrated for their engineering co-op programs and would therefore serve as natural exemplars for innovative work-based learning efforts. These estimates are rough because every co-op experience is different. Some students may not be working full time, and the duration of a co-op during different terms may vary. The assumptions used to calculate on-the-job training hours are provided in the figure note.

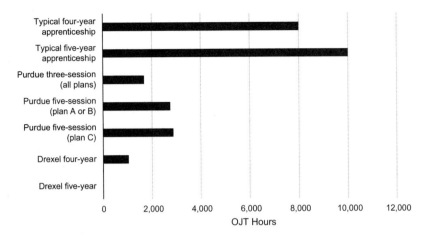

Figure 20.1   On-the-job-training length, apprenticeship, and engineering co-ops.

NOTE: Purdue co-op lengths come from https://opp.purdue.edu/programs/CO-OP.html. Drexel co-op lengths come from https://drexel.edu/scdc/co-op/undergraduate/. Calculations of hours for both Purdue and Drexel assume standard fifteen-week fall and spring semesters, a twelve-week summer semester, and forty-hour work weeks.

Purdue's five-session co-op plan and Drexel's four-year plan would meet the minimum 2,000-hour on-the-job training requirement for a registered apprenticeship, assuming students worked full time during their co-ops. Purdue's three-session co-op plan would not meet the requirement because it generates only 1,680 co-op hours. Similarly, Drexel's four-year plan generates only 1,040 co-op hours and would therefore not meet Department of Labor requirements.

Even though the Purdue five-session plan and the Drexel five-year plan meet requirements, they still involve dramatically fewer on-the-job training hours than typical four- and five-year apprenticeships. The reason for the discrepancy is of course that a full schedule of classes in a bachelor's degree program is spread out over several years to accommodate study time and the social and extracurricular aspects of the college experience. A time dilation results from translating semesters in higher education into RTI hours in the world of registered apprenticeship. This crowds out potential on-the-job training hours that would normally fill up most of the time in a four- or five-year apprenticeship.

Although this type of bachelor's-level engineering apprenticeship programs is still speculative, it is worth considering how such a program might be formally organized. In unionized apprenticeships in the building trades, it is common for many different employers to hire from the same pool of apprentices. Since many employers draw from the same pool of apprentices, it is most appropriate for an umbrella organization like a joint labor-management organization to sponsor the program, rather than an individual employer. Employers sign on to the "group program" but are not themselves a program sponsor. Similarly, in an engineering co-op program, many employers form partnerships with the engineering department and hire from a common pool of students. These employers might find it more appropriate to sign on to a group engineering apprenticeship program rather than serve as individual sponsors themselves.

These are not the only models, of course. In this book, for example, ideas for apprenticeships in the United States can be found in the chapter by Mary Alice McCarthy.

Conclusions

The essence of this chapter is twofold. First, an ABET-accredited engineering program with a substantial co-op component could theoretically be registered as an apprenticeship program without any changes to the existing curriculum. Second, these hypothetical registered engineering apprenticeship programs would be heavily weighted toward RTI hours and away from on-the-job training hours, compared to a standard four- or five-year apprenticeship. This reweighting would require a radical change in how registered apprenticeships typically balance on-the-job training and RTI, although it would not conflict with any existing regulations or ABET accreditation standards.

This model would require the most compromise and adaptation from the Department of Labor and the least compromise and adaptation from either ABET or the engineering programs themselves. This seems appropriate, since it is the apprenticeship system that is interested in broadening its reach, not the four-year college system. A rebalancing of on-the-job training and RTI would not be the first radical change to registered apprenticeships in recent years. Two other changes that are at least as significant include the introduction of competency-based apprenticeship programs to accommodate nontraditional occupations[7] and the recent introduction of industry-recognized apprenticeship programs to accommodate sponsor concerns that the traditional registration process was too rigid and burdensome.[8]

Ideally a successful pilot of the model would encourage ABET and entrepreneurial four-year colleges to experiment with new instructional models in the future, including accepting even more on-the-job training/co-op hours for credit in lieu of classroom instruction.

21 THE AGILITY IMPERATIVE

The Future of Work and Business–Higher Education Partnerships

Jason A. Tyszko and Robert G. Sheets

ABSTRACT

This chapter first addresses the concept of agility in the business community and its implications for the future of work and learning. Next, the chapter examines the agility imperative in the context of business–higher education partnerships and explores four major considerations: how businesses—in a dynamic labor economy—can provide faster, better, and clearer information to education partners about changing in-demand competencies that require shorter lead times; the evolution of new work-and-learn models and platforms that blend employment and education; the rise of cross-functional, interdisciplinary teams in driving innovation; and worker agility and the need for open education pathways that promote equity and opportunity.

HOW BUSINESSES COMPETE and how work is performed are changing in ways that will have major implications for business and higher education partnerships. Businesses will increasingly compete on innovation and agility in a rapidly changing global economy. They will compete on how well they can leverage new business practices and technologies to develop new business models, products, and services.[1] Businesses will also compete on how effective they are in changing the organization of work at all levels—full-time, contract, contingent, or otherwise—consistent with business model and process innovation. Finally, they will compete on how well they maintain an innovative and agile workforce and how quickly and effectively workers at all levels can drive innovation and learn and apply new skills.[2]

This "agility imperative" will also create the need for more agile partnerships between businesses and talent development and sourcing partners, including higher education. This will unlock opportunities for businesses and higher education to explore new types of partnerships that can provide shared value for business, higher education, and students and workers alike.

Competing on Agility and the Future of Work and Learning

Competing on agility will drive major changes in how work is performed in a rapidly changing economy. Rather than slowing down, the pace of change in how work is performed will only accelerate, requiring constant upskilling and reskilling of workers and the closer integration of work and learning.[3] In previous eras and economies, change within industries, jobs, and employment relationships was slow, steady, and predictable. In today's economy and workplaces, however, disruptive change is now the defining feature, and success in the new economy will depend on the agility of workers who will be on the front lines of navigating change. This agility imperative will have significant implications for the future of work and learning and for the future of business and higher education partnerships.

Competing on Agility

The agility imperative is equal parts innovation and adaptability. Innovation is the development and implementation of new ideas, solutions, methods, and processes that create shared societal value.[4] This value can materialize in many ways, including business productivity and economic growth and solutions to environmental, energy, health, and safety problems. The most powerful innovations are when scientific and technological advances (e.g., artificial intelligence, or AI) and new thinking from other disciplines (e.g., design thinking) enable major transformations of business models, products, services, and processes. Although innovation can appear to be spontaneous, it is more often the result of disciplined and deliberate actions taken by teams and networks that result in the fast and continuous generation of new ideas and new ways of doing business. It also involves rapid and effective execution and implementation.

Adaptability generally refers to the ability of businesses to move quickly and effectively in anticipating, adapting to, and leveraging change. This includes responding quickly and successfully to market changes, whether they are innovations driven internally by the business themselves or externally by peer companies or the industry writ large. Adaptability also involves resiliency and the capacity to come back quickly from setbacks.[5] Adaptability is essential if companies are to remain relevant and competitive in a dynamic economy where competitive advantage and market leadership position has an ever-decreasing half-life.

As with innovation, agility is achieved by creating agile cultures, organizations, and work and learning processes.[6] It also involves creating agile organizational alliances and partnerships, including partnerships in sourcing, developing, and transitioning talent. As a result, competing on innovation and agility will have major implications for the future of work and learning.

The Future of Work and Learning

Leading businesses will increasingly compete on agility in an innovation-based economy. This has major implications for how work is organized and reorganized in a dynamic and disruptive economy. It also has major implications for how learners are prepared for this new world of work and how workers, at every level, navigate change and opportunity.

To date, the future-of-work literature has emphasized the impact of automation and AI on work tasks and jobs. For example, a report by McKinsey predicted that up to 45 percent of work activities could be automated by available and demonstrated technologies.[7] What is sometimes not addressed is how these leading technologies will enable major business model and process innovations that result in new forms of business organization and new ways of doing business. What needs greater emphasis is how technology innovation joins with business innovation to create the future of work in more open and networked enterprises.

Business and technological innovations, coupled with the need to be more agile, prompt constant changes in the organization of work and related work-and-learning requirements. They also are creating stronger pressures to better integrate work and learning. In addition, they are changing traditional employment relationships and shifting more responsibilities to workers in managing their own careers and attaining the skills needed to remain competitive. In many companies, the traditional employment relationship characterized by stable organizational roles, career pathways, and employment security is a thing of the past. The traditional top-down and closed business enterprise has given way to a more open and networked enterprise that is more agile and responsive to constant disruption.

We now turn to the implications of the future of work for business–higher education partnerships, both for preparing learners for the new economy and for sustaining the skills, competitiveness, and mobility of current workers.

Creating More Agile Business–Higher Education Partnerships

Agile businesses require agile partnerships. How businesses compete and how work is performed in an innovation-based economy has major implications for how higher education organizes its own major business functions and operations. It also provides significant opportunities for businesses and higher education to explore new approaches for building more agile partnerships consistent with how businesses are driving innovation and adaptability in the new economy. In exploring these new approaches, business and higher education should work together to address several relevant considerations.

Better Real-Time Information and Shorter Lead Times

More agile business–higher education partnerships require businesses to provide faster, clearer, and more actionable information to higher education on rapidly changing skill and competency requirements for current and future workers. The importance of this challenge can be clearly seen in the growing concern among leading employers that they cannot currently respond quickly enough to rapidly changing skill requirements that have shorter "half-lives."

The beginning of a solution for employers is starting to take shape with the US Chamber of Commerce Foundation's recently launched Job Data Exchange or JDX.[8] The JDX is attempting to support an improved data standard for jobs to make competencies, credentials, and other hiring requirements more searchable, discoverable, and comparable on the web. In addition, the JDX will provide a mechanism to send data on changing job requirements directly to education and workforce partners.

However, better real-time information will not make a difference unless talent development and sourcing partners have the ability to act quickly and more nimbly in adapting their education and training programs. This will require shorter amounts of time to make modifications or changes in programs and curricula. To date, universities and colleges have responded quickly to changing skill requirements through their corporate partnerships and noncredit programs. However, that is typically not always the case with for-credit degree and certificate programs that are major sources of future talent. More agile partnerships will require businesses to work with universities and colleges to achieve shorter lead times by reengineering how they develop and update their education and training programs based on dynamic information from employers.

New Work-and-Learn Models and Platforms

More agile partnerships also will require new approaches for integrating work and learning that leverage leading technologies. Competing on agility requires workers to constantly learn by doing and take a more active role in determining what knowledge and skills they need and how to apply them very close to the work they are doing on a day-to-day basis. This will require more work-centered and learner-centered approaches for both businesses and higher education. It also requires experimentation with new types of learning system platforms that can provide more comprehensive and direct support to learners beyond just online instruction.

New work-and-learn models also require a data infrastructure that supports employers in documenting and verifying learning attained while on the job or as part of a work-based learning experience (e.g., internships). In an agile business–higher education partnership, employers are part of the delivery of education, which means that all learning must count, be competency based, and be portable across employer human resource information systems, learning management systems, and student information systems.

Driving Innovation and the Growing Role of Interdisciplinary, Cross-Functional Teams

To date, business and higher education partnerships have focused mainly on addressing new skill requirements for critical job roles, whether they be within traditional disciplines (e.g., accounting) or newer interdisciplinary domains (e.g., data science). However, these partnerships are still based largely on traditional forms of organizing work that are based on business functions and related disciplines that are now undergoing major changes.

The most powerful forms of innovation occur at the interfaces of disciplines and functions that cut across organizational boundaries and reach all levels of workers.[9] This type of innovation work requires team members to have both depth and breadth of skills. Employees need deep expertise in their primary job but also need the breadth to leverage the expertise of other team members from different professional and disciplinary backgrounds. This breadth requires not just broader education and training but also extensive experience in working as members of cross-functional teams using leading innovation methods, tools, and practices that span traditional professional and disciplinary boundaries. One promising strategy is for business–higher education partnerships to promote both depth and breadth by supporting innovation challenge projects that bring together student teams from multiple programs (e.g., business and engineering).[10]

Expanding Equity and Opportunity through More Agile and Open Career and Education Pathways

Business and higher education partnerships also must explore how to empower talent at all levels. Employers are increasingly interested in working with higher education to enable workers to better navigate more open career and education pathways both within and outside their companies. In the age of agility, workers are the new entrepreneurs and must be more proactive in pursuing career advancement opportunities as well as more resilient in responding to changing job requirements.

Employers are also increasingly on the front lines of providing career and education guidance that includes redesigning their tuition aid and training programs to provide more opportunities to workers, especially for frontline employees who have not been successful in accessing and completing traditional higher education programs and pathways. Agile and open career and education pathways that combine work experience with learning hold the promise of providing alternative, high-quality career pathways and opportunities that advance credentialing and upward mobility in ways that close the equity gap.

There are other models, of course. In this book, for example, the chapter by Brian Fitzgerald and colleagues from the Business–Higher Education Forum outlines a different type of partnership for sharing relevant career-education information between business and higher education. LaVerne Srinivasan and colleagues from the Carnegie Corporation of New York propose multisector partnerships, perhaps including education, government, and the business sector, to help bridge the gap between the skills that employers want and the ones taught in higher education.

Conclusion

This chapter has argued that the agility imperative will create the need for more agile business–higher education partnerships that have the potential to provide shared value for business, higher education, and students and workers, and to provide expanded opportunity and equity in the new global economy. To realize this potential, leading businesses and higher education partners should now begin exploring these new more agile partnerships based on the four major considerations presented here, with the intent of creating shared value and advancing opportunity and equity in the new economy.

22 DEMAND FOR THE "BLENDED DIGITAL PROFESSIONAL"

Brian K. Fitzgerald, Isabel Cardenas-Navia, and Janet Chen

ABSTRACT

Recent market intelligence from the Business–Higher Education Forum (BHEF) demonstrates the demand for professionals across a wide range of functions within organizations who can secure data (cybersecurity skills), access data (cloud computing skills), analyze and visualize data (data analytics), develop or use computer systems to learn from data (artificial intelligence/machine learning), and make data-driven decisions (broad understanding of digital technology). This strong demand for digital technology skills across all sectors is expected to increase over the coming years. BHEF launched the National Higher Education and Workforce Initiative (HEWI) in 2012 to use the latest digital market intelligence to create business–higher education partnerships and assist higher education in responding rapidly to increasing demand for professionals across all disciplines with digital skills. To date, HEWI has supported more than three dozen business–higher education partnerships and created more than fifty new digital credentials ranging from undergraduate concentrations, minors, and majors, to graduate certificates and professional science master's programs. This chapter profiles the work of BHEF and its proven partnership model.

THE EXPLOSION of digital technologies is changing the nature of work and reinventing the roles of professionals across all business sectors, nonprofits, and research enterprises. Rapid advances in artificial intelligence (AI), the Internet of Things, and other emerging technologies are changing the nature of the types of jobs that need to be done. The impact of these technologies is felt in all sectors, from communications to travel, and professionals must adapt their talents to thrive in this new digital era. According to the World Economic Forum, at least 133 million new roles will be generated by 2022 as a result of the new division of labor between humans, machines, and algorithms.[1]

Professionals now need deep expertise in a primary discipline *and* a foundational knowledge of digital technology skills. The Business–Higher Education Forum (BHEF), a nonprofit membership organization comprised of Fortune 500 C-suite executives and leading university presidents dedicated to advancing innovative education and workforce solutions and improving US competitiveness, commissioned Burning Glass Technologies to examine in-demand skills in the job market by drawing from a set of more than 150 million unique US job postings, dating back to 2007.[2] The research identified fourteen skills that have become foundational in the new economy, which converge in three interrelated groups: human, business enabler, and digital building block skills.

- *Human skills* apply social, creative, and critical intelligence. These skills appear on many lists of sought-after "soft skills."
- *Business enabler skills* are required across job families. These skills enable individuals to bridge the capabilities of digital technologies with broader business goals, allowing the other skills to be put to work in practical situations.
- *Digital building block skills* leverage digital tools to add value and align with functional domains that are critical to the digital economy.

The blended digital professional combines these three foundational skill areas with domain knowledge (Figure 22.1). These employees have the expertise necessary to become more adaptable to future disruption, increase their earning power, and improve their long-term career prospects. BHEF's partnerships and pathways are designed to develop the blended digital professional for the twenty-first-century digital economy.

Other models offer approaches that complement ours. In other chapters in this book, for example, Jason A. Tyszko and Robert G. Sheets describe a job-data exchange where business and higher education could share information on skills and competencies, and LaVerne Srinivasan and colleagues from the Carnegie Corporation of New York suggest multisector partnerships, which might include education, government, and the business sector, to help bridge the gap between the skills that employers want and the ones taught in higher education.

BHEF's National Higher Education and Workforce Initiative

BHEF launched the National Higher Education and Workforce Initiative (HEWI) in 2012 to use the latest market intelligence to create business–higher education partnerships and assist higher education in responding to increasing demand for professionals across all disciplines with digital skills. To date, the initiative has supported more than three dozen business–higher education partnerships and created more than fifty new digital credentials ranging from undergraduate concentrations, minors and majors, to graduate certificates and professional science master's programs.

As part of this initiative, BHEF developed a proven model—the Partnership Implementation Process—that consists of eight essential steps to guide the development of business-led engagement with higher education (Figure 22.2). The Partnership Implementation Process serves as a common framework

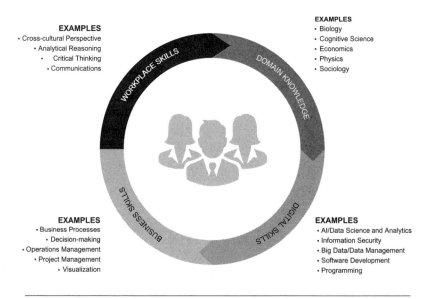

EXAMPLES
• Cross-cultural Perspective
• Analytical Reasoning
• Critical Thinking
• Communications

EXAMPLES
• Biology
• Cognitive Science
• Economics
• Physics
• Sociology

WORKPLACE SKILLS

DOMAIN KNOWLEDGE

BUSINESS SKILLS

DIGITAL SKILLS

EXAMPLES
• Business Processes
• Decision-making
• Operations Management
• Project Management
• Visualization

EXAMPLES
• AI/Data Science and Analytics
• Information Security
• Big Data/Data Management
• Software Development
• Programming

All professionals will need a foundational skill set that mixes digital skills, business skills, 21st-century workplace skills, and domain knowledge.

Figure 22.1   The blended digital professional

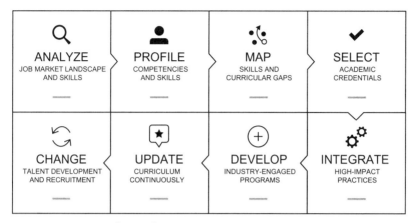

Figure 22.2   Partnership implementation process

for moving partnerships from needs assessment to changed hiring practices that are adaptable, replicable, and scalable, and is guided by BHEF in its role as a third-party facilitator. The process considers five corporate levers—corporate/executive leadership, corporate philanthropy, employee engagement, core competencies and expertise, and research and development facilities—to keep the relationship strategic and not merely transactional.

Business–Higher Education Collaborations Support Pathways to Develop Blended Digital Professionals

The District of Columbia, Maryland, and Virginia region (DMV) is home to the third largest digital technology (DT) workforce in the United States, but DMV companies are unable to fill more than 35,000 DT-oriented jobs in the region.[3] The need for employees with digital skills is growing throughout the United States, but it poses a particular challenge in the DMV: the *Washington Post* reported that in the past few years the number of DT workers in the DMV has grown only 3 percent, which is below the national growth rate of 12 percent.[4] Furthermore, the DMV is expected to add at least 227,000 new jobs requiring at least high or medium DT skills between 2017 and 2027.[5] This demand will not be met exclusively through university education: in 2017, there were 26,000 openings across twenty key tech occupations in the region, but only 16,000 completions of related degrees or certificates.[6] More than 4,700 job openings are available in occupations that require DT skills.[7]

A key component to solving the DT workforce demands in the DMV is to align the region's many companies and higher education institutions. BHEF, in partnership with the Greater Washington Partnership and the Business Roundtable, facilitated a consortium between large employers and leading higher education institutions in the DMV to align their efforts in creating new pathways for professionals to gain DT skills in areas including data science and analytics, cybersecurity (cyber), cloud computing (cloud), networking/IT (IT), and artificial intelligence/machine learning (AI/ML).

Since the consortium's formal launch in April 2018, members have made significant progress in developing pathways for students to gain DT credentials. Consortium companies discussed areas in which they had substantial need for talent; they identified the areas of data analytics, cyber, AI/ML, and cloud. After further analysis, companies refined the DT skills needs at their organizations to two different digital skill sets:

- The *Generalist* DT skill set is intended to enable individuals pursuing careers that incorporate a DT component. A credential incorporating the Generalist skill set or competencies should be accessible and relevant to any individual regardless of major or academic background. The competencies for the Generalist credential are generally focused on data analytics and data security.
- The *Specialist* DT skill set is intended to enable individuals pursuing STEM (science, technology, engineering, and mathematics) careers with a meaningful DT component. A credential incorporating one of the Specialist skill sets would complement a traditional STEM degree by offering the opportunity to develop DT skills in AI/ML, data science and analytics, cyber, and/or cloud.

Throughout the spring and summer of 2018, BHEF and the Greater Washington Partnership facilitated a series of meetings bringing together company subject-matter experts and faculty in each of these areas to develop competency maps for the Generalist skill set and for the AI/ML, data science and analytics, and cyber Specialist skill sets. These competencies are detailed learning outcomes that enable universities to set uniform assessment standards for the competencies. This approach offers companies an assurance that credentials from different universities would provide the same foundational education in DT.

During the same time period, BHEF worked with universities to map the learning outcomes from the competency maps into existing curricula. This exercise showed that although many universities in the consortium offered curricula covering the majority of the learning outcomes from the Generalist and Specialist competency maps, no university offered students a feasible pathway to gain their STEM degree as well as develop a complementary DT skill set in AI/ML, data science and analytics, or cyber. For undergraduates to have the opportunity to gain the full suite of DT skills valued by employers, universities would need to modify, add to, and/or highlight a series of existing courses.

Over the spring and fall of 2018, consortium partners worked to develop and implement the Generalist DT credential. University faculty and administrators developed new courses, adapted existing courses, and worked through their institutional processes to launch a new credential. Company subject-matter experts and executives volunteered to review curricula for new and adapted university courses, as well as committed to offering DT students a series of opportunities—including mentoring, internships, and guaranteed resume review for open positions—to participate in the new credentials.

As a result of these efforts, two consortium partners, George Mason University and Virginia Commonwealth University, enrolled students in their new Generalist DT credential offerings in January 2019.[8] Four additional consortium partners—American University, Georgetown University, University of Richmond, and Virginia Tech—launched their new Generalist DT credentials in September 2019, with others planning to follow in January 2020. These credentials will be available as minors, concentrations, and certificates to undergraduate (and some graduate) students at these institutions. University partners in the consortium are also developing courses to offer Specialist DT credentials to STEM majors. The first of those credentials were scheduled to be launched in January 2020.

The successful development of the Generalist and Specialist DT credentials required significant efforts by company leaders and subject-matter experts and university leaders and faculty, as well as intermediaries BHEF, the Greater Washington Partnership, and the Business Roundtable.

The collaboration model developed in the DMV demonstrates a powerful replication model that brings together companies and higher education institutions to develop and continuously refine educational credentials for students to gain digital technology skills. It is also an opportunity to develop a feedback loop between employers and higher education institutions that signals changes in talent demand and hiring practices and improves the work-readiness of graduates.

23 A COHERENT APPROACH TO CONNECT EDUCATION AND THE FUTURE OF WORK

LaVerne Srinivasan, Elise Henson, and Farhad Asghar

ABSTRACT

Fundamental goals for American public education are to ensure that each student is prepared to be an active participant in a robust democracy and to be successful in the global economy. This requires coordinated efforts among government, philanthropy, the business community, and the education sector. However, as our nation's economic and labor market opportunities evolve, the lack of alignment among K–12, higher education, and the world of work is further exposed and compromises our resilience and success. Our institutions are working to meet the opportunities and demands of the future of work in relative isolation. We must encourage systematic connections that reach across the educational, political, and economic domains to holistically prepare students for life, work, and citizenship. This demands a redesign of educational and employment options for all students. We must ask tough questions about what contributions are needed from each sphere today to prepare the workforce of tomorrow.

TODAY'S HIGH SCHOOL STUDENTS are arriving at college underprepared: 40 percent fail to graduate from four-year institutions, and 68 percent fail to graduate from two-year institutions.[1] Yet the future of work will require higher—not lower—college graduation rates. Already, our economy has 16 million recession- and automation-resistant middle-income jobs that require some postsecondary credential, as well as 35 million jobs that require a bachelor's degree or higher.[2] Nearly half of American employers say they are struggling to fill positions—the highest number in more than a decade—citing dearths of applicants, experience, and both technical and soft skills as their biggest challenges.[3]

As our nation's economic and labor market opportunities evolve, this lack of alignment among K–12, higher education, and the world of work will become further exposed and will compromise our resilience and success as a country. At present, students without access to higher education already experience less mobility and lower lifetime salaries.[4] Looking forward, if K–12 and higher education do not redesign their approaches to reach a broader set of students, we might experience even greater labor shortages and income disparities. If we want to alleviate these issues and prepare students for the careers of the future, it is imperative that we close the chasm between K–12 and higher education.

In this chapter, rather than discussing granular tactics for improving education, we examine the system as a whole—specifically, we examine the issue of fragmentation. Those attempting to reform the education system are familiar with the ways in which it is fragmented. Many have experienced the unintended consequences that come from working in isolation and proceeding with untested assumptions, especially during efforts to scale innovations or foster long-term sustainability. We believe the solution is to work more integratively: to resist the temptation to tackle siloed, singular components and instead collaborate on large-scale transformations designed around a unified vision.

That vision, when considering American public education, is to prepare each student for active participation in a robust democracy and success in an advanced global economy. Accomplishing this demands an approach that reaches across educational, political, and economic domains to seamlessly prepare students for life, work, and citizenship. It demands the redesign of educational and career pathways to allow for cross-pollination among all sectors, from business to government to philanthropy—and it demands asking tough questions about what each sphere must contribute today to prepare the workforce of tomorrow.

Higher education can play a unique role because it has the ability to reach in several directions: toward both K–12 schools and educators, and businesses and future employers. Since it is often under the control of the state, higher education can also reach across to the governor, mayor, and other decision- and policymakers. As such, higher education can do more than effect change within a single institution; instead, it can help to enact networks and policies across an entire city or state. In short, to prepare students to become citizens of the world—who also have economic opportunities in the future workplace—stakeholders must abandon their traditional silos and work together to achieve coherence.

The Case for Coherence

Linear, laser-focused strategies are appropriate when consequences are predictable, contexts are similar, and results are easily measured and few in number. But in the world of education, where contexts are diverse, the level of transformation needed is enormous, and the number of stakeholders is high, linear approaches to change do not work. They accomplish superficial, rather than meaningful, improvements and can lead to missteps and frustration.

To create longer-term solutions at scale, we must accept that education is a complex social system, and design strategies for change around that fundamental fact. Thus, if our goal is to move toward twenty-first-century teaching and learning that better prepares young people for the dynamic world of work, traditional top-down, isolated, programmatic approaches will not succeed. Rather, to effect broad change, we must be thoughtful, flexible, and inclusive, and we must consider myriad factors, including the vantage points and resources of all stakeholders.

Three Design Principles for Coherence

In one attempt to catalyze this shift, Carnegie Corporation of New York launched the Integration Design Consortium in 2017. The corporation extended grants to five organizations to design and implement two-year projects aimed at reducing fragmentation in education and advancing equity. During our collaboration with these initiatives—which each focused on different disciplines, such as human-centered design, systems thinking, and change management—we saw several themes emerge again and again. Irrespective of the project or context, these principles seemed to be influential in making progress toward coherence. For those striving for educational change, we believe these three principles can serve as a foundation upon which to design innovative solutions, and a lens through which to envision ways of thinking and working differently.

Cultivating a Shared Purpose

Rather than assuming that everyone engaged in educational improvement has similar priorities, deliberate attempts must be made to develop a shared understanding of what students need most during their journeys through the system. The work of defining this purpose cannot be done in an isolated manner; instead, a collective vision should be cocreated by various stakeholders, then anchored by thoughtful implementation planning. Developing a cohesive vision has multiple benefits, including increasing broad buy-in and helping individuals understand how their actions can lead to change at scale.

One promising initiative that exemplifies this approach is the Cowen Institute at Tulane University, which shares its purpose of advancing youth success with a multitude of stakeholders in its home city of New Orleans. In addition to disseminating salient research and implementing several direct service programs, the Cowen Institute develops and leads citywide collaboratives focused on promoting access to and persistence in college and careers. These include the New Orleans College Persistence Collaborative and the College and Career Counseling Collaborative, bringing together counselors and practitioners from high schools and community-based organizations across New Orleans under the common goal of increasing students' access to and persistence in college and careers. By engaging in a shared review and understanding of data centered on the needs of all students, these communities of learning play an important role in cultivating a shared sense of purpose across a diversity of organizations and institutions. At the same time, they provide members with professional development, the opportunity to share best practices, and a means of engaging in collective problem-solving centered on improving college and career success for New Orleans youth.

Cocreating Inclusive Environments

This principle, which has its roots in user-centered design, encourages the consideration of various points of view when developing policies, prioritizing input from those who will be directly affected by the outcome. It also urges individuals to assess their own beliefs before creating policies that reverberate through the entire system, and advocates the shifting of power structures so that those most affected have the opportunity to share their perspectives and play a role in the decision-making process. It is only by identifying the actors in the system, understanding their perspectives, and using their input that we can create inclusive and effective programs.

Transforming Postsecondary Education in Mathematics (TPSE Math) is one example of a movement to create an inclusive postsecondary environment. It focuses on a discipline that has traditionally been a barrier to student success: math. In one study of fifty-seven community colleges across several states, 59 percent of students were assigned to remedial math courses upon enrollment, and, of those, only 20 percent completed a college-level math course within three years.[5] Through TPSE Math, leading mathematicians have convened stakeholders across the country to change mathematics education at community colleges, four-year colleges, and research universities so that it better meets the needs of a diverse student body and their diverse future careers. For example, TPSE has provided significant support in the national movement to develop multiple mathematics pathways for students. The goal is for every student to have the opportunity to take a rigorous entry-level mathematics course relevant to his or her field of study and future career and to significantly reduce the time for underprepared students to complete their first college-level math course. This results in more inclusive math departments and courses that focus on success for all students, not only those who will go on to be math majors or to remain in academia. TPSE has also promoted cross-sector engagement by facilitating conversations about effective and innovative practices—including the connections between college mathematics and the world of work—and then sharing those learnings across institutions. These math departments are supporting a rich set of interdisciplinary academic experiences and pathways designed to prepare students with the mathematical knowledge and skills needed for engagement in society and the workforce.

Building Capacity That Is Responsive to Change

To create infrastructure and processes that will be effective over the long term, it is crucial to acknowledge and accept the dynamic nature of the education system. This means prioritizing relationships and trust, and viewing a project's initial implementation as the first of multiple iterations and trials, each of which considers the potential impact on different stakeholders. This is crucial because achieving broader coherence across the education system can seem daunting, so it is more manageable to identify a specific gap or disconnect to address, such as the transition from college to career.

Focusing on particular barriers and trying out solutions before prescribing them at scale acknowledges the dynamism of the sector and the complexities of coherence, while making meaningful progress on issues that matter.

The University Innovation Alliance (UIA), for instance, takes an agile, human-centered approach to increasing the number and diversity of college graduates in the United States. Since its founding in 2014, this national coalition of eleven public research universities has produced 29.6 percent more low-income bachelor's degree graduates per year, amounting to nearly 13,000 graduates annually. The UIA estimates that the total will reach 100,000 by the 2022–2023 academic year.[6] True to the nature of the research institutions leading the work, the UIA accomplishes this through experimentation and iteration. One area of focus for the network has been ensuring student success beyond graduation through redesigning college-to-career supports to better ensure students find gainful employment upon graduation. The project uses design thinking, with its rapid prototyping of ideas and short feedback cycles, in service of reimagining career services to better support low-income students, first-generation students, and students of color. The process of innovation starts with understanding the perspective of students and the current practices on campuses; providing career services professionals with the capacity, time and connections they need to generate new campus solutions; and engaging employers and other stakeholders in the redesign. This approach is consistent with the vision of the UIA, that "by piloting new interventions, sharing insights about their relative cost and effectiveness, and scaling those interventions that are successful[,] . . . [its] collaborative work will catalyze systemic changes in the entire higher education sector."[7]

Two other relevant models can be found elsewhere in this book. Jason A. Tyszko and Robert G. Sheets describe a job-data exchange where information on skills and competencies could be shared between employers and higher education. Brian Fitzgerald and colleagues from the Business–Higher Education Forum outline a different type of partnership for sharing relevant career-education information between business and higher education.

An Integrative Pathway to the Future

Strides in educational coherence are being made on a regional level, too. Tennessee and Colorado, for example, have adopted holistic cradle-to-career solutions that intentionally plan for the duration of their residents' lifetimes, and the Central Ohio Compact has mobilized K–12, higher education, community-based organizations, and local industry with the goal of helping 65 percent of local adults earn a postsecondary credential by 2025.[8] Each of these initiatives exemplifies the design principles described earlier, by considering the experiences of key actors and employing a multistakeholder approach that includes policymakers—factors crucial to enacting change on a systemic level.

Though these projects are promising, they are not enough. In most of the country, education, employment, and economic reform remain isolated in both policy and practice. If we continue down this path, limiting ourselves to what is possible within each of our silos, our mutual interests will soon be consumed by our differences. For the revolutionary changes that the future demands, we must move beyond this fragmented way of thinking and working, and accept that history's boundaries no longer apply. The examples described in this chapter show us what can be achieved when we take a coherent approach to connecting education and the future of work, harnessing integrative design principles to foster progress, flexibility, and inclusivity. To improve today and prepare for the future, we must build on these ideas together. We must embrace a user-centered approach that is designed around our ultimate goal: empowering and preparing our nation's youth for fulfilling, engaged lives and productive careers, now and for decades to come.

CONCLUSION

DEBATES ABOUT THE FUTURE OF WORK are rife with disagreement about the scale of the changes that are coming. Some raise alarms about automation rendering humans obsolete, while others take a more measured position that humans will need to learn new ways of working with machines, but that they will still have a valued role in the workplace. Given these differing visions, there are many potential solutions to address the learning needs of workers facing a future that is largely unpredictable.

The contributors to this book present viewpoints that reveal key tensions between traditional approaches to skill development and the innovative, transformational change that the future of work will demand. These debates give rise to six themes that align visions for the future along continuums in the following areas:

- Disruption versus transformation
- Credentials versus skills
- Technical skills versus human skills
- Vocational education versus liberal arts
- Learning versus unlearning
- Higher education solutions versus employer solutions

In this concluding chapter we discuss these areas of debate and conclude by revisiting the book's overarching question of what is higher education's special role in addressing employment needs in the future of work.

Disruption versus Transformation

The term *disruption* connotes the sense that changes to industries and jobs will be radical and potentially difficult. In this vision of change, automation portends massive job losses as workers are forced to make a difficult switch to new lines of work. *Transformation*, by contrast, conveys the idea that the coming changes will be gentler and easier to navigate than some observers predict. Jobs may change by incorporating new technologies, but a radical restructuring of the labor market will be largely avoided.

The chapter by Lewis, Young, Shaffner, and Arbit illustrates the drastic impact of disruption in its portrayal of a community of fragile workers who are chronically unemployed as a direct result of the collapse of the manu-facturing economy in Ypsilanti, Michigan. The men they describe cannot envision a work life separate from industrial manufacturing and view the growth of technology in everyday work as a threat. The "back to the future" perspective of these men defines good jobs and good futures by what was successful in the past vis-à-vis the local manufacturing economy rather than a forward-looking vision that embraces change. Their relationship to nearby higher education is weak, if not nonexistent, as they are caught in the middle of two realities—that of a decaying industrial economy in Ypsilanti and that of a thriving knowledge-based economy in the nearby college town of Ann Arbor. This dire reality provides a call to action for colleges and employers to serve the needs of fragile workers so that they can have a productive role in current and future economic realities.

In contrast to Lewis et al., Lund and Hancock depict a gentler scenario of transformation. McKinsey's research predicts that job losses and gains will mostly balance each other out. Rather than massive unemployment, the likelier scenario is that automation will induce extensive transfor-mation of existing roles. With this gentler version of change in mind, they predict that demand for social-emotional skills will grow about as fast as the demand for advanced technological skills. Their sugges-tions for educational solutions to changing workforce needs suggest that modest adjustments to existing higher education approaches should be sufficient to address the new workforce needs. Among these solutions are expanding existing credentials to reach more and diverse students, including lifelong learners, and better aligning higher education to meet workforce needs.

Robinson's reflections on the technological transitions he has witnessed over the course of his career support the idea that the changes coming in the future of work will be more transformational than disruptive. Technology has transformed day-to-day work in previous eras, it continues to do so today, and will continue into the future. Indeed, Robinson's observation that the theme of the "future of work" has been around for many decades suggests that workplace transformation instigated by technology is nothing new. Rather, it is an enduring state of affairs that has always demanded continuous learning beyond a bachelor's degree.

Credentials versus Skills

Today's employers are starting to transition away from traditional higher education degrees as the premier indicator that workers possess the skills and knowledge needed for success on the job. As employers rely less on college degrees, the question emerges of how they can identify skills in the absence of a traditional credential. Pittinsky argues that, while traditional liberal arts degrees still have a value in preparing workers with foundational skills in communications, analytical thinking, and numeric literacy, employers also care about technical skills, which have a short half-life and require constant refreshing through certifications and other forms of non-degree study. Trumbore, too, describes the value of alternative credentials in her discussion of Wharton's online credit-bearing short courses that result in microcredentials. These kinds of alternative credentials solve the problem that on-campus residential degrees are time intensive, expensive, and often not the best solution for those who seek educational options that can be pursued while people continue to work.

Apprenticeships are one promising solution that is reemerging as the value of traditional degrees wanes. McCarthy's chapter presents apprenticeships as a solution to the current disconnect between credentials and skills that addresses the needs of education and employers. Apprenticeships can effectively address the high cost of higher education as well as the need for continuous learning that is connected to work. However, to advance apprenticeships as a large-scale solution, models need to be developed so that apprenticeships lead to higher education degrees, which are still necessary for entry to high-level careers. As Kuehn describes, registered apprenticeships in the European model provide a training option that incorporates classroom-based and on-the-job training while learners are paid employees of the company. Elevating apprenticeships to the bachelor's-degree level would help "guarantee workers high-quality jobs and ensure the stream of innovations that propel the modern economy."

Technical Skills versus Human Skills

In emphasizing automation, artificial intelligence, and machine learning, deliberations about the future of work place great importance on technological innovations and the skills people will need in order to contend with them. These discussions typically diminish the enduring importance of human skills, whose importance several contributors note. In describing Upjohn's approach to creating a human-centered organization, Ray, Hong, and White argue that galvanizing individuals and teams around a worthy mission is critical. Workers increasingly seek more than a paycheck or external validation of achievements, such as good performance evaluations; they now seek fulfillment through pursuing a worthy purpose and personal and professional growth.

Both Ray and Ulica discuss the importance of balancing the global and the local. Ray notes the importance of empowering local teams around the world while also maximizing the global scale of a multinational corporation. Ulica argues for the importance of geographic knowledge, which enables workers to understand and interact with foreign cultures. Economic globalization compels interactions across countries and cultures, which makes knowledge of cultural diversity, societies, and environments paramount for the future of work. Likewise, Bell-Rose and Ollen document the importance of diversity in the workplace and highlight the important role of employers and higher education institutions in creating environments that nurture an appreciation of differences so that all can achieve their potential.

Vocational Education versus Liberal Arts

Related to the debate between technical skills and human skills is the dynamic between vocational education and liberal arts. Higher education is based on the liberal arts model, with vocational preparation reserved for lower-order educational options. While many employers still perceive value in liberal arts, particularly for preparing learners to adapt throughout their careers, a sizable segment of employers now claim that a liberal arts approach does not adequately prepare students with the immediate skills needed for the workforce. Braunstein supports this perspective in his discussion of the citizen developer. As everyday workers are brought closer to technology, they are empowered with the tools needed to create their own technology solutions, making technological literacy a foundational skill for all lines of work.

The good news is that many higher education institutions are incorporating programs that infuse career readiness into the liberal arts curriculum, as Mayer describes. Incorporating applied learning and technology skills into the curriculum, offering bootcamps, and partnering with employers to provide work-relevant training are a few of the ways that liberal arts institutions integrate career preparation into their offerings. Otter takes a different perspective on the disconnect between liberal arts education and workforce preparation. She diagnoses the root of the problem as the organization of higher education into silos by academic discipline. What is needed for success in the future of work is a greater focus on interdisciplinary thinking that integrates essential skills, technological literacy, and application of competencies in ways that are relevant to the complex problems and projects that exist in the real world.

Learning versus Unlearning
The future of work necessitates change at the level of individual workers, as well as for employers and higher education institutions. The recurrent theme of change calls for an examination of what it takes for change to occur and how it can be navigated successfully.

Dede describes the need for unlearning entrenched practices and ways of doing things to allow learning and upskilling for new roles. Unlearning strategies must be integrated into occupational upskilling for transformational change to occur. This need for unlearning echoes in Zhu, Alonso, and Taylor's discussion of the resistance of workers to technological change. Those who resist retraining and upskilling do so out of a belief that it undermines their current value to employers. Without the willingness or ability to unlearn now-obsolete skills, the potential of these workers to acquire new skills and identities is limited.

Evidence of the importance of embracing new ways of doing things is found in Schejbal's chapter on transforming higher education to meet the needs of learners across their lifespans. He argues that institutional culture is a hard barrier to overcome because university faculty bring an individualistic perspective to curriculum development that is based on their area of expertise. To bring curricular coherence to the liberal arts, joint ownership of the entire curriculum is required, which depends on the willingness of faculty to compromise their individual academic interests.

The need for continual learning and unlearning is inescapable in the future of work. As the pace of technological and industry change accelerates, today's workers should expect to revisit education throughout their lives. This is true in all industries, including STEM fields, as Gazi and Baker discuss in their chapter. STEM knowledge changes especially quickly, necessitating the need for professional, continuing, and online education for STEM workers. The increased need for training and retraining in the future of work demands new ways of thinking about higher education across the lifespan. Rascoff and DeVaney propose a stronger shift toward alumni learning models by higher education institutions. They argue that a commitment to perpetual learning of alumni can be a new social contract for higher education that serves as a recurring source of value for alumni in service of their ongoing success. They claim a clear need for "renewable intellectual energy" as skills change rapidly and industries transform. Work-based learning has limits because employers lack the long-term horizon of developing the human capital of individual workers, while higher education is suited to take the long view in supporting success of their alumni.

Higher Education versus Employer Solutions

Discussions throughout this book reveal a range of potential solutions to solve the gap between what employers want and what higher education delivers. True change at scale requires partnerships among higher education, employers, and other relevant partners, rather than siloed efforts that fail to reach across organizations or sectors. Srinivasan, Henson, and Asghar note that linear strategic solutions do not work for diffuse issues such as education with diverse contexts, an enormous need for transformation, and a high number of stakeholders. Multisector partnerships are necessary to unify our fragmented systems of learning and work. Accomplishing this vision requires coordination across education, government, and the business sector. Weiner extends this idea with his contention that K–12 education needs to certify students in an array of work-relevant competencies and mindsets, including collaboration, teamwork, and problem solving. To begin developing these skills in higher education is too late.

A large-scale, coordinated solution is aspirational and a worthy goal to work toward. At the same time, more focused partnership models are effective. Tyszko and Sheets underscore the need for improved information sharing between employers and higher education. The US Chamber of Commerce Foundation's Job Data Exchange provides real-time information sharing on skills and competencies, in order to promote agile partnerships between business and higher education. The Business–Higher Education Forum, too, sees a solution in the form of stronger partnerships between employers and higher education institutions. Fitzgerald, Cardenas-Navia, and Chen describe the National Higher Education and Workforce Initiative that supports business–higher education partnerships and the creation of digital credentials. The partnership implementation process entails corporate leadership, philanthropy, employee engagement, core competencies and expertise, and research and development activities to build deep, strategic partnerships that go beyond short-term engagements. These strategic partnerships generate a continuing feedback loop to share information between employers and higher education institutions, resulting in improved talent management and work readiness of graduates.

Heitzlhofer offers a novel approach to solving the dilemma of scaling retraining at a level necessary to address large-scale retraining needs. To scale retraining, companies must collaborate and coordinate their retraining efforts across companies. Learning and development teams have the potential to be a bridge across companies, rather than operating as clandestine operations whose secrets are closely guarded from their competitors.

The Way Forward: The Imperative for Higher Education Solutions

So, then, what is the special role of higher education in solving the skills gap in the future of work? A strong foundation in liberal arts education remains relevant for the future of work because of its effectiveness in developing the ability to learn, think critically, communicate, and problem solve. At the same time, colleges and universities need to pay specific attention to the development of technical skills and less easily measured competencies, such as leadership and adaptability. Improving how knowledge and competencies are documented and signaled to employers through credentials is an area that warrants careful focus as traditional university degrees are increasingly competing with other forms of training, such as apprenticeships, bootcamps, and applied learning activities outside of the formal curriculum.

Expanding access to more and diverse students of all ages is imperative for building a strong pool of trained talent that is prepared to move into professional roles. The future of work demands workers with diverse talents and perspectives who are globally minded, able to work in many cultural contexts and with diverse groups of people. Developing creative ways to engage with learners across their lifespans will enable workers to adapt as conditions change.

The core of the solution resides in strengthening the relationship between higher education and employers. Clearly, higher education needs to make a more robust, intentional, and coordinated effort to engage with employers in order to address future workforce needs. Improvements in information sharing, employment-oriented curricula, and cocurricular offerings will address employers' needs for skilled talent who are able to adapt and will improve the employment prospects of graduates. These efforts are central not only for workers and employers but also for higher education so that it remains relevant amid the shifting relationship between education and employment in the future.

NOTES

Introduction

1. Daisuke Wakabayashi, "Google's Shadow Work Force: Temps Who Outnumber Full-Time Employees," *New York Times*, May 28, 2019, https://www.nytimes.com/2019/05/28/technology/google-temp-workers.html.

2. H. James Wilson and Paul R. Daugherty, "Collaborative Intelligence: Humans and AI Are Joining Forces," *Harvard Business Review*, July 1, 2018, https://hbr.org/2018/07/collaborative-intelligence-humans-and-ai-are-joining-forces.

3. "15 More Companies That No Longer Require a Degree—Apply Now," Glassdoor Blog, August 14, 2018, https://www.glassdoor.com/blog/no-degree-required/; Corinne Purtill, "Apple, IBM, and Google Don't Care Anymore If You Went to College," Quartz at Work, August 23, 2018, https://qz.com/work/1367191/apple-ibm-and-google-dont-require-a-college-degree/.

4. Vanessa Fuhrmans, "How a Company's Aging Workforce Retrained Itself for the Cloud," *Wall Street Journal*, October 27, 2019, https://www.wsj.com/articles/how-a-companys-aging-workforce-retrained-itself-for-the-cloud-11572192001.

5. Paul Fain, "Interview with IBM Official about the Company's 'New-Collar' Push to Look beyond College Degrees," *Inside Higher Ed*, October 29, 2019, https://www.insidehighered.com/digital-learning/article/2019/10/29/interview-ibm-official-about-companys-new-collar-push-look.

6. Lauren Thomas, "Walmart Is Going after High School Students in War for Talent," CNBC, June 4, 2019, https://www.cnbc.com/2019/06/03/walmart-is-going-after-high-school-students-in-war-for-talent.html.

7. J. Manyika, S. Lund, M. Chui, J. Bughin, J. Woetzel, P. Batra, R. Ko, & S. Sanghvi, "Jobs Lost, Jobs Gained: Workforce Transitions in a Time of Automation," McKinsey & Company, 2017.

8. Jörg Goldhahn, Vanessa Rampton, and Giatgen A. Spinas, "Could Artificial Intelligence Make Doctors Obsolete?" *BMJ* 363 (2018): k4563, https://doi.org/10.1136/bmj.k4563.

9. Stefan Hall, "Can You Tell If This Article Was Written by a Robot? 7 Challenges for AI in Journalism," World Economic Forum, January 15, 2018, https://www.weforum.org/agenda/2018/01/can-you-tell-if-this-article-was-written-by-a-robot-7-challenges-for-ai-in-journalism/.

10. C. Dede & J. Richards (Eds.), *The 60-Year Curriculum: New Models for Lifelong Learning in the Digital Economy*, New York: Routledge, 2020.

11. Strada Education Network and Gallup, 2017 *College Student Survey: A Nationally Representative Survey of Currently Enrolled Students* (Washington, DC: Gallup, 2017).

Chapter 1

Equipping a New Generation with the Skills Needed in the Automation Age

1. Frank Levy and Richard J. Murnane, *The New Division of Labor: How Computers Are Creating the Next Job Market* (Princeton, NJ: Princeton University Press, 2005).

2. See, for example, "How Americans See Automation and the Workplace in 7 Charts," Pew Research FactTank, April 8, 2019, https://www.pewresearch.org/fact-tank/2019/04/08/how-americans-see-automation-and-the-workplace-in-7-charts/; EU Directorate-General for Communication, *Special Eurobarometer 419: Public Perceptions of Science, Research and Innovation*, 2014, https://data.europa.eu/euodp/en/data/dataset/S2047_81_5_419_ENG.

3. Jacques Bughin, "Why AI Isn't the Death of Jobs," *MIT Sloan Management Review*, May 24, 2018.

4. J. Manyika, S. Lund, M. Chui, J. Bughin, J. Woetzel, P. Batra, R. Ko, and S. Sanghvi, *Jobs Lost, Jobs Gained: What the Future of Work Will Mean for Jobs, Skills, and Wages*, McKinsey Global Institute, December 2017, https://www.mckinsey.com/featured-insights/future-of-work/jobs-lost-jobs-gained-what-the-future-of-work-will-mean-for-jobs-skills-and-wages.

5. Michael Chui, James Manyika, and Mehdi Miremadi, "Four Fundamentals of Workplace Automation," *McKinsey Quarterly*, November 2015.

6. McKinsey Global Institute, *Skill Shift: Automation and the Future of the Workforce*, May 2018, https://www.mckinsey.com/featured-insights/future-of-work/skill-shift-automation-and-the-future-of-the-workforce.

7. McKinsey Global Institute, *Skill Shift*.

8. "Deep-Learning Machine Listens to Bach, Then Writes Its Own Music in the Same Style," *MIT Technology Review*, December 14, 2016.

9. Schools in some countries have at various times sought to make such skills part of the school curriculum. Some German federal states, for example, mark or have marked pupils for nonacademic traits including diligence, endurance, and reliability. However, some teachers' unions and others criticize the practice as being inappropriate and subjective. "Verkopfte Debatte," *Die Zeit*, September 4, 2003.

10. Mark Muro, Sifan Liu, Jacob Whiton, and Siddharth Kukarni, *Digitalization and the American Workforce*, Brookings Institution, November 2017, https://www.brookings.edu/research/digitalization-and-the-american-workforce/.

11. McKinsey Global Institute, *Skill Shift*.

12. Anna Feldman, "STEAM Rising: Why We Need to Put the Arts into STEM Education," *Slate*, June 16, 2019, https://slate.com/technology/2015/06/steam-vs-stem-why-we-need-to-put-the-arts-into-stem-education.html.

13. Sharon Lacey, "Integrating the Arts and Humanities at MIT, Then and Now," MIT blog post, June 20, 2018, https://arts.mit.edu/integrating-the-arts-and-humanities-at-mit-then-and-now/.

14. Michael Conway, Kweilin Ellingrud, Tracy Nowski, and Renee Wittemyer, *Closing the Tech Gender Gap through Philanthropy and Corporate Social Responsibility*, September

2018, McKinsey & Company, https://www.mckinsey.com/industries/high-tech/our-insights/closing-the-tech-gender-gap-through-philanthropy-and-corporate-social-responsibility.

15. Julia Angwin, Jeff Larson, Surya Mattu, and Lauren Kirchner, "Machine Bias," *ProPublica*, May 2016, https://www.propublica.org/article/machine-bias-risk-assessments-in-criminal-sentencing; Joy Buolamwini and Timnit Gebru, "Gender Shades: Intersectional Accuracy Disparities in Commercial Gender Classification," *Proceedings of Machine Learning Research* 1 (2018): 1–15, http://proceedings.mlr.press/v81/buolamwini18a.html. See also Jake Silberg and James Manyika, *Tackling Bias in Artificial Intelligence (and in Humans)*, McKinsey Global Institute, June 2019, https://www.mckinsey.com/featured-insights/artificial-intelligence/tackling-bias-in-artificial-intelligence-and-in-humans.

16. Japanese robotics professor Masahiro Mori coined the term "uncanny valley" in a 1970 essay to characterize the unsettling feeling people may experience when facing humanoid robots. For an English translation see Masahiro Mori, "The Uncanny Valley," *IEEE Spectrum*, June 12, 2012.

17. See JFF, www.jff.org.

18. www.ptech.org.

19. Celeste Carruthers, "5 Things to Know about the Tennessee Promise Scholarship," Brookings Institution, May 6, 2019, https://www.brookings.edu/blog/brown-center-chalkboard/2019/05/06/five-things-to-know-about-the-tennessee-promise-scholarship/.

20. Western Governors University, "WGU, EIU-UHW, and Healthcare Employers Partner to Reinvent Workforce Education for Tens of Thousands of California Students" (press release), April 16, 2019.

21. Arizona State University, "Starbucks College Achievement Plan: Education Meets Opportunity," https://edplus.asu.edu/what-we-do/starbucks-college-achievement-plan; AT&T, "Start Up Your Computers, Class Is Now in Session," January 15, 2014, https://about.att.com/newsroom/georgia_tech_launches_first_massive_online_degree_program.html.

22. Grace Oldham, "ASU Plans For-Profit Venture to Increase Corporate Partnerships in Education Offerings," *The State Press*, March 23, 2019.

23. See, for example, OECD, *Reskilling: How Difficult Is It?* OECD Forum 2018, https://www.oecd-forum.org/users/67300-anne-lise-prigent/posts/39838-oecd-forum-2018-reskilling-how-difficult-is-it.

24. "Employee Training Rendered Personal for the Walmart Family," *The Blueprint*, https://blueprint.box.com/employee-training-walmart-academy; Charisse Jones, "Walmart's Expanding the Chance to Go to College for a Dollar a Day to More of Its Workers," *USA Today*, June 5, 2019.

25. www.georgiaquickstart.org.

26. See Michigan Ross alumni career services, https://michiganross.umich.edu/our-community/alumni/alumni-advantage/career-resources/career-services.

27. Matthew Rascoff and Eric Johnson, "Reimagining College as a Lifelong Learning Experience," *Chronicle of Higher Education*, August 28, 2016.

Chapter 2

The Role of Citizen Developers in Developing Technological Literacy

1. Marc Andreessen, "Why Software Is Eating the World," *Wall Street Journal*, August 20, 2011.

2. See, for example, Gerald C. Kane, Doug Palmer, Anh Nguyen Phillips, David Kiron, and Natasha Buckley, "Coming of Age Digitally," *Deloitte Insights*, June 5, 2018, www2.deloitte.com/us/en/insights/focus/digital-maturity/coming-of-age-digitally-learning-leadership-legacy.html.

3. For a succinct review of some of these challenges, see Beth Bohstedt and Sundi Richard, "Digital Agility: Embracing a Holistic Approach to Digital Literacy in the Liberal Arts," *EDUCAUSE Review*, January 8, 2020, https://er.educause.edu/blogs/2020/1/digital-agility-embracing-a-holistic-approach-to-digital-literacy-in-the-liberal-arts.

4. "Vocational," *Merriam-Webster* [online dictionary], www.merriam-webster.com/dictionary/vocational.

5. See, for example, Samuel Castiglione, Pamela Leconte, and Frances Smith, *The Revised Position Paper of the Interdisciplinary Council on Vocational Evaluation and Assessment*, 2018, http://vecap.org/wp-content/uploads/2018/11/V22-The-Revised-Position-Paper-of-the-I-C-.pdf.

6. Alex Gay, "How Digital Literacy Affects the Modern Workforce," *Adobe Blog*, March 14, 2019, https://theblog.adobe.com/how-digital-literacy-affects-the-modern-workforce/.

7. For one perspective on the most important inventions of all time, see Devon Scott-Leslie, "Top 100 Famous Inventions and Greatest Ideas of All Time," *Cad Crowd*, March 31, 2020, www.cadcrowd.com/blog/top-100-famous-inventions-and-greatest-ideas-of-all-time/.

8. See, for example, Lewis Chou, "9 Data Visualization Tools That You Cannot Miss in 2019," *Medium*, September 10, 2019, https://towardsdatascience.com/9-data-visualization-tools-that-you-cannot-miss-in-2019-3ff23222a927.

9. Stephen D. Simpson, "The Death of the Trading Floor," *Investopedia*, June 25, 2019, www.investopedia.com/financial-edge/0511/the-death-of-the-trading-floor.aspx.

10. Ibid.

11. Techopedia, "Software Development Life Cycle (SDLC)," April 3, 2020, https://www.techopedia.com/about.

12. Alison Doyle, "Important Job Skills for Software Engineers," The Balance/Careers, July 09, 2019, www.thebalancecareers.com/software-engineer-skills-list-2062483.

13. Drew Gilpin Faust, "The Role of the University in a Changing World," Harvard University, June 30, 2010, https://www.harvard.edu/president/speech/2010/role-university-changing-world.

Chapter 3

The Future of Work

1. Hart Research Associates (on behalf of the Association of American Colleges & Universities), *Fulfilling the American Dream: Liberal Education and the Future of Work*, July 2018, 12, https://www.aacu.org/sites/default/files/files/LEAP/2018EmployerResearchReport.pdf.

2. Hart Research Associates, *Fulfilling the American Dream*, 13.

3. Hart Research Associates, *Fulfilling the American Dream*, 16–17.

4. Oliver Wyman, *Parchment Market Study: Adjacent TAM*, July 2019, 55–59.

5. Michael Roth, "Closing Keynote. Parchment Summit on Innovating Academic Credentials," March 2017, http://www.parchmentsummit.com/summit-videos-2017/.

6. George Anders, "That 'Useless' Liberal Arts Degree Has Become Tech's Hottest Ticket," *Forbes*, July 29, 2015, https://www.forbescom/sites/georgeanders/2015/07/29/liberal-arts-degree-tech/#42c08538745d.

7. "The Role of Higher Education in Career Development and Employer Perceptions," *Chronicle of Higher Education*, December 2012, p. 15.

8. Hart Research Associates, *Fulfilling the American Dream*, 8.

Chapter 4
Why Geography Is So Important

1. For more on Salopek's remarkable journey, see the National Geographic Society website "About the Out of Eden Walk," www.nationalgeographic.org/projects/out-of-eden-walk/about/.

2. Rania Abouzeid, "Thousands of Refugee Children Are Stranded on Europe's Doorstep," *National Geographic*, October 23, 2017, https://www.nationalgeographic.com/photography/proof/2017/10/unaccompanied-minors-refugees-serbia-afghanistan-pakistan-children-migration/.

3. Ibid.

4. Vicki Phillips and Lina Gomez, "The Power of Geography," *Edtech Mindset*, December 2019, 42n2, accessed June 15, 2020 at www.mindcet.org/uploads/2020/01/MindCET_Magazine_issue-9.pdf.

5. Jonathan Foley, "A Five-Step Plan to Feed the World" [website], *National Geographic Magazine*, accessed June 22, 2020 at www.nationalgeographic.com/foodfeatures/feeding-9-billion/.

6. "What Is Geo-Literacy" [website], National Geographic Society, accessed June 15, 2020 at www.nationalgeographic.org/media/what-is-geo-literacy/.

7. Council on Foreign Relations and National Geographic Society, *What College-Aged Students Know about the World: A Survey on Global Literacy*, September 2016, accessed April 15, 2020 at https://drive.google.com/file/d/0B2AUpoucQL4jQXhzOWt4QjBfMFk/view.

8. Kevin Qualey, "If Americans Can Find North Korea on a Map, They're More Likely to Prefer Diplomacy," *New York Times*, July 5, 2017, accessed June 22, 2020 at www.nytimes.com/interactive/2017/05/14/upshot/if-americans-can-find-north-korea-on-a-map-theyre-more-likely-to-prefer-diplomacy.html.

9. Perspectives in this section are those of my colleague, Alex Tait, Geographer at the *National Geographic Society*.

10. Bureau of Labor Statistics, US Department of Labor, *Occupational Outlook Handbook*, Cartographers and Photogrammetrists, April 10, 2020, accessed June 15, 2020 at www.bls.gov/ooh/architecture-and-engineering/cartographers-and-photogrammetrists.htm.

11. "GIS (Geographic Information System)" [website], National Geographic Society, accessed June 15, 2020 at www.nationalgeographic.org/encyclopedia/geographic-information-system-gis/.

12. ESRI, *Geography Matters: An ESRI White Paper* (Redlands, CA: ESRI, 2008), accessed June 22, 2020 at www.esri.com/library/whitepapers/pdfs/geography-matters.pdf.

Chapter 5
Enabling a High-Performing, Human-Centered Organization in Pfizer's Upjohn Division

1. Robert D. Putnam, *Bowling Alone: The Collapse and Revival of American Community* (New York: Simon & Schuster, 2000).

2. OECD, *PISA 2015 Results. Volume III: Students' Well-Being* (Paris: PISA, OECD Publishing, 2017), https://www.oecd-ilibrary.org/education/pisa-2015-results-volume-iii_9789264273856-en.

3. LinkedIn, "Inside the Mind of Today's Candidate; 13 Insights That Will Make You a Better Recruiter," 2017, https://business.linkedin.com/content/dam/me/business/en-us/talent-solutions/resources/pdfs/inside-the-mind-of-todays-candidate.pdf.

4. Tracy Brower, "Secrets of the Most Productive People," *Fast Company*, February 16, 2019, https://www.fastcompany.com/90308095/why-you-should-stop-trying-to-achieve-work-life-balance.

5. J. Clifton and J. Harter, *It's the Manager: Gallup Finds the Quality of Managers and Team Leaders Is the Single Biggest Factor in Your Organization's Long-Term Success* (Omaha, NE: Gallup Press, 2019).

6. Clifton and Harter, *It's the Manager.*

7. At Pfizer, the term *colleague* is preferred over *employee.*

8. D. Sull and C. Sull, "With Goals, FAST Beats SMART," *MIT Sloan Management Review*, June 5, 2018, https://sloanreview.mit.edu/article/with-goals-fast-beats-smart/.

9. G. Vielmetter and Y. Sell, *Leadership 2030: The Six Megatrends You Need to Understand to Lead Your Company into the Future* (New York: AMACOM, 2014).

10. Peter Drucker, *The Effective Executive* (New York: Harper Wiley, 2015).

Chapter 6

How the Future of Work Impacts the Workforce of Technical Organizations

1. See, for example, Sarah Kessler, "Automation Anxiety Dates Back to the Late 16th Century," *Quartz*, August 12, 2029, https://qz.com/1681832/the-history-of-the-future-of-work/. Also, "A Retrospective on the History of Work" [undated web site], Atlassian, https://www.atlassian.com/history-of-work.

2. See, for example, "Lead in the New," *Commercial Aerospace Insight Report*, Accenture, March 2019, https://www.accenture.com/_acnmedia/accenture/redesign-assets/dotcom/documents/global/1/accenture-commercial-aerospace-insight-report.pdf. Also, Joachim Kirsch, "The New Value Chain: Greater Efficiency in the Aviation Industry," *Aircraft Interiors International*, January 17, 2018, https://www.aircraftinteriorsinternational.com/features/the-new-value-chain-a-greater-efficiency-in-the-aviation-industry.html.

3. See, for example, Tsedal Neeley, "Global Teams That Work," *Harvard Business Review*, October 2015, https://hbr.org/2015/10/global-teams-that-work. Also, Emma Buckby, "6 Tips to Make a Global Team Work," *Communicaid*, February 1, 2017, https://www.communicaid.com/cross-cultural-training/blog/6-tips-make-global-team-work/.

4. See, for example, "Professional Certification (Computer Technology)," *Wikipedia*, https://en.wikipedia.org/wiki/Professional_certification_(computer_technology); and "Adult Learners: Who They Are & What They Want from College," *EAB Daily Briefing*, October 23, 2019, https://eab.com/insights/daily-briefing/adult-learner/adult-learners-who-they-are-what-they-want-from-college/.

5. "APPEL Has Evolved over Time to Meet NASA's Evolving Needs for Training." See https://appel.nasa.gov/about-us/history/.

6. See, for example, John Jarrell, "The Future of Digital Technology in the Aviation Industry," *International Airport Review*, October 2, 2018, https://www.internationalairportreview.com/article/76057/future-digital-technology/; and Larry Marchand, "The Future Flight Path of Aerospace Technology," *SME*, October 1, 2019, https://www.sme.org/technologies/articles/2019/october/the-future-flight-path-of-aerospace-technology/.

7. Roger Forsgren, personal interview, April 22, 2020.

8. See, for example, Robert Ubell, "How Online Education Went from Teaching Reform to Economic Necessity for Colleges," *EdSurge*, March 5, 2020, https://www.edsurge.com/news/2020-

03-05-how-online-education-went-from-teaching-reform-to-economic-necessity-for-colleges.

9. See, for example, Michael Ryschkewitsch, Dawn Schaible, and Wiley Larson, "The Art and Science of Systems Engineering," NASA, January 18, 2009, https://appel.nasa.gov/wp-content/uploads/2013/05/Art_and_Sci_of_SE_LONG_1_20_09.pdf; and "SELP Program Overview," NASA APPEL Knowledge Services, https://appel.nasa.gov/developmental-programs/seldp-overview/seldp-program-overview/.

10. John M. Mann, "The Times They Are a Changing: Changes in the Workplace in the Last 20 Years," The Alexander Group, June 26, 2019, https://tagsearch.com/insights/articles/changes-in-the-workplace-in-the-last-20-years.

11. Daniel Greenspan, "Best Computer Jobs for the Future," *IT Career News*, December 20, 2019, https://www.itcareerfinder.com/brain-food/blog/entry/best-computer-jobs-for-the-future.html.

Chapter 7
Corporate Learning and Development Has a Vital Role to Play in the Robotics Revolution—Is It Ready?

1. Mark Muro, Robert Maxim, and Jacob Whiton, with contributions from Ian Hathaway, *Automation and Artificial Intelligence: How Machines Are Affecting People and Places*, Brookings Institution, January 2019, https://www.brookings.edu/wp-content/uploads/2019/01/2019.01_BrookingsMetro_Automation-AI_Report_Muro-Maxim-Whiton-FINAL-version.pdf.

2. Susan Lund, James Manyika, Liz Hilton Segel, André Dua, Bryan Hancock, Scott Rutherford, and Brent Macon, *The Future of Work in America: People and Places, Today and Tomorrow*, McKinsey Global Institute, July 2019, https://www.mckinsey.com/featured-insights/future-of-work/the-future-of-work-in-america-people-and-places-today-and-tomorrow.

3. Timothy Aeppel, "U.S. Companies Put Record Number of Robots to Work in 2018," Reuters, February 27, 2019, https://www.reuters.com/article/us-usa-economy-robots/u-s-companies-put-record-number-of-robots-to-work-in-2018-idUSKCN1QH0K0.

4. Khari Johnson, "DHL Will Invest $300 Million to Quadruple Robots in Warehouses in 2019," *VentureBeat*, November 29, 2018, https://venturebeat.com/2018/11/29/dhl-will-invest-300-million-to-quadruple-robots-in-warehouses-in-2019/.

5. UCSF Medical Center at Mission Bay, "High-Tech 'TUG' Robots Will Do Heavy Lifting at Mission Bay," n.d., http://www.ucsfmissionbayhospitals.org/articles/high-tech-tug-robots-do-heavy-lifting-at-mission-bay.html.

6. Vesselina Stefanova Ratcheva and Till Leopold, "5 Things to Know about the Future of Jobs," World Economic Forum, September 2018, https://www.weforum.org/agenda/2018/09/future-of-jobs-2018-things-to-know/.

7. Ratcheva and Leopold, "5 Things to Know," 2018.

8. Northeastern University and Gallup, "U.S., U.K. and Canadian Citizens Call for a Unified Skills Strategy for the AI Age," Northeastern University, 2019, https://www.northeastern.edu/gallup/#_ga=2.76113117.932416699.1568327085-1498293726.1568327085.

9. Ellyn Shook and Mark Knickrehm, "Reworking the Revolution," Accenture, 2018, https://www.accenture.com/_acnmedia/pdf-69/accenture-reworking-the-revolution-jan-2018-pov.pdf#zoom=50, 9.

10. Pablo Illanes, Susan Lund, Mona Mourshed, Scott Rutherford, and Magnus Tyreman, *Retraining and Reskilling Workers in the Age of Automation*, McKinsey Global Institute, January 2018, https://www.mckinsey.com/~/media/McKinsey/Featured%20Insights/Future%20of%20 Organizations/Retraining%20and%20reskilling%20workers%20in%20the%20age%20of%20au- tomation/Retraining-and-reskilling-workers-in-the-age-of-automation.ashx, 2.

11. Ratcheva and Leopold, "5 Things to Know," 2018.

12. Illanes et al., *Retraining and Reskilling Workers*, 5.

13. Susan Caminiti, "AT&T's $1 Billion Gambit: Retraining Nearly Half Its Workforce for Jobs of the Future," CNBC, March 13, 2018, https://www.cnbc.com/2018/03/13/atts-1-billion-gambit- retraining-nearly-half-its-workforce.html.

14. Anne Fisher, "'Upskilling' Your Workforce? Start by Measuring the Skills They Have Now," *Fortune*, June 22, 2019, https://fortune.com/2019/06/22/upskilling-training-workforce-measure-skills/.

15. Amazon.com, Inc., "Amazon Pledges to Upskill 100,000 U.S. Employees for In-Demand Jobs by 2025," July 11, 2019, https://press.aboutamazon.com/news-releases/news-release-details/ amazon-pledges-upskill-100000-us-employees-demand-jobs-2025.

16. Lauren Debter, "Amazon Surpasses Walmart as the World's Largest Re- tailer," *Forbes*, May 15, 2019, https://www.forbes.com/sites/laurendebter/2019/05/15/ worlds-largest-retailers-2019-amazon-walmart-alibaba/#2717c1734171.

17. Lund et al., *The Future of Work in America*, 52.

18. John Ydstie, "Robust Apprenticeship Program Key to Germany's Manufac- turing Might," NPR, January 4, 2018, https://www.npr.org/2018/01/04/575114570/ robust-apprenticeship-program-key-to-germanys-manufacturing-might.

19. Ydstie, "Robust Apprenticeship Program."

20. CareerBuilder, "Nearly Three in Four Employers Affected by a Bad Hire, According to a Recent CareerBuilder Survey," December 7, 2017, http://press.careerbuilder.com/2017-12- 07-Nearly-Three-in-Four-Employers-Affected-by-a-Bad-Hire-According-to-a-Recent-Career- Builder-Survey.

21. Alisha Green, "Just How Long Do Employees Stay at Uber, Dropbox and Salesforce?" *San Francisco Business Times*, April 10, 2018, https://www.bizjournals.com/sanfrancisco/ news/2018/04/10/employee-retention-big-bay-area-tech-companies.html.

Chapter 8

Supporting Unlearning to Enable Upskilling

1. Lynda Gratton and Andrea Scott, *The 100-Year life: Living and Working in an Age of Longevity* (London: Bloomsbury Information, 2016).

2. Chris Dede, "The 60 Year Curriculum: Developing New Educational Models to Sup- port the Agile Labor Market," *Evolllution*, October 19, 2018, https://evolllution.com/reve- nue-streams/professional_development/the-60-year-curriculum-developing-new-educational -models-to-serve-the-agile-labor-market/.

3. Thomas S. Kuhn, *The Structure of Scientific Revolutions*, 3rd ed. (Chicago, IL: University of Chicago Press, 1996).

4. C. Brook, M. Pedler, C. Abbott, and J. Burgoyne, "On Stopping Those Things That Are Not

Getting Us to Where We Want to Be: Unlearning, Wicked Problems and Critical Action Learning," *Human Relations* 69, no. 2 (2016): 369–389.

5. J. Bailenson, *Experience on Demand: What Virtual Reality Is, How It Works, and What It Can Do* (New York: Norton, 2018); M. Slater and M. V. Sanchez-Vives, "Enhancing Our Lives with Immersive Virtual Reality," *Frontiers in Robotics and AI* 3 (2016): 74.

6. C. Dede, J. Jacobson, and J. Richards, "Introduction: Virtual, Augmented, and Mixed Realities in Education," in *Virtual Reality, Augmented Reality, and Mixed Reality in Education*, eds. D. Liu, C. Dede, R. Huang, and J. Richards (Hong Kong: Springer, 2017), 1–18.

Chapter 9

Higher Education's Changing Faces

1. Rovy Branon, "Learning for a Lifetime," *Inside Higher Ed*, November 16, 2018, https://www.insidehighered.com/views/2018/11/16/why-longer-lives-require-relevant-accessible-curricula-throughout-long-careers.

2. Lynda Gratton and Andrew Scott, *The 100-Year Life: Living and Working in an Age of Longevity* (London: Bloomsbury Information, 2016).

3. Paul Irving, "When No One Retires," *Harvard Business Review*, November 7, 2018, https://hbr.org/cover-story/2018/11/when-no-one-retires.

4. Joseph B. Fuller, Judith K. Wallenstein, Manjari Raman, and Alice de Chalendar, "Your Workforce Is More Adaptable Than You Think," *Harvard Business Review* (May–June 2019): 118–126.

5. Nelson Baker, "The Future of Work: Matching Skills with Workforce Demand" (podcast), Georgia Tech Professional Education, n.d., https://www.linkedin.com/posts/gtprofessionaleducation_highereducation-activity-6540224039187730432-aTsW.

6. Michael Beer, Magnus Finnström, and Derek Schrader, "Why Leadership Training Fails—and What to Do about It," *Harvard Business Review* (October 2016): 50–57.

7. Deloitte, *Business Partners Needed: Results of Deloitte's* 2013 *Global Finance Talent Survey*, 2013, https://deloitte.wsj.com/cfo/files/2013/07/Deloitte-global-finance-talent-survey-report-2013.pdf.

8. Beer et al., "Why Leadership Training Fails," 50–57.

9. Chip Cutter, "Amazon Prepares to Retrain a Third of Its U.S. Workforce," *Wall Street Journal*, July 11, 2019, https://www.wsj.com/articles/amazon-to-retrain-a-third-of-its-u-s-workforce-11562841120.

10. US Bureau of Labor Statistics, "Employee Tenure Summary," *Economics New Release*, September 20, 2018, https://www.bls.gov/news.release/tenure.nro.htm.

11. Neil Howe, "The Graying of Wealth," *Forbes*, March 16, 2018, https://www.forbes.com/sites/neilhowe/2018/03/16/the-graying-of-wealth/#28864335302d.

12. John Gramlich, "Looking Ahead to 2050, Americans Are Pessimistic about Many Aspects of Life in U.S.," Pew Research Center, March 29, 2019, https://www.pewresearch.org/fact-tank/2019/03/21/looking-ahead-to-2050-americans-are-pessimistic-about-many-aspects-of-life-in-u-s/.

13. Georgia Institute of Technology Commission on Creating the Next in Education, *Deliberate Innovation, Lifetime Education*, April 2018, https://provost.gatech.edu/sites/default/files/documents/deliberate_innovation_lifetime_education.pdf.

14. Debabish Dutta, Lalit Patil, and James B. Porter, Jr., *Lifelong Learning Imperative in Engineering:*

Sustaining American Competitiveness in the 21st Century (Washington, DC: National Academies Press, 2012), https://www.nap.edu/read/13503/chapter/1.

15. Joshua Goodman, Julia Melkers, and Amanda Pallais, "Can Online Delivery Increase Access to Education?" *Journal of Labor Economics* 37, no. 1 (2018): 1–34.

16. Yakut Gazi, "Alternative, Stackable, and Microcredentials: Where Are We Headed?" *EDUCAUSE Review*, October 19, 2016, https://er.educause.edu/blogs/2016/10/alternative-stackable-and-microcredentials-where-are-we-headed.

Chapter 10

The Future of Business Education

1. World Economic Forum, *The Future of Jobs Report* 2018 (Geneva, Switzerland: World Economic Forum, 2018).

2. Bryan Edward Penprase, "The Fourth Industrial Revolution and Higher Education," in *Higher Education in the Era of the Fourth Industrial Revolution* (New York: Springer, 2018), 207–29.

3. Peter H. Cappelli, "Skill Gaps, Skill Shortages, and Skill Mismatches," *ILR Review* 68, no. 2 (2015): 251–90.

4. Penprase, "The Fourth Industrial Revolution and Higher Education."

5. Mie Buhl and Lars Birch Andreasen, "Learning Potentials and Educational Challenges of Massive Open Online Courses (MOOCs) in Lifelong Learning," *International Review of Education* 64, no. 2 (2018): 151–60.

6. Buhl and Andreasen, "Learning Potentials and Educational Challenges."

7. Coursera, *Global Skills Index (GSI)*, https://www.coursera.org/gsi.

8. Laura Pappano, "The Year of the MOOC," *New York Times*, November 14, 2012.

9. Fiona Hollands and Aasiya Kazi, "MOOC-Based Alternative Credentials: What's the Value for the Learner?" *EDUCAUSE Review*, June 3, 2019, https://er.educause.edu/articles/2019/6/mooc-based-alternative-credentials-whats-the-value-for-the-learner.

10. Hollands and Kazi, "MOOC-Based Alternative Credentials."

11. Chen Zhenghao, Brandon Alcorn, Gayle Christensen, Nicholas Eriksson, Daphne Koller, and Ezekiel Emanuel, "Who's Benefiting from MOOCs, and Why?" *Harvard Business Review* 25 (2015): 44.

12. René F. Kizilcec, Chris Piech, and Emily Schneider, "Deconstructing Disengagement: Analyzing Learner Subpopulations in Massive Open Online Courses," in *Proceedings of the Third International Conference on Learning Analytics and Knowledge* (New York: ACM, 2013), 170–79; Daphne Koller, Andrew Ng, Chuong Do, and Zhenghao Chen, "Retention and Intention in Massive Open Online Courses: In Depth," *EDUCAUSE Review* 48, no. 3 (2013): 62–63; Saijing Zheng, Mary Beth Rosson, Patrick C. Shih, and John M. Carroll, "Understanding Student Motivation, Behaviors and Perceptions in MOOCs," *Proceedings of the 18th ACM Conference on Computer Supported Cooperative Work & Social Computing–CSCW '15*, 2015. doi:10.1145/2675133.2675217.

13. Kizilcec et al., "Deconstructing Disengagement."

14. Jessie Brown and Martin Kurzweil, *The Complex Universe of Alternative Postsecondary Credentials and Pathways* (Cambridge, MA: American Academy of Arts & Sciences, 2017).

15. Kelsey Gee, "More Universities Shut Down Traditional M.B.A. Programs as Popularity Wanes,"

Wall Street Journal, June 5, 2019, https://www.wsj.com/articles/more-universities-shut-down-traditional-m-b-a-programs-as-popularity-wanes-11559727000.

16. René F. Kizilcec and Sherif Halawa, "Attrition and Achievement Gaps in Online Learning," in *Proceedings of the Second (2015) ACM Conference on Learning@Scale* (New York: ACM, 2015), 57–66.

17. Tawanna R. Dillahunt, Sandy Ng, Michelle Fiesta, and Zengguang Wang, "Do Massive Open Online Course Platforms Support Employability?" In *Proceedings of the 19th ACM Conference on Computer-Supported Cooperative Work & Social Computing–CSCW '16*, 2016. doi:10.1145/2818048.2819924.

18. Susan Adams, "This Company Could Be Your Next Teacher: Coursera Plots a Massive Future for Online Education," *Forbes*, February 21, 2019, https://www.forbes.com/sites/susanadams/2018/10/16/this-company-could-be-your-next-teacher-coursera-plots-a-massive-future-for-online-education/#521d83bb2a39.

19. Yuan Wang, Luc Paquette, and Ryan Baker, "A Longitudinal Study on Learner Career Advancement in MOOCs," *Journal of Learning Analytics* 1, no. 3 (2014): 203–6; Alyssa Friend Wise and Yi Cui, "Unpacking the Relationship between Discussion Forum Participation and Learning in MOOCs: Content Is Key, in *Proceedings of the 8th International Conference on Learning Analytics and Knowledge* (New York: ACM, 2018), 330–39; Juan Miguel L. Andres, Ryan S. Baker, Dragan Gašević, George Siemens, Scott A. Crossley, and Srećko Joksimović, "Studying MOOC Completion at Scale Using the MOOC Replication Framework," in *Proceedings of the 8th International Conference on Learning Analytics and Knowledge* (New York: ACM, 2018), 71–78.

20. Oleksandra Poquet, Nia Dowell, Christopher Brooks, and Shane Dawson, "Are MOOC Forums Changing?" in *Proceedings of the 8th International Conference on Learning Analytics and Knowledge* (New York: ACM, 2018), 340–49.

21. Tawanna R. Dillahunt, Brian Zengguang Wang, and Stephanie Teasley, "Democratizing Higher Education: Exploring MOOC Use among Those Who Cannot Afford a Formal Education," *International Review of Research in Open and Distributed Learning* 15, no. 5 (2014).

22. Poquet et al., "Are MOOC Forums Changing?"

23. Wang et al., "A Longitudinal Study on Learner Career Advancement in MOOCs."

24. Zhenghao et al., "Who's Benefiting from MOOCs, and Why?"; Dillahunt et al., "Democratizing Higher Education."

25. Kizilcec and Halawa, "Attrition and Achievement Gaps in Online Learning."

26. Zhenghao et al., "Who's Benefiting from MOOCs, and Why?"

27. Dillahunt et al., "Democratizing Higher Education"; Dillahunt et al., "Do Massive Open Online Course Platforms Support Employability?"

28. Gee, "More Universities Shut Down Traditional M.B.A. Programs."

29. Natasha Lomas, "FutureLearn Takes $65M from Seek Group for 50% Stake in UK Online Degree Platform," *TechCrunch*, April 29, 2019, https://techcrunch.com/2019/04/29/futurelearn-takes-65m-from-seek-group-for-50-stake-in-uk-online-degree-platform/.

30. Emily Tate, "Coursera Pushes into Unicorn Status after Raising Another $103M," *EdSurge*, May 28, 2019, https://www.edsurge.com/news/2019-04-25-coursera-pushes-into-unicorn-status-after-raising-another-103m.

Chapter 11

Back to the Future

1. It has been argued that Ann Arbor's status as such a place is due to its historic investments in research and technological development. See Francesca Levy, "America's Most Livable Cities," *Forbes*, April 29, 2010, https://www.forbes.com/2010/04/29/cities-livable-pittsburgh-lifestyle-real-estate-top-ten-jobs-crime-income.html#28ca085e6346.

2. J. Manyika, S. Lund, M. Chui, J. Bughin, J. Woetzel, P. Batra, R. Ko, and S. Sanghvi, *Jobs Lost, Jobs Gained: What the Future of Work Will Mean for Jobs, Skills, and Wages*, McKinsey Global Institute, December 2017, https://www.mckinsey.com/featured-insights/future-of-work/jobs-lost-jobs-gained-what-the-future-of-work-will-mean-for-jobs-skills-and-wages.

3. Manyika et al., *Jobs Lost, Jobs Gained*.

4. Joseph Aoun, *Robot-Proof: Higher Education in the Age of Artificial Intelligence* (Cambridge, MA: MIT Press, 2018).

5. Association of American Colleges and Universities, "Liberal Education and America's Promise," https://www.aacu.org/leap.

6. Earl Lewis, "Towards a 2.0 Compact for the Liberal Arts," *Daedalus* (Fall 2019), https://www.amacad.org/publication/toward-20-compact-liberal-arts.

7. Joseph Aoun, "Introduction," in *Robot Proof: Higher Education in the Age of Artificial Intelligence* (Cambridge, MA: MIT Press, 2018); Scott Page, *Diversity Bonus* (Princeton, NJ: Princeton University Press, 2017).

8. Cathy Davidson, *The New Education* (New York: Basic Books, 2017), 3, 8–9.

9. Lewis, "Towards a 2.0 Compact for the Liberal Arts."

10. See *Branches from the Same Tree: The Integration of the Humanities and Arts with Sciences, Engineering, and Medicine in Higher Education* (Washington, DC: National Academies of Sciences, Engineering, and Medicine, 2018).

Chapter 12

Evolution of the Liberal Arts

1. Michael T. Nietzel, "Whither the Humanities: The Ten-Year Trend in College Majors," *Forbes*, January 7, 2019, https://www.forbes.com/sites/michaeltnietzel/2019/01/07/whither-the-humanities-the-ten-year-trend-in-college-majors/#49eb6f9264ad.

2. Robert Matz, "The Myth of the English Major Barista," *Inside Higher Ed*, July 26, 2016, https://www.insidehighered.com/views/2016/07/06/cultural-implications-myth-english-majors-end-working-permanently-starbucks-essay.

3. Examples include Michelle R. Weise, Andrew R. Hanson, Rob Sentz, and Yustina Saleh, *Robot-Ready: Human+ Skills for the Future of Work* (Indianapolis, IN: Strada Institute for the Future of Work and Emsi, 2018); Scott Hartley, *The Fuzzy and the Techie: Why the Liberal Arts Will Rule the Digital World* (Boston: Mariner Books, 2018); Joseph Aoun, *Robot-Proof: Higher Education in the Age of Artificial Intelligence* (Cambridge, MA: MIT Press, 2018); Deloitte Global and the Global Business Coalition for Education, "Preparing Tomorrow's Workforce for the Fourth Industrial Revolution" (Johannesburg: Creative Services at Deloitte, 2018); and John Stakehouse, Jill Brra,

Anna Klimbovskaia, and Andrew Aulthouse, *Humans Wanted: How Canadian Youth Can Thrive in the Age of Disruption* (Toronto: Royal Bank of Canada, 2018).

4. Weise et al., *Robot-Ready*, 7.

5. Weise et al., *Robot-Ready*, 9.

6. Hartley, *The Fuzzy and the Techie*, 208.

7. Weise et al., *Robot-Ready*, 3.

8. Salesforce.org, "Rewiring for an Automated Future: Thought Leaders Discuss Ways Colleges Can Better Prepare the Workers of Tomorrow," *Chronicle of Higher Education*, https://www.chronicle.com/paid-article/becoming-robot-proof/191.

9. Aoun, *Robot-Proof*, 84.

10. Aoun, *Robot-Proof*, 185.

11. Aoun, *Robot-Proof*, 85.

12. Clark University, "The Clark Experience," https://www.clarku.edu/academics/undergraduate-overview/the-clark-experience/.

13. Clark University, "Problems of Practice Courses," https://www.clarku.edu/academics/undergraduate-overview/curriculum/problems-of-practice-courses/.

14. Clark University, "Career Preparation," https://www.clarku.edu/after-clark/career-preparation/.

15. Arizona State University Humanities Lab, "What Is the Humanities Lab?" https://humanities.lab.asu.edu/.

16. Arizona State University Humanities Lab, "There Are No Easy Answers," https://humanities.lab.asu.edu/about/.

17. Clayton Christensen, "Clayton Christensen Interview with Mark Suster at Startup Grind 2013," interview by Mark Suster, YouTube, February 20, 2013. Video, 31:29, https://www.youtube.com/watch?v=KYVdf5xyD8I.

18. Richard Price and Alan Dunagan, "Betting on Bootcamps: How Short-Course Training Programs Could Change the Landscape of Higher Ed," Christensen Institute (April 2019), 3.

19. Lindsay McKenzie, "Code Switch," *Inside Higher Ed*, November 28, 2018, https://www.insidehighered.com/news/2018/11/28/liberal-arts-college-and-boot-camp-team-offer-new-computer-science-degree.

20. Trilogy Education Services, "Meet Trilogy Education," https://www.trilogyed.com/about/.

21. "Program Overview," Summer of Code 2019, accessed June 8, 2019, https://www.summerofcode2019.com/program-details.

22. "Frequently Asked Questions," Summer of Code 2019, accessed June 8, 2019, https://www.summerofcode2019.com/faq2.

23. Lindsay McKenzie, "Coding Curriculum in a Box," *Inside Higher Ed*, June 5, 2019, https://www.insidehighered.com/news/2019/06/05/nonprofit-boot-camp-infiltrates-college-computer-science-curricula.

24. Rebecca Lurye, "Infosys and Trinity College Working to Make Digital Scientists Out of Liberal Arts Grads," *Hartford Courant*, April 1, 2019, https://www.courant.com/business/hc-biz-hartford-infosys-trinity-pilot-20190331-k4qmswky4zhmhjulhuy6gyobtm-story.html.

25. "Curriculum," Sweet Briar College, accessed June 8, 2019, https://sbc.edu/reset/curriculum/.

26. "CORE 110—Design Thinking," Sweet Briar College, accessed June 8, 2019, http://catalog. sbc.edu/preview_course_nopop.php?catoid=9&coid=6201.

27. "CORE 160—STEM in Society," Sweet Briar College, accessed June 8, 2019, http://catalog. sbc.edu/preview_course_nopop.php?catoid=9&coid=6205.

28. "CORE 170—Decisions in a Data-Driven World," Sweet Briar College, accessed June 8, 2019, http://catalog.sbc.edu/preview_course_nopop.php?catoid=9&coid=6206.

29. United States Military Academy Curriculum Slide, United States Military Academy Academic Presentation, October 23, 2019.

30. Lori Varlotta, "Designing a Model for the New Liberal Arts," *Liberal Education* 104, no. 4 (Fall 2018), https://www.aacu.org/liberaleducation/2018/fall/varlotta.

31. Varlotta, "Designing a Model for the New Liberal Arts," https://www.aacu.org/ liberaleducation/2018/fall/varlotta.

32. Varlotta, "Designing a Model for the New Liberal Arts," https://www.aacu.org/ liberaleducation/2018/fall/varlotta.

33. Emily Tate, "'Tech and Trek,'" *Inside Higher Ed*, February 22, 2017, https://www.inside-highered.com/digital-learning/article/2017/02/22/ohio-college-invests-tech-enhance-learning.

Chapter 13

The Evolution of Liberal Education in a Technology-Mediated, Global Society

1. "Liberal Education and America's Promise," Association of American Colleges and Universities, https://www.aacu.org/leap.

2. Lumina Foundation, "Degree Qualifications Profile," http://degreeprofile.org/.

3. Herbert A. Simon, "What We Know about Learning," http://158.132.155.107/posh97/private/ learning/learning-simon.htm.

4. OECD, *The Future of Education and Skills: Education 2030*, https://www.oecd.org/education/2030/E2030%20Position%20Paper%20(05.04.2018).pdf.

5. Anthony P. Carnevale and Nicole Smith, "New Market Forces Create Demand for New Skills," *Human Resource Development International* 16, no. 5 (2013), https://cew.georgetown.edu/ wp-content/uploads/2014/11/HRDI.Editorial.pdf.

6. Carnevale and Smith, "New Market Forces Create Demand for New Skills."

7. Willard Dix, "A Liberal Arts Degree Is More Important Than Ever," *Forbes*, November 16, 2016, https://www.forbes.com/sites/willarddix/2016/11/16/a-liberal-arts-degree-is-more -important-than-ever/#44e1049c339f.

8. Mimi Roy, "Liberal Arts Education in India: The Past, Present and the Future," *Higher Education Review*, https://www.thehighereducationreview.com/opinion/last-word/-liberal-arts-education-in-india-the-past-present-and-the-future-fid-28.html.

9. Roy, "Liberal Arts Education in India."

10. Fareed Zakaria, *In Defense of a Liberal Education* (New York: Norton, 2015), 92.

11. Tan Chorh Chuan quoted in "NUS and Yale to Create Singapore's First Liberal Arts College," *YaleNews*, March 31, 2011, https://news.yale.edu/2011/03/31/ nus-and-yale-create-singapore-s-first-liberal-arts-college.

12. Hart Research Associates (on behalf of the Association of American Colleges and Uni-

versities), *Fulfilling the American Dream: Liberal Education and the Future of Work*, https://www.aacu.org/research/2018-future-of-work.

13. Tony Golsby-Smith, "Want Innovative Thinking? Hire from the Humanities," *Harvard Business Review* (March 2011), https://hbr.org/2011/03/want-innovative-thinking-hire.

Chapter 14

The Core and the Adult Student

1. "How Many Nonprofit Colleges and Universities Have Closed Since 2016?" *Education-Dive*, August 2, 2019, https://www.educationdive.com/news/tracker-college-and-university-closings-and-consolidation/539961/.

2. David P. Haney, "Cash, Trends and Denial," *Inside Higher Ed*, May 23, 2019, https://www.insidehighered.com/views/2019/05/23/early-warning-signs-financial-trouble-institutions-often-miss-opinion.

3. For example, the University of Georgia reduced the number of state colleges and universities from thirty-five down to twenty-eight, and the University of Wisconsin merged its thirteen two-year arts and science campuses with its thirteen comprehensive and doctoral institutions.

4. Nathan D. Grawe, *Demographics and the Demand for Higher Education* (Baltimore, MD: Johns Hopkins University Press, 2018).

5. Daniel Yankelovich, "Ferment and Change: Higher Education in 2015," *Chronicle of Higher Education*, November 25, 2005, https://www.chronicle.com/article/FermentChange-Higher/14934.

6. A. Carnevale, N. Smith, and M. Melton, *Learning While Earning*, Center on Education and the Workforce, 2015, https://1gyhoq479ufd3yna29x7ubjn-wpengine.netdna-ssl.com/wp-content/uploads/Working-Learners-Report.pdf.

7. Yankelovich, "Ferment and Change."

8. National Center for Education Statistics, "Back to School Statistics," https://nces.ed.gov/fastfacts/display.asp?id=372.

9. University of California Berkeley, Office of Planning and Analysis.

10. University of Central Florida, "UCF Facts 2018–19," https://www.ucf.edu/about-ucf/facts/.

11. "Tulane University Final Official Counts By Primary School—Fall 2018," https://registrar.tulane.edu/sites/registrar.tulane.edu/files/2018_FALL_OFFICIAL_ENROLLMENT.pdf.

12. "Northwestern University Common Data Set 2018–2019," https://enrollment.northwestern.edu/pdf/common-data/2018-19.pdf.

13. Association of American Colleges and Universities, "Statement on Liberal Education," October 1, 1998.

14. Martha Nussbaum, "Liberal Education and Global Community," 2004, https://www.aacu.org/publications-research/periodicals/liberal-education-global-community.

15. Martha Nussbaum quoted in Colleen Flaherty, "Saving the Liberal Arts," *Inside Higher Ed*, May 20, 2016, https://www.insidehighered.com/news/2016/05/20/scholars-consider-how-save-liberal-arts.

16. University of Wisconsin-Madison, "Guide 2019–2020," https://guide.wisc.edu/undergraduate/#requirementsforundergraduatestudytext.

17. Stanford University, "Stanford Undergrad," https://undergrad.stanford.edu/academic

-planning/degree-requirements/general-education-requirements-undergrads.

18. Central Michigan University, "2019–2020 Undergraduate Bulletin," http://cmich. smartcatalogiq.com/2019-2020/Undergraduate-Bulletin/General-Education-Requirements _Competencies-UP/I-Introduction.

19. S. Hurtado, K. Eagan, J. H. Pryor, H. Whang, and S. Tran, *Undergraduate Teaching Faculty: The 2010–2011 HERI Faculty Survey*, 2012, https://www.heri.ucla.edu/monographs/HERI-FAC2011-Monograph.pdf.

20. J. L. Ratcliff, D. K. Johnson, and J. G. Gaff, "Editors' Notes," *New Directions for Higher Education* 125 (2004): 1–8.

21. University of Kentucky, "The UK Core General Education Requirements," http://www.uky. edu/registrar/sites/www.uky.edu.registrar/files/ukcorecoursesf2019.pdf, 1.

22. University of Kentucky, "The UK Core General Education Requirements," 2.

23. University of Kentucky, "The UK Core General Education Requirements," 3.

24. University of Kentucky, "The UK Core General Education Requirements," 4.

25. James L. Ratcliff, "Quality and Coherence in General Education," in *Handbook of the Undergraduate Curriculum*, ed. J. Gaff, J. Ratcliff, and associates (San Francisco, CA: Jossey-Bass, 1996), 144.

26. A. T. Kronman, *Education's End: Why Our Colleges and Universities Have Given Up on the Meaning of Life* (New Haven, CT: Yale University Press, 2007), 89–90.

27. S. A. Snook and J. C. Connor, "The Price of Progress: Structurally Induced Inaction," in *Organization at the Limit: Lessons from the Columbia Disaster*, ed. W. Starbuck and M. Farjoun (Malden, MA: Blackwell, 2005), 178–201.

28. R. Hollingsworth, "The Snare of Specialization," *Bulletin of the Atomic Scientists* 40, no. 6 (1984): 34–37.

29. See, for example, Presidential Commission on the Space Shuttle Challenger Accident, *Report of the Presidential Commission on the Space Shuttle Challenger Accident*, 1986, https:// history.nasa.gov/rogersrep/genindex.htm; J. Reason, *Managing the Risks of Organizational Accidents* (New York: Taylor & Francis, 2016); and K. H. Roberts and R. G. Bea, "When Systems Fail," *Organizational Dynamics* 29 (2001): 179–91.

30. For example, C. Perrow, "The President's Commission and the Normal Accident," in *The Accident at Three Mile Island: The Human Dimension*, ed. D. L. Sills, C. P. Wolf, and V. B. Shelarski (Boulder, CO: Westview Press, 1982); and L. Heimann, "Repeated Failures in the Management of High-Risk Technologies," *European Management Journal* 23, no. 1 (2005): 105–17.

31. Snook and Connor, "The Price of Progress," 184.

32. Lumina Foundation, "What Is Tuning," *Degree Qualification Profile*, http://degreeprofile. org/wp-content/uploads/2014/12/What-is-Tuning.pdf.

33. For example, the Utah System of Higher Education began curricular tuning in 2009. See Norman Jones, "'Tuning' the Disciplines," *Liberal Education* 98, no. 4 (2012).

34. *College Learning for the New Global Century* (Washington, DC: Association of American Colleges and Universities, 2008).

35. Jordan Friedman, "U.S. News Data: The Average Online Bachelor's Student," *U.S. News & World Report*, April 4, 2017, https://www.usnews.com/higher-education/online-education/ articles/2017-04-04/us-news-data-the-average-online-bachelors-student.

36. "A Major Step: What Adults without Degrees Say About Going (Back) to College," Public Agenda, https://www.publicagenda.org/files/PublicAgenda_Main_Findings_Adults%20Without%20Degrees.pdf.

Chapter 15

Perpetual Learning as Alumni Engagement

1. Council for Advancement and Support of Education, *Voluntary Support of Education: Key Findings from Data Collected for the* 2017–18 *Academic Fiscal Year for U.S. Higher Education*, 2018, https://www.case.org/system/files/media/file/2018%20VSE%20Research%20Brief.pdf.

2. Annual Giving Network, "Class Exodus," November 25, 2015, https://annualgiving.com/2015/11/25/class-exodus-2/.

3. David J. Deming and Kadeem Noray, "STEM Careers and Technological Change," September 2018, https://scholar.harvard.edu/files/ddeming/files/demingnoray_stem_sept2018.pdf.

Chapter 16

Harnessing the Power and Potential of Diversity and Inclusion

1. Sandra L. Colby and Jennifer M. Ortman, "Projections of the Size and Composition of the U.S. Population: 2014 to 2060," *Current Population Reports*, P25-1143. Washington, DC: US Census Bureau.

2. Mary Bennett, "A Breakdown of the Five Generations of Employees in the Workplace," Navex Global, February 7, 2017, https://www.navexglobal.com/blog/article/formal-introduction-five-generations-employees-your-workforce/.

3. Maureen E. Devlin, *The Power and Potential of Diversity and Inclusion: A Compendium Based on the TIAA Institute's* 2016 *Higher Education Leadership Conference* (New York: TIAA Institute, 2017).

4. Diversity Best Practices, *Building a Diverse, Future Ready Talent Pool* (New York: Diversity Best Practices, 2019).

5. The Hispanic and Latino ethnic categories used throughout this chapter should be considered interchangeable. The relevant category for the National Center for Education Statistics (NCES) and its Integrated Postsecondary Education Data System (IPEDS) is "Hispanic or Latino." Note that the Latino/Latina/Latinx group encompasses more people and cultures than the Hispanic group. Because widely accepted definitions and usage standards for statistical purposes do not yet exist, the categories continue to be used interchangeably, and we have maintained the usage of our sources.

6. "Disparities at State Flagships," *Hechinger Report*, January 29, 2018, https://hechingerreport.org/disparities-state-flagships/.

7. J. Oliver Schak, Charlie Bentley, Andrew Howard Nichols, and Will Del Pilar, *Broken Mirrors II: Latino Student Representation in Public State Colleges and Universities* (Washington, DC: The Education Trust, 2019).

8. D. Shapiro, A. Dundar, F. Huie, P. K. Wakhungu, A. Bhimdiwala, and S. E. Wilson, *Completing College: A National View of Student Completion Rates–Fall* 2012 *Cohort* (Signature Report No. 16) (Herndon, VA: National Student Clearinghouse Research Center, 2018).

9. Association of American Colleges and Universities, *A Vision for Equity* (Washington, DC: As-

sociation of American Colleges and Universities, 2018); Diversity Best Practices, *Building a Diverse, Future Ready Talent Pool*; and US Department of Education, *Advancing Diversity and Inclusion in Higher Education: Key Data Highlights Focusing on Race and Ethnicity and Promising Practices*, November 2016, https://www2.ed.gov/rschstat/research/pubs/advancing-diversity-inclusion.pdf.

10. American Academy of Arts & Sciences, *The Future of Undergraduate Education: The Future of America* (Cambridge, MA: American Academy of Arts & Sciences, 2017).

11. Devlin, *The Power and Potential of Diversity and Inclusion.*

12. Association of American Colleges and Universities, *National Survey of AAC&U Member Chief Academic Officers* (Washington, DC: Association of American Colleges and Universities, 2015).

13. S. Carlson, *The Future of Work: How Colleges Can Prepare Students for the Jobs Ahead* (Washington, DC: Chronicle of Higher Education, 2017).

14. Lauren A. Rivera, *Pedigree: How Elite Students Get Elite Jobs* (Princeton, NJ: Princeton University Press, 2015).

15. Bennett, "A Breakdown of the Five Generations of Employees in the Workplace."

16. P. D. Eckel and C. A. Trower, *Boards and Institutional Diversity: Missed Opportunities, Points of Leverage* (New York: TIAA Institute, 2016).

17. W. G. Tierney and M. Lanford, *Cultivating Strategic Innovation in Higher Education* (New York: TIAA Institute, 2016).

Chapter 17
Public Education and the Future of Work

1. Muro, M., et al., *Automation and Artificial Intelligence: How Machines Are Affecting People and Places*, The Metropolitan Policy Program at Brookings, p. 5, January 2019 ("Almost no occupation will be unaffected by the adoption of currently available technologies. . . . 'Routine,' predictable physical and cognitive tasks will be the most vulnerable to automation in the coming years."), https://www.brookings.edu/wp-content/uploads/2019/01/2019.01_BrookingsMetro_Automation-AI_Report_Muro-Maxim-Whiton-FINAL-version.pdf.

2. Radin, J., et al., "Closing the Employability Skills Gap: The Answer Is Simpler Than You May Think," *Deloitte Insights*, January 28, 2020 ("Now, possibly more than ever, there appears to be an impetus for employees to bring their 'soft' skills—such as creativity, leadership, and critical thinking—to work. While traditionally referred to as 'soft skills' in reality these capabilities are critical to delivering business value and adapting hard skills as workforce needs change.").

3. Jandt, Fred E. *An Introduction to Intercultural Communication: Identities in a Global Community*, Table 7.1, SAGE Publications, 2012 (indicating United States is the most individualistic culture among 50 countries studied) (available online at https://www.sagepub.com/sites/default/files/upm-binaries/11711_Chapter7.pdf).

4. Noguera, P., Darling-Hammond, L., and Friedlaender, D., *Equal Opportunity for Deeper Learning*, Jobs for the Future, October 2015 (quoting Harvard Professor Jal Mehta's contention that "students in more affluent schools and top tracks are given the kind of problem-solving education that befits the future managerial class, whereas students in lower tracks and higher-poverty schools are given the kind of rule-following tasks that mirror much of factory and other working class work.").

5. Deming, David, *The Growing Importance of Social Skills in the Labor Market*, Harvard University and National Bureau of Economic Research, 2017 (documenting trends that more jobs require teamwork and social-emotional skills, and that higher wages are associated with these competencies).

6. Marr, B., "The Ten Vital Skills You Will Need for the Future of Work," *Forbes*, April 29, 2019 (citing World Economic Forum research that emotional intelligence, interpersonal communication interpersonal communication, and facility in understanding and navigating cultural diversity among the top skills sought by employers).

7. Jones, S., and Bouffard, S., "Social and Emotional Learning in Schools: From Programs to Strategies," *Social Policy Report*, v. 26, no. 4, 2012 ("SEL programs are rarely integrated into classrooms and schools in ways that are meaningful, sustained, and embedded in the day-to-day interactions of students, educators, and school staff.").

8. Freeland Fisher, J., *Not Just What You Know but Who You Know Matters*, Education Next, Harvard University, August 29, 2018 ("Today, even under the new Every Student Succeeds Act, our education system focuses the majority of its energy on getting better and better at delivering and measuring what students know. . . . The system in turn vastly undervalued children and young adults' access to meaningful networks, which leads to stark gaps in access to mentors, supportive adults, industry experts and diverse peer groups."), https://www.educationnext.org/not-just-what-but-who-you-know-matters-freeland-fisher-excerpt/.

9. Johnson, H., and Wiener, R, *This Time with Feeling: Integrating Social-Emotional Development with College- and Career-Ready Standards*, The Aspen Institute, March 2017 (citing strategies for embedding the building of social-emotional competencies into academic instruction).

10. "Getting Ready for the Future of Work," *McKinsey Quarterly*, September 2017 ("For workers of the future, then, the ability to adapt their skills to the changing needs of the workplace will be critical. Lifelong learning must become the norm—and at the moment, the reality falls far short of the necessity."), https://www.mckinsey.com/business-functions/organization/our-insights/getting-ready-for-the-future-of-work.

11. Florida, R. *How Diversity Leads to Economic Growth*, City Lab, December 2011 (citing economic research showing that "diversity spurs economic development and homogeneity slows it down."), https://www.citylab.com/life/2011/12/diversity-leads-to-economic-growth/687/.

12. M. Muro, R. Maxim, and J. Whiton, *Automation and Artificial Intelligence: How Machines Are Affecting People and Places*, Brookings Institution, 2019, https://www.brookings.edu/research/automation-and-artificial-intelligence-how-machines-affect-people-and-places/.

13. Lund, S., et al., *The Future of Work in America*, McKinsey Global Institute, July 2019, p. 124 ("women represent 47 percent of the displaced workers in our midpoint automation scenario, while men are 53 percent. Based on the current gender share of occupations, our modeling suggests that women could capture 58 percent of net job growth through 2030").

14. National Institute for Education Statistics, U.S. Department of Education, "Degrees Conferred by Postsecondary Institutions, by Level of Degree and Sex of Student: Selected Years, 1869–70 through 2025–26" (Table 318.10), https://nces.ed.gov/programs/digest/d15/tables/dt15_318.10.asp.

15. Hansen, C., "Report: STEM Degrees Rise, but Disparities Remain," *U.S. News & World Report*, Nov. 29, 2017 (noting that men earn proportionally more STEM bachelor degrees, but approximately the same number overall because more women earn bachelor degrees, but that men earn

many more associate degrees in STEM fields), https://www.usnews.com/news/education-news/
articles/2017-11-29/report-stem-degrees-rise-but-disparities-remain.

16. National Assessment of Educational Progress, *NAEP Report Card: Technology & Engineering Literacy (TEL), Highlights from the* 2018 *Assessment*, https://www.nationsreportcard.gov/
tel_2018_highlights/.

17. U.S. Census Bureau, U.S. Department of Commerce, "America's Education: Population Age 25 and over by Educational Attainment," 2017, https://www.census.gov/library/visualizations/2017/comm/americas-education.html.

Chapter 18

Developing Workers for the Workplace

1. K. Schwab, *The Fourth Industrial Revolution: What It Means, How to Respond* (Geneva, Switzerland: World Economic Forum, 2016).

2. J. Manyika, S. Lund, M. Chui, J. Bughin, J. Woetzel, P. Batra, R. Ko, and S. Sanghvi, *Jobs Lost, Jobs Gained: What the Future of Work Will Mean for Jobs, Skills, and Wages*, McKinsey Global Institute, December 2017, https://www.mckinsey.com/featured-insights/future-of-work/
jobs-lost-jobs-gained-what-the-future-of-work-will-mean-for-jobs-skills-and-wages.

3. Census Bureau (2018). "Older People Projected to Outnumber Children for first Time in U.S. History." Press Release CB18–41. Retrieved from https://www.census.gov/newsroom/
press-releases/2018/cb18-41-population-projections.html.

4. D. A. Spencer, "Fear and Hope in an Age of Mass Automation: Debating the Future of Work," *New Technology, Work and Employment* 33 (2018): 1–12.

5. P. E. Meehl, "Causes and Effects of My Disturbing Little Book," *Journal of Personality Assessment* 50 (1986): 370–75.

6. Standing, G. (1984). "The Notion of Technological Unemployment," *International Labor Review*, 123, 127–147.

7. C. B. Frey and M. A. Osborne, "The Future of Employment: How Susceptible Are Jobs to Computerization?" *Technological Forecasting and Social Change* 114 (2017): 254–80; Spencer, "Fear and Hope in an Age of Mass Automation."

8. J. B. Rodell and J. W. Lynch, "Perceptions of Employee Volunteering: Is It 'Credited' or 'Stigmatized' by Colleagues?" *Academy of Management Journal* 59 (2016): 611–35.

9. Chip Cutter, "Amazon Prepares to Retrain a Third of Its U.S. Workforce," *Wall Street Journal*, July 11, 2019, https://www.wsj.com/articles/amazon-to-retrain-a-third-of-its-u-s-workforce-11562841120.

10. J. Jones, R. Johnson-Murray, V. Streets, A. Alonso, and S. D. Waters, "Driving Workforce Readiness: The Case for Community-Based HR Initiatives," in *Handbook of Organizational Community Engagement and Outreach*, eds. J. A. Allen and R. Reiter-Palmon (Cambridge, UK: Cambridge University Press, 2019).

Chapter 19

Past as Prologue

1. See Roy Bahat, "Findings of Shift: The Commission on Work, Workers, and Technology," Shift Commission, May 16, 2017, https://shiftcommission.work/findings-of-shift-the
-commission-on-work-workers-and-technology-a071bc169dfo.

2. Alec Tyson and Shiva Maniam, "Behind Trump's Victory: Divisions by Race, Gender, Education," Pew Research Center, November 9, 2016, https://www.pewresearch.org/fact-tank/2016/11/09/behind-trumps-victory-divisions-by-race-gender-education/.

3. See "The Rising Cost of Not Going to College," Pew Research Center, February 11, 2014, https://www.pewsocialtrends.org/2014/02/11/the-rising-cost-of-not-going-to-college/.

4. Burning Glass, *Moving the Goalposts: How Demand for a Bachelor's Degree Is Reshaping the Workforce*, September 2014, https://www.burning-glass.com/wp-content/uploads/Moving_the_Goalposts.pdf.

5. National Center for Education Statistics, "Table 104.10: Rates of High School Completion and Bachelor's Degree Attainment among Persons Age 25 and over, by Race/Ethnicity and Sex, Selected Years, 1910 through 2017," *Digest of Education Statistics*, https://nces.ed.gov/programs/digest/d17/tables/dt17_104.10.asp.

6. See National Student Clearinghouse Research Center, *Completing College: A National View of Student Completion Rates–Fall 2011 Cohort*, December 2017, https://nscresearchcenter.org/wp-content/uploads/SignatureReport14_Final.pdf.

7. Anthony P. Carnevale, Martin Van Der Werf, Michael C. Quinn, Jeff Strohl, and Dmitri Repnikov, *Our Separate and Unequal Public Colleges: How Public Colleges Reinforce White Privilege and Marginalize Black and Latino Students* (Washington, DC: Center on Education and the Workforce, Georgetown University, 2018), https://cew.georgetown.edu/cew-reports/sustates/.

8. US Department of Labor, Employment and Training Administration, "Registered Apprenticeship National Results, Fiscal Year (FY) 2018," September 3, 2019, https://www.doleta.gov/oa/Data_statistics.cfm.

9. Robert Lerman, Lauren Eyster, and Kate Chambers, *The Benefits and Challenges of Registered Apprenticeship: The Sponsors' Perspective* (Washington, DC: The Urban Institute, March 2009), http://webarchive.urban.org/UploadedPDF/411907_registered_apprenticeship.pdf.

10. See US Department of Labor, "Registered Apprenticeship National Results."

11. Daniel Jacoby, "Apprenticeship in the United States," Economic History Association, https://eh.net/encyclopedia/apprenticeship-in-the-united-states/.

12. Jacoby, "Apprenticeship in the United States."

13. National Apprenticeship Service (UK), "A Guide to Higher and Degree Apprenticeships," April 2018, https://assets.publishing.service.gov.uk/government/uploads/system/uploads/attachment_data/file/699399/Higher_and_degree_apprenticeship_fact_sheet-090418.pdf.

14. For a formal definition of degree apprenticeship, see Mary Alice McCarthy, Iris Palmer, and Michael Prebil, "Connecting Apprenticeship and Higher Education," New America, December 6, 2017, https://www.newamerica.org/education-policy/policy-papers/eight-recommendations-connecting-apprenticeship-and-higher-ed/.

15. Matt Krupnick, "U.S. Quietly Works to Expand Apprenticeships to Fill White-Collar Jobs," *The Hechinger Report*, September 27, 2016, https://hechingerreport.org/u-s-quietly-works-to-expand-apprenticeships-to-fill-white-collar-jobs/.

16. US Department of Labor, Bureau of Labor Statistics, "Information Security Analysts," https://www.bls.gov/ooh/computer-and-information-technology/information-security-analysts.htm.

17. Laura Bate, "Cybersecurity Workforce Development: A Primer," New America, November 1, 2018, https://www.newamerica.org/cybersecurity-initiative/reports/cybersecurity-workforce-development/.

18. Harper College, "Cyber Security/Networking," https://www.harperapprenticeships.org/news/apprenticeship/cyber-security/.

19. "Nearly One in Five New Nurses Leaves First Job within a Year, According to Survey of Newly-Licensed Registered Nurses," Robert Wood Johnson Foundation, September 4, 2014, https://www.rwjf.org/en/library/articles-and-news/2014/09/nearly-one-in-five-new-nurses-leave-first-job-within-a-year--acc.html.

20. Norton Healthcare, "Student Nurse Apprenticeship Program," https://nortonhealthcare.com/careers/career-areas/nursing/apprenticeship.

21. Institute of Medicine and National Research Council, *Transforming the Workforces for Children Birth through Age 8: A Unifying Foundation* (Washington, DC: National Academies Press, 2015), https://www.nap.edu/catalog/19401/transforming-the-workforce-for-children-birth-through-age-8-a.

22. "Average Early Childhood Educator (ECE) Hourly Pay," PayScale, https://www.payscale.com/research/US/Job=Early_Childhood_Educator_(ECE)/Hourly_Rate.

23. Emily Workman, "Earning while Learning with Early Educator Apprenticeship Programs," New America, February 21, 2019, https://www.newamerica.org/education-policy/reports/earning-while-learning-with-early-educator-apprenticeship-programs/.

24. Michael Prebil, "Solid Foundations: Four State Policy Approaches for Supporting College-Connected Apprenticeships," New America, September 17, 2019, https://www.newamerica.org/education-policy/reports/solid-foundations-four-state-policy-approaches-supporting-college-connected-apprenticeships/.

25. Code of Virginia § 23.1-2907.1 Policy for Award of Academic Credit for Apprenticeship Credentials, https://law.lis.virginia.gov/vacode/title23.1/chapter29/section23.1-2907.1/.

26. See Ivy Tech Community College, "State Programs," https://www.ivytech.edu/apprenticeships-state/index.html.

27. Benjamin Collins, "Apprenticeship in the United States: Frequently Asked Questions," Congressional Research Service, January 29, 2016, https://fas.org/sgp/crs/misc/R44174.pdf.

Chapter 20

Bachelor's-Level Registered Apprenticeship for Engineers

1. Debbie Reed, Albert Yung-Hsu Liu, Rebecca Kleinman, Annalisa Mastri, Davin Reed, Samina Sattar, and Jessica Ziegler, *An Effectiveness Assessment and Cost-Benefit Analysis of Registered Apprenticeship in 10 States: A Report to the U.S. Department of Labor, Employment and Training Administration* (Oakland, CA: Mathematica Policy Research, 2012); Kevin Hollenbeck and Wei-Jang Huang, *Net Impact and Benefit-Cost Estimates of the Workforce Development System in Washington State.* Upjohn Institute Technical Report No. 16–033 (Kalamazoo, MI: The W.E. Upjohn Institute for Employment Research, 2016).

2. Daniel Kuehn, Ian Hecker, and Alphonse Simon, *Registered Apprenticeship in Science and Engineering* (Washington, DC: The Urban Institute, 2019).

3. Kuehn et al., *Registered Apprenticeship in Science and Engineering.*

4. Author's calculations from the Registered Apprenticeship Partners Information Data System (RAPIDS), the federal administrative data for the apprenticeship system. States included are Alaska,

Alabama, Arkansas, Arizona, California, Colorado, Florida, Georgia, Idaho, Illinois, Indiana, Iowa, Kentucky, Louisiana, Michigan, Mississippi, Missouri, North Dakota, Nebraska, New Hampshire, New Jersey, New Mexico, Nevada, Ohio, Oklahoma, Pennsylvania, South Carolina, South Dakota, Tennessee, Texas, Utah, West Virginia, and Wyoming.

5. Only a portion of 1999 is represented in the administrative data.

6. Kuehn et al., *Registered Apprenticeship in Science and Engineering*.

7. Robert Lerman, Fredrica Kramer, and Juan Pedroza, *Retrospective on Registered Apprenticeship: A Review of Program Initiatives and Their Policy Implications: A Report to the Office of Apprenticeship, U.S. Department of Labor* (Washington, DC: The Urban Institute, 2008).

8. Tamar Jacoby and Robert Lerman, *Industry Driven Apprenticeship: What Works, What's Needed* (Washington, DC: Opportunity America, 2019).

Chapter 21

The Agility Imperative

1. Robert Atkinson and Steven Ezell, *Innovation Economics: The Race for Global Advantage* (New Haven, CT: Yale University Press, 2012); Tony Davila, Marc Epstein, and Robert Shelton, *Making Innovation Work: How to Manage It, Measure It, and Profit from It* (Saddle River, NJ; Wharton School Publishing, 2006); Stephen Denning, *The Age of Agile: How Smart Companies Are Transforming the Way Work Gets Done* (New York, NY: AMACON, American Management Association, 2018); Linda Holbeche, *The Agile Organization: How to Build an Engaged, Innovative, and Resilient Business* (London, UK: Kogan Page, 2018); John Kao, *Innovation Nation: How America Is Losing Its Innovation Edge, Why It Matters and What We Can Do to Get It Back* (New York, NY: Free Press, 2007).

2. Robert Sheets and Jason Tyszko, *Competing on Innovation: Implications for Building the Middle-Skill Talent Pipeline*, prepared for National Academies Board on Science, Technology, and Economic Policy, The Supply Chain for Middle-Skilled Jobs: Education, Training, and Certification Pathways (Washington, DC, 2015).

3. World Economic Forum, *The Future of Jobs: Employment, Skills and Workforce Strategy for the Fourth Industrial Revolution. Global Challenge Insight Report* (Geneva, Switzerland: World Economic Forum, 2016).

4. Sheets and Tyszko, *Competing on Innovation*.

5. Holbeche, *The Agile Organization*.

6. Holbeche, *The Agile Organization*.

7. Michael Chui, James Manyika, and Mehdi Miremadi, "Four Fundamentals of Workplace Automation," McKinsey Quarterly, November 2015, https://www.mckinsey.com/business-functions/mckinsey-digital/our-insights/four-fundamentals-of-workplace-automation.

8. Andrew Reamer, Robert Sheets, and Jason Tyszko, *Clearer Signals: Building an Employer-Led Job Registry for Talent Pipeline Management* (Washington, DC: U.S. Chamber of Commerce Foundation, 2017); "Job Data Exchange (JDX)," U.S. Chamber of Commerce Foundation, accessed December 1, 2019, https://www.uschamberfoundation.org/workforce-development/JDX.

9. Sheets and Tyszko, *Competing on Innovation*.

10. Sheets and Tyszko, *Competing on Innovation*.

Chapter 22
Demand for the "Blended Digital Professional"

1. Miguel Milano, "The Digital Skills Gap Is Widening Fast: Here's How to Bridge It," The World Economic Forum, March 12, 2019, https://www.weforum.org/agenda/2019/03/the-digital-skills-gap-is-widening-fast-heres-how-to-bridge-it/.

2. Will Markow, Debbie Hughes, and Andrew Bundy, *The New Foundational Skills of the Digital Economy* (Washington, DC: Business-Higher Education Forum, 2018), http://www.bhef.com/sites/default/files/BHEF_2018_New_Foundational_Skills.pdf.

3. Markow et al., *The New Foundational Skills of the Digital Economy*.

4. Markow et al., *The New Foundational Skills of the Digital Economy*.

5. Greater Washington Partnership, "Capital CoLAB Expansion Areas: Fact Base," 2019.

6. Greater Washington Partnership, "Capital CoLAB Expansion Areas."

7. Greater Washington Partnership, "Capital CoLAB Expansion Areas."

8. N. Anderson, "Businesses and Universities Team Up on a New Digital Technology Credential," *Washington Post*, May 19, 2019, https://www.washingtonpost.com/local/education/businesses-and-universities-team-up-on-a-new-digital-technology-credential/2019/05/19/f7152632-726a-11e9-9f06-5fc2ee80027a_story.html.

Chapter 23
A Coherent Approach to Connect Education and the Future of Work

1. National Center for Education Statistics, "Undergraduate Retention and Graduation Rates," May 2019, https://nces.ed.gov/programs/coe/indicator_ctr.asp.

2. Anthony P. Carnevale, Jeff Strohl, Neil Ridley, and Artem Gulish, "Three Educational Pathways to Good Jobs," Georgetown University, 2018, https://cew.georgetown.edu/cew-reports/3pathways/, 10.

3. Manpower Group, "Solving the Talent Shortage: Build, Buy, Borrow and Bridge," 2018, https://go.manpowergroup.com/talent-shortage-2018#thereport, 5–7.

4. Jennifer Ma, Matea Penda, and Meredith Welch, "Education Pays 2016: The Benefits of Higher Education for Individuals and Society," College Board, 2016, https://trends.collegeboard.org/sites/default/files/education-pays-2016-full-report.pdf, 3–4.

5. T. Bailey, D. W. Jeong, and S. W. Cho, "Referral, Enrollment, and Completion in Developmental Education Sequences in Community Colleges," *Economics of Education Review* 29, no. 2 (2010): 255–70.

6. The University Innovation Alliance, "Our Results," http://www.theuia.org/#about.

7. The University Innovation Alliance, "Vision and Prospectus," http://www.theuia.org/sites/default/files/UIA-Vision-Prospectus.pdf.

8. Central Ohio Compact, "Central Ohio's Most Critical Challenge," http://centralohiocompact.org/what-is-the-compact/our-challenge/.

ABOUT THE CONTRIBUTORS

Alexander Alonso
Chief Knowledge Officer, Society for Human Resource Management
Alexander Alonso, PhD, SHRM-SCP, is the Society for Human Resource Management's (SHRM's) chief knowledge officer leading operations for SHRM certification, research functions, SHRM's Paragon Labs, and SHRM Foundation. During his career, he has led numerous global business initiatives with the aim of unleashing human potential through evidence-based management. His works have been published in top peer-reviewed journals and he has published several books including *The Price of Pettiness*, a guide to enhancing workplace culture. His works have been recognized by groups such as the American Psychological Association for their contribution to real-world issues and have received more than $10 million in research funding from well-known foundations. Dr. Alonso serves as a columnist analyzing major trends in the workforce for *The Industrial Psychologist* and *HR Magazine*. In addition, he has served on several professional society boards including the SIOP and the Personnel Testing Council of Metropolitan Washington.

Julie Arbit
Research Associate, Center for Social Solutions
at the University of Michigan
Julie Arbit is a research associate at the University of Michigan Center for Social Solutions where she focuses on the future of work, and water, equity, and security. She is also an MS student in environmental policy and planning at the University of Michigan. Research interests include a

policy-driven approach to sustainable agriculture, conservation, food and water access, and social/environmental justice within fragile human and natural ecosystems. She hopes to integrate foundations of research methodology, data science and visualization, and policy and case study toward a career in sustainable development.

Farhad Asghar

Program Officer for Pathways to Postsecondary Success,
Carnegie Corporation of New York

Farhad Asghar is the program officer for Pathways to Postsecondary Success at the Carnegie Corporation of New York, where he manages the Pathways to Postsecondary Success portfolio. Farhad oversees grantmaking aimed at creating flexible pathways for students with the goal of completing college and preparing for careers. Farhad brings to his role a history of managing programs, strategic partnerships, and fundraising initiatives. He served as the executive director of Community Partnerships for the College Board's Access to Opportunity initiative. Prior to that, Farhad was the associate vice president for development and external relations, and the associate dean of Bank Street College of Education. Farhad also served as the director of Liberty LEADS, a highly successful college access program. Farhad holds a BA in English literature and secondary education from Brooklyn College and an MPA from NYU's Wagner School of Public Service.

Nelson C. Baker

Dean, Professional Education, Georgia Institute of Technology

Nelson C. Baker, PhD, is the dean of Professional Education at the Georgia Institute of Technology and professor in the university's School of Civil and Environmental Engineering. As dean, Dr. Baker leads a multifaceted operation including the Global Learning Center, Georgia Tech-Savannah, the Language Institute, and Georgia Tech's extensive professional education programs in STEM- and business-related subjects. Dr. Baker also oversees educational outreach programs and serves as the interface between Georgia Tech's professional education activities and the industries, corporations, government agencies, and professional societies that benefit from them. Under Dr. Baker's leadership, Georgia Tech Professional Education has steadily expanded, now serving more than 36,000 learners worldwide and 2,600 organizations each year. Dr. Baker graduated from the Georgia

Institute of Technology in 1980 with a BCE in Civil Engineering. He earned his MS and PhD degrees in civil engineering from Carnegie Mellon University in 1985 and 1989 respectively.

Stephanie Bell-Rose
Senior Managing Director, Corporate Strategy
and Head of the TIAA Institute, TIAA
Stephanie Bell-Rose leads the TIAA Institute, which produces research and insights on financial security and organizational effectiveness issues for the education, nonprofit, and public sectors. Prior to joining TIAA, she served as president of the Goldman Sachs Foundation, and as General Counsel and program officer at the Andrew W. Mellon Foundation. Bell-Rose currently serves on the boards of trustees of the Knight Foundation, the Public Welfare Foundation, and the Association of Black Foundation Executives, and is on the board of overseers of Columbia University's School of Professional Studies. She earned her AB, JD, and MPA degrees from Harvard University.

Lance Braunstein
Managing Director, BlackRock
Lance Braunstein is the head of the Aladdin Product Group at BlackRock. He oversees the product development and operation for Aladdin. Prior to BlackRock, Lance was the chief information officer at E*TRADE. He joined E*TRADE when they acquired OptionsHouse where he was the CIO. Prior to OptionsHouse, Mr. Braunstein spent seven years at Goldman Sachs and ten years at Morgan Stanley. Mr. Braunstein earned his BA in mathematics from the University of Rochester, an MS in atmospheric science from Colorado State University, and an MBA in finance from the Wharton School at the University of Pennsylvania.

Isabel Cardenas-Navia
Director of Research, Workcred
Dr. Isabel Cardenas-Navia is Workcred's director of research, in which she advances Workcred's research agenda to examine workforce credentialing issues and needs. Previously, Dr. Cardenas-Navia was the vice president of programs, and the director of emerging workforce programs, with the Business–Higher Education Forum. Through her career, she has led and facilitated projects bringing together Fortune 500 employers and higher education institutions;

produced novel research on workforce issues in emerging technical fields; and led the development and implementation of a national strategic plan, capacity building tools, and best practices for partnerships between businesses and higher education institutions in data science and analytics.

Janet Chen

Director, Business–Higher Education Forum
Janet Chen is a director at the Business–Higher Education Forum (BHEF). She supports the creation of strategic business–higher education partnerships and regional talent ecosystems in high-demand, emerging fields to increase diversity of talent, including capturing insights through case studies and thought-leadership publications. Prior to joining BHEF, Chen served as director of programs for the Advisory Committee on Student Financial Assistance, advising Congress and the secretary of education on higher education and student aid policy. Chen earned her master's degree in higher education from the Harvard Graduate School of Education and her bachelor's degree in social policy from Northwestern University.

Chris Dede

Wirth Professor in Learning Technologies, Harvard University
Chris Dede is the Timothy E. Wirth Professor in Learning Technologies at Harvard's Graduate School of Education. His fields of scholarship include emerging technologies, policy, and leadership. In 2007, he was honored by Harvard University as an outstanding teacher, and in 2011 he was named a Fellow of the American Educational Research Association. His coedited books include: *Teacher Learning in the Digital Age: Online Professional Development in STEM Education*; *Virtual, Augmented, and Mixed Realities in Education*; *Learning Engineering for Online Education: Theoretical Contexts and Design-Based Examples*; and *The 60-Year Curriculum: New Models for Lifelong Learning in the Digital Economy*.

James DeVaney

Associate Vice Provost for Academic Innovation and Founding Executive Director for the Center for Academic Innovation, University of Michigan
James leads university-wide programs and initiatives designed to shape the future of learning. He is the founding executive director of the University of

Michigan Center for Academic Innovation which seeks to extend academic excellence, expand public purpose, and end educational privilege. He is also the associate vice provost for academic innovation where he works at the intersection of strategy, design, policy, and technology. Previously, James cofounded Huron Consulting Group's global education and digital education practices and provided council to more than sixty universities in more than fifteen countries across the Middle East, North Africa, Europe, Australia, and North America.

Christine Farrugia
Director of Research Initiatives, School of
Professional Studies, Columbia University
Christine Farrugia, PhD, is director of Research Initiatives at the Columbia University School of Professional Studies where she leads research on the future of work, lifelong learning, and educational access. Previously, she was research director at the Institute of International Education (IIE) where she led Open Doors, a large-scale annual survey of international educational exchange in the United States. She has collaborated and consulted extensively with higher education institutions, associations, and national governments on students' educational and career pathways, international academic mobility, and data-driven planning.

Brian K. Fitzgerald
Chief Executive Officer, Business–Higher Education Forum
Dr. Brian K. Fitzgerald, an internationally recognized leader in creating innovative talent solutions, has served as the Business–Higher Education Forum's (BHEF) chief executive officer since 2005. Under his leadership, BHEF developed and implemented a long-term strategic plan, through which BHEF has formed dozens of successful partnerships between the nation's leading business and academic institutions to create new talent development solutions in high-demand emerging fields and utilized insights from case studies and cutting-edge market intelligence to influence thought-leaders and policymakers. His work has been widely published, and he regularly presents the organization's latest market intelligence to business and academic audiences.

Yakut Gazi

Associate Dean, Learning Systems, Georgia Institute of Technology

Yakut Gazi, PhD, has worked at higher education institutions in the US, Qatar, Turkey, and Spain in a variety of faculty and administration roles since 1993. She has taught courses in educational technology, foundations of distance learning, psychology of learning, theories of learning, and predictive analytics in higher education. She has presented at regional, national, and international conferences and is the author or coauthor of books, book chapters, journal articles, and proceedings. Dr. Gazi has her PhD in educational psychology from Texas A&M University, and an MA in educational sciences and a BS in teaching chemistry, both from Bogazici University in Turkey.

Bryan Hancock

Partner, McKinsey & Company

Bryan Hancock is a partner in the Washington, DC, office of McKinsey & Company, and he is the global leader of McKinsey's talent practice. He is a coauthor of the McKinsey Global Institute report "The Future of Work in America." Bryan serves a wide range of public, private, and social sector clients—including those focused on education and workforce development in the context of the future of work. He has served multiple higher education institutions on their organization and strategy. In addition, Bryan serves a wide range of talent-intensive businesses, as well as investors and companies in the human capital management sector

Uli Heitzlhofer

Senior Director of People Learning & Development, Lyft

Uli started his career as an HR generalist in Germany. In 2011, he joined Google as performance management program manager. Recognizing his passion for L&D, he joined Google's Executive Development team in 2013. Over the next one and a half years, he learned the ins and outs of learning programs before shifting focus to a global scale by joining Google's Manager Development team, targeting experienced managers. After six and a half years at Google, Uli joined Lyft as head of People Learning & Development. Since then, he redesigned Lyft's Performance Management system, overhauled the entire L&D portfolio, and placed People Development on the company-wide agenda.

Elise Henson
Program Analyst, Carnegie Corporation of New York
Education Program, Carnegie Corporation of New York
Elise Henson is a program analyst within the Carnegie Corporation of New York's Education program, where she supports grantmaking in the Integration, Learning, and Innovation portfolio. In her position, she manages grantee relations, contributes to internal projects, and supports and informs program strategy. Ms. Henson has extensive experience working in education and youth development. Prior to joining the Carnegie Corporation, she worked at generationOn, the youth division of Points of Light, where she launched and led a new branch of a national program to inspire, equip, and mobilize young people to volunteer in their communities through afterschool clubs. Ms. Henson also has four years of experience as a classroom teacher; she taught middle and high school math, language arts, social studies, and science at small international schools in the Marshall Islands and Nigeria, and English as a Second Language in Nicaragua. She holds a master's degree in international educational development from Teachers College, Columbia University, and a bachelor's degree in biology from Williams College.

Lu Hong
Senior Vice President, Human Resources, Pfizer Upjohn
Lu Hong leads HR for Pfizer's Upjohn business comprising 12,000 colleagues on a mission to relieve the burden of noncommunicable diseases with trusted, quality medicines for every patient, everywhere in the world. Lu Hong joined Pfizer in 1993. Previously, she led HR for the Asia Pacific region covering sixteen markets responsible for about $10 billion in annual revenue and progressed later to lead Global HR Operations for the company. Having lived and worked in the US, Japan, and China, Lu Hong is fulfilled by working creatively with globally diverse leaders to combine efforts while valuing the uniqueness of every individual.

Neil Irwin
Senior Economics Correspondent, New York Times
Neil Irwin is senior economic correspondent at the *New York Times* and author of *How to Win in a Winner-Take-All World* and *The Alchemists.* Irwin writes frequently about global economic trends; the changing nature

of work and employment; financial markets and monetary policy; and how these big-picture shifts affect everyone who is trying to make their way in the modern economy. Irwin was a founding staff member of The Upshot, the *Times*'s site for analytical and explanatory journalism. He was previously a reporter and columnist at the *Washington Post,* where he led coverage of the global financial crisis. He often analyzes economic trends on television and radio, including appearances on the PBS Newshour, CBS This Morning, BBC America, MSNBC, CNBC, CNN, and public radio's "Marketplace." Irwin has an MBA from Columbia University, where he was a Knight-Bagehot Fellow in Economic and Business Journalism. He has served on the fellowship's advisory board since 2017. His undergraduate studies were at St. Mary's College of Maryland, where he served on the board of trustees from 2007 to 2013.

Daniel Kuehn

Senior Research Associate, the Urban Institute
Dr. Kuehn is a labor economist with the Urban Institute's Income and Benefits Policy Center. His research focuses on apprenticeship, job training, the science and engineering workforce, and diversity and inclusion. Dr. Kuehn holds a bachelor's degree in economics from the College of William and Mary, a master's degree in public policy from George Washington University, and a PhD in economics from American University.

Ramon Laguarta

Chairman and CEO, PepsiCo
Ramon L. Laguarta is the chairman of the board of directors and chief executive officer of PepsiCo. Ramon, a twenty-four-year PepsiCo veteran, has served as CEO since October 2018, and chairman of the board since February 2019. Prior to becoming CEO, Ramon was president of PepsiCo. Between 2015 and 2017, Ramon served as chief executive officer of the sector formerly known as Europe Sub-Saharan Africa (ESSA), one of PepsiCo's most complex businesses, with responsibility for leading the company's beverage, food, and snacks business in Europe and Sub-Saharan Africa. Prior to serving as CEO of ESSA, Ramon held a variety of positions of increasing responsibility in Europe, including leading the acquisition and successful integration of the company's dairy business in Russia. Before

joining PepsiCo in 1996, he worked for Chupa Chups, S.A., a Spanish leading confectionery company, where he held a number of international roles in Asia, Europe, the Middle East, and the United States. In addition to being a member of the PepsiCo board of directors, Ramon also currently serves as a director of Visa Inc. Ramon is a native of Barcelona and holds an MBA from ESADE Business School in Spain and a master's in international management (M&M) from Thunderbird School of Global Management.

Earl Lewis

Director and Founder, Center for Social Solution; Thomas C.
Holt Distinguished University Professor of History, Afroamerican
and African Studies, and Public Policy, University of Michigan
Earl Lewis is the founding director of the University of Michigan Center for Social Solutions and the Thomas C. Holt Distinguished University Professor of History, Afroamerican and African Studies, and Public Policy. He is president emeritus of the Andrew W. Mellon Foundation, a past president of the Organization of American Historians, a member of the Council on Foreign Relations, and a fellow of the American Academy of Arts and Sciences.

Susan Lund

MGI Partner, McKinsey Global Institute
Susan Lund is a PhD economist and partner at the McKinsey Global Institute, the economics research arm of the global consulting firm. She leads research and works with clients on issues related to the workforce, technology, and globalization.

Christopher Mayer

Associate Dean for Strategy and Initiatives,
United States Military Academy at West Point
Christopher Mayer, PhD, is associate dean for Strategy & Initiatives and associate professor at the United States Military Academy at West Point. His responsibilities at West Point include strategic planning, advancing strategic initiatives, and teaching philosophy courses. His research focus includes ethics and how higher education needs to adapt to prepare students for the future of work and develop them into future-ready leaders.

He is an evaluator and workshop leader for the Middle States Commission on Higher Education, a contributor to the Center for Higher Education Leadership newsletter, and a reviewer for the Quality Assurance Commons for Higher and Postsecondary Education.

Mary Alice McCarthy
Director, Center on Education and Labor at New America
Dr. Mary Alice McCarthy leads the Center on Education and Labor at New America (CELNA). The center is dedicated to expanding pathways to postsecondary education and high-quality jobs for the growing population of nontraditional and historically disadvantaged students. CELNA reaches across the traditional silos of higher education, career and technical education, and workforce development to identify strategies for strengthening connections between learning, work, and economic mobility. Prior to joining New America, Dr. McCarthy worked at the US Departments of Education and Labor. She has a PhD in political science from the University of North Carolina.

Anne Ollen
Senior Director, TIAA Institute, TIAA
Anne Ollen has responsibility for the TIAA Institute's higher education program, building and sharing knowledge in two broad areas: academic workforce trends and issues and higher education organizational effectiveness. Anne leverages the institute's pillars of work—research, partnerships, convenings, and strategic communications—to bring distinctive value to its stakeholders. Prior to joining the institute as it was launched in 1998, Anne led the development of TIAA financial education seminars targeting benefits administrators, women, retirees, and those just starting their careers. She earned a BA from the College of Mount Saint Vincent and an MA from Queens College, CUNY.

Kelly Otter
Dean, School of Continuing Studies, Georgetown University
Dr. Kelly Otter is dean of Georgetown University's School of Continuing Studies (SCS). In this role, she oversees professional graduate programs; liberal studies programs at the undergraduate, master's, and doctoral levels;

professional certificates and custom education; and summer and special programs. She previously served in academic leader roles at Northeastern University, the University of Pittsburgh, the College of New Rochelle, and New York University. Her portfolio comprises academic program development, international education and partnerships, the design and management of technology-mediated education infrastructures and programs, veteran support services, and adult and workforce education. Dr. Otter is a member of the University Professional and Continuing Education Association (UPCEA) and has taught in the fields of media studies and interdisciplinary research.

Matthew Pittinsky

Chief Executive Officer, Parchment; Cofounder, Blackboard
Matthew Pittinsky, PhD is the CEO of Parchment and cofounder and former executive chairman and CEO of Blackboard Inc. Matthew is an assistant research professor of sociology at Arizona State University. He serves on the boards of the Woodrow Wilson Graduate School of Teaching and Learning, CampusLogic, and Picmonic. In 2012, Teachers College at Columbia University awarded Matthew with the President's Medal of Excellence to recognize his impact and innovation in the field of education technology and entrepreneurship. Among his academic and professional publications, Matthew cowrote and edited *The Wired Tower*, which addressed e-learning and the internet's impact on education.

Matthew Rascoff

Associate Vice Provost for Digital Education and Innovation,
Duke Learning Innovation
Matthew Rascoff is associate vice provost for Digital Education and Innovation at Duke University, where he leads Duke Learning Innovation. He was previously vice president and founder of the Office of Learning Technology & Innovation for the University of North Carolina system. Rascoff launched JSTOR's first international office in Berlin, where he was a Fellow of the Bertelsmann and Robert Bosch Foundations. He led product management teams at Wireless Generation, an education technology company, and launched their office in Durham, North Carolina. Earlier in his career he helped establish Ithaka S+R, a nonprofit that develops

collaborative strategies and research for higher education and the arts. After undergraduate studies at Columbia University Rascoff did graduate work at Bogazici University in Istanbul on a Fulbright Scholarship. He earned an MBA from Harvard Business School and represented the state of North Carolina as a German Marshall Memorial Fellow.

Amrit Ray
Global President, R&D and Medical, Pfizer Upjohn, Pfizer, Inc.
Dr. Amrit Ray is a physician researcher and corporate executive known for advancing medical breakthroughs and championing patient-focused, ethical policies. Dr. Ray is global president of R&D and Medical at Pfizer Upjohn and has international medical research experience across multiple diseases. He was previously chief medical officer for pharmaceuticals at Johnson & Johnson and a hospital doctor in Britain's National Health Service. His contributions to health care have been recognized by patients, governments, and public health groups. He publishes widely on how medical innovation can positively impact patients and society. Dr.Ray holds BSc and medical degrees from Edinburgh University, and an MBA from Dartmouth.

Gregory L. Robinson
Director, James Webb Telescope Program, National
Aeronautics and Space Administration (NASA)
Gregory L. Robinson is program director for the James Webb Space Telescope. He focuses on increasing development efficiency, management processes, contractor performance, and mission success. Mr. Robinson was formerly the NASA Science Mission Directorate, deputy associate administrator for programs. In this role he ensured high performance during development and operations of 114 science flight projects. He was deputy director of NASA's John Glenn Research Center; and NASA's deputy chief engineer prior to that. Mr. Robinson also served as deputy assistant administrator for systems at NOAA's National Environmental Satellite, Data, and Information Service, leading the acquisition and management of all satellite systems. He spent eleven years in various leadership positions at NASA's Goddard Space Flight Center.

David Schejbal
President, Excelsior College
David Schejbal became president of Excelsior College in August 2020. Schejbal is a leading voice in adult and nontraditional higher education, and with his leadership, the college remains student focused. Throughout his career, Schejbal's primary focus has been on making education accessible, affordable, and flexible for all students. He previously served as vice president and chief of digital learning at Marquette University. Prior to joining Marquette, he was dean of continuing education, outreach, and e-learning at the University of Wisconsin-Extension, working across all twenty-six campuses of the system to extend the resources of the university to communities throughout the nation. He was president of the University Professional and Continuing Education Association (UPCEA) from 2015 to 2016. Presently, he is cochair of the Board of Visitors of the U.S. Army War College.

Justin Shaffner
Research Associate, University of Michigan Center for Social Solutions
Justin Shaffner is a research associate at the University of Michigan Center for Social Solutions where he focuses on the future of work, water equity and security, and the Third Slavery Project. His doctoral research at the University of Cambridge focused on the politics of resource extraction in the Pacific. Recent publications include *Cosmopolitics: The Collected Papers of the Open Anthropology Cooperative, Volume I* (OAC Press, 2016, coedited with Huon Wardle), and "Hope and Insufficiency: Capacity Building in Ethnographic Comparison," special issue of *The Cambridge Journal of Anthropology* (2017, 35:1, co-edited with Rachel Douglas-Jones).

Robert Sheets
Research Professor, the George Washington University
Robert Sheets is a research professor at the George Washington University's Institute of Public Policy. He is a researcher and consultant in education, workforce development and economic development policy and labor market information at the federal and state levels. Sheets received his BA and MA from the University of Missouri at Columbia and his PhD from the University of Illinois at Urbana-Champaign.

LaVerne Evans Srinivasan
*Vice President, Carnegie Corporation of New York's National Program;
Program Director, Education, Carnegie Corporation of New York*
LaVerne Evans Srinivasan is the vice president of Carnegie Corporation of New York's National program and program director for Education. At the Carnegie Corporation she oversees grantmaking and amplifying activities aimed at engaging parents and communities, improving teaching and leadership for learning, advancing innovative learning environment designs, providing K–12 pathways to college and career success, and fostering integrated approaches to innovation and learning. A graduate of Harvard College and Harvard Law School, Srinivasan joined Carnegie Corporation in 2014, arriving with extensive experience in senior-level leadership roles in the areas of urban district change, nonprofit education reform, and educational technology. She served as a deputy chancellor of the New York City Department of Education where among other accomplishments, she designed and implemented Project Home Run, a strategically redesigned and streamlined system for recruiting, hiring, and placing teachers and school principals that greatly increased the teacher talent available to high-needs schools and which has been replicated nationwide.

Johnny C. Taylor, Jr.
President and CEO, Society for Human Resource Management
Johnny C. Taylor, Jr., SHRM-SCP, is president and CEO of SHRM, the Society for Human Resource Management. With over 300,000 members in 165 countries, SHRM is the largest HR professional association in the world, impacting the lives of 115 million workers. Mr. Taylor is a sought-after voice on all matters affecting work. He is frequently asked to testify before Congress and authors the weekly "Ask HR" column in *USA Today*. He is a member of the White House American Workforce Policy Advisory Board and was appointed by President Trump as chair of the President's Advisory Board on Historically Black Colleges and Universities. He serves on the boards of the University of Miami, Jobs for America's Graduates, and the American Red Cross.

Anne Trumbore

Executive Director, Digital, Executive Education,
Lifelong Learning, the Darden School, University of Virginia
Anne currently serves as executive director of Digital, Executive Education, and Lifelong Learning at the Darden School, University of Virginia. Previously, Anne established and led Wharton Online, a strategic, revenue-producing, digital learning initiative of the Wharton School, University of Pennsylvania. As an early stage employee at Coursera, NovoEd, and Stanford's Online High School, Anne helped pioneer new forms of student-centered online education. She analyzes data to understand learner needs, initiates and supports research projects, and frequently presents at conferences and universities. Her work has resulted in a number of publications on online pedagogy and history, the future of higher education, and the future of work. She is under contract with Princeton University Press for a book on the history of technology in higher education.

Jason A. Tyszko

Vice President, Center for Education and Workforce,
US Chamber of Commerce Foundation
Jason A. Tyszko is vice president at the US Chamber of Commerce Foundation where he advances policies and programs that preserve America's competitiveness and enhance the career readiness of youth and adult learners. Tyszko's prior experience focused on coordinating interagency education, workforce, and economic development initiatives. In 2009, he served as a policy adviser to Illinois Governor Pat Quinn's administration. In addition, Tyszko was deputy chief of staff and senior policy adviser to the Illinois Department of Commerce and Economic Opportunity. Tyszko received his master of arts from the University of Chicago and his bachelor of arts from DePaul University.

Michael L. Ulica

President and Chief Operating Officer, National Geographic Society
As president and chief operating officer at the National Geographic Society (NGS), Michael Ulica implements the institution's global strategy, which invests in groundbreaking scientists, explorers, educators, and storytellers to illuminate and protect the wonder of our world. Ulica also oversees the

society's day-to-day operations. Since joining National Geographic in 2006, Ulica has held a variety of leadership roles. Most recently, he served as executive vice president and chief operating and financial officer where he oversaw all operational, administrative, and financial functions, including serving as the society's treasurer. He is a graduate of Virginia Polytechnic Institute and State University, where he earned a BS in finance.

Lauren Weber

Reporter, Wall Street Journal

Lauren Weber writes about careers and the workplace for the *Wall Street Journal*, with a special interest in stories that explore the intersection of macroeconomic trends and the on-the-ground practices of workers and employers. In 2017, Weber wrote "Contracted," an award-winning series of stories about the evolution of contracting and contingent work. Weber arrived at the *Wall Street Journal* in 2011 after a stint as a private investigator. She has also been a staff reporter at Reuters and Newsday, and her freelance work has appeared in the *New York Times, Los Angeles Times*, and other newspapers. Weber is the author of "In Cheap We Trust," a cultural history of frugality and cheapness in the United States. She is a graduate of Wesleyan University and Baruch College-CUNY, and was a Knight-Bagehot fellow at Columbia University.

Trish White

Change Consultant, EcoCreate Ltd.

Trish White is a change consultant drawing on twenty-five years in organizational development, leadership, and coaching. Following a brief period teaching economics, Trish began her career with Pfizer in Ireland and went on to lead HR teams for Australia, New Zealand, Hong Kong, Taiwan, and Pakistan. Afterwards, she relocated to New York assuming responsibility for Global Talent Management and the development program for Pfizer's C-level executive successors. Examination of those experiences and an MSc in organizational change generated the impetus to establish a consultancy practice back at home in Ireland. Trish conducts much of her international work virtually.

Ross Wiener

Executive Director, Education & Society Program and
Vice President, the Aspen Institute
As executive director of the Education & Society Program, Ross leads a team of educators and analysts to inspire, inform, and influence positive change in public education. Prior to Aspen, Ross was policy director at the Education Trust, a nonprofit that advances equity in public education, and also served as a trial attorney in the US Department of Justice, Civil Rights Division. Ross graduated from University of Wisconsin-Madison and George Washington University Law School and clerked for Judge Kermit Lipez on the US Court of Appeals for the First Circuit.

Joseph Williams

Senior Reporter, Business Insider
Joseph Williams is senior reporter on the enterprise technology desk at *Business Insider*, covering emerging tech like artificial intelligence, quantum computing, and virtual reality. He is interested in innovative startups, industry leaders with a strong point of view on the future of the technologies, lawmakers carving out the path forward on policy frameworks, and everything in between. Williams also runs *Business Insider*'s Innovation Inc. series, which gives readers an in-depth look at how legacy companies like Walmart, JPMorgan Chase, and FedEx are undergoing their own digital transformations and adopting AI, VR, and other tech.

Jason Wingard

Dean Emeritus and Professor, School of Professional Studies,
Columbia University
Dr. Jason Wingard is a leading executive and academic in the areas of organizational strategy, leadership development, and the future of work. He currently serves as dean emeritus and professor of human capital management of the Columbia University School of Professional Studies. He is also founder and chairman of the Executive Board, a boutique management consulting firm. Dr. Wingard has published widely on the topic of strategy and leadership, including *Learning to Succeed: Reinventing Corporate Education in a World of Unrelenting Change* (2015); and *Learning for Life: How Continuous Education Will Keep Us Competitive in the Global Knowledge Economy* (2016).

Alford A. Young, Jr.

Arthur F. Thurnau Professor of Sociology, Afroamerican and African Studies, Gerald R. Ford School of Public Policy (by courtesy); Edgar G. Epps Collegiate Professor of Sociology and Afroamerican Studies; Associate Director, Center for Social Solutions University of Michigan

Young studies how low-income African Americans construct understandings of various aspects of social reality (especially, notions of social mobility, social inequality, social structure, and good jobs and work opportunity in America). He has published *The Minds of Marginalized Black Men: Making Sense of Mobility, Opportunity, and Future Life Chances* (Princeton University Press, 2004), *Are Black Men Doomed?* (Polity Press, 2018), and *From the Edge of the Ghetto: African Americans and the World of Work* (Rowman and Littlefield Publishers, 2019). Young also coordinates an initiative entitled the Scholars Network on Masculinity and the Well-Being of African American Men.

Susan Zhu

Assistant Professor of Management, Gatton College of Business and Economics

Susan Zhu is a assistant profesor of management at Gatton College of Business and Economics. From 2018 to 2020, she was research fellow in the Department of Research and Insights at the Society for Human Resource Management (SHRM) and a visiting scholar in the McDonough School of Business at Georgetown University. Susan's research focuses on recruitment, staffing, and leader decision-making, and her work has been published in various top journals. Susan has previously worked at IBM, where she consulted on selection, employee engagement, and organizational change projects for a variety of clients. Susan received her PhD in industrial and organizational psychology from University of Connecticut and BA in psychology and biology from Wake Forest University.

INDEX

201; sponsors of, 195; United Kingdom
apprenticeships as model for, 196–98; as
weighted toward RTI hours over on-the-
job training hours, 200, 201
apprenticeships for STEM workers, 194–95;
current forms of, 195, 196; programs
leading to college degree, 195; and
reimagining of STEM education, 195. *See
also* apprenticeships for engineers leading
to college degree
apprenticeships in current U.S. system: certificates ("journey cards") awarded in, 189;
history of, 186, 187–88; law regulating,
187; as separate from formal education
system, 187, 188; success of, 187
apprenticeships leading to college degree: and
authority for registering of apprenticeship
programs, 192; college credit for on-the-
job learning as issue in, 192; examples
of current programs, 189–91, 226–27;
as necessary in modern economy, 189,
226; policy and legal changes required
for, 191–92, 193; responsibility for cost
of, as issue, 191–92; in United Kingdom,
196–98, *197*
Arizona State University: Humanities Lab
offering real-world application of knowledge, 115; Starbucks Freshman Academy
at, 89
artificial intelligence (AI): education in,
design by task force of professionals,
71; impact on jobs, 3, 18–19, 67, 75, 93,
171–72, 205, 210–11; impact on jobs,
by gender, 175; impact on jobs, by race,
174; need to retrain workers displaced
by, 63; public's mixed reaction to, 18; and
shifts in demand across skill categories,
19–21, *20*
Ashoka University (India): blended liberal
arts program including arts and sciences,
126; as model for globalization of liberal
arts, 126
Asians: college enrollment rates, 160, *161*; as

percentage of faculty, *165*; six year college
outcomes *vs.* other races, 161, *164*
Association of American Colleges and
Universities (AAC&U): and LEAP, 138;
"Statement on Liberal Education," 131
athletics, and teamwork skills, 173
AT&T: and college-business collaborations,
26; employee upskilling program, 69, 87
automation: impact on jobs, 1–2, 3, 11–
12, 18–19, 93, 107, 111, 171–72, 205;
necessity of engaging with, 29–30; need
to retrain workers displaced by, 63, 143;
productivity increases from, as unrealized
so far, 11; public's mixed reaction to, 18;
and shift in demand across skill categories, 19–21, *20*

badging. *See* microcredentialing and badging
BHEF. *See* Business-Higher Education Forum
bias: implicit, unlearning through immersive
media experiences, 83, *83*; liberal arts
education and, 127–28; susceptibility of
algorithms and machine-learning to, 127
blended digital professionals: business–
higher education partnerships for training of, 213–16; as model future employee,
211; set of skills possessed by, 211, *212*
boards of trustees, need for increased diversity in, 168–70
bootcamps: increase in, 185; partnerships
with colleges and universities, 116–17
Broken Mirrors II (Education Trust), 160
Bureau of Labor Statistics, U.S., 88
business education: need to explore options
for, 102; online models for, 92–93; traditional, as costly and undemocratic, 91.
See also microcredentialing and badging
business enabler skills, as one of three types
of most-desired skills, 211
Business-Higher Education Forum (BHEF),
211–15, 230
business–higher education partnerships: as
best approach to closing skills gap, 4, 229,

development of high-order competencies,
122–23, 228
internet, and increased productivity in engineering, 62. *See also* online learning
internships: as credential valued by employers, 40; in liberal arts programs emphasizing real-world application of knowledge,
115; as tool for increasing diversity and
inclusion, 166; unpaid, as financially
impossible for many, 188; upskilling of
workers through, 182
IT. *see* information technology
Ivy Technical Community College (Indiana),
apprenticeship programs at, 192

Job Data Exchange (JDX), 206, 230
job security, decline in, 12, 51
job seekers, and retraining, obstacles to, 182
job tenure, average: in technology industry,
71; in U.S., 88
journalism, AI and, 3
judgment, as valued skill in modern workplace, 172
just-in-time training, value in fast-changing
economy, 107

K-12 education for future of work: and
assessment, new forms of, 177; broader
access to higher education as goal of,
218; career-technical education (CTE) as
misguided approach to, 174; as engines of
opportunity, 178; fusing of learning and
development in, 174; lifelong learning,
adaptability, and teamwork as focus of,
172, 176; necessary focus on needed skills,
229; need for radical change, 172; need to
address immediately, 171; need to align
with market needs, 218; political activism
as component in, 176, 177; and project-
based learning, 176; and racial and gender
equity, 174–76; social-emotional skills
training in, 173–74; teamwork and adaptability training in, 172–73

K-12 education of present: focus on individual acquisition of knowledge, 172, 173;
perpetuation of class inequality, 172,
250n4; perpetuation of racial inequality,
174–75; stifling of individuality and
creativity, 173

leadership: as foundation of success in all
industrial sectors, 123; increased importance in times of rapid change, 60; role in
increasing diversity and inclusion, 167–70
leadership skills: increasing demand for, 20;
need for evaluation and documentation
of, 230; as valued in modern workplace, 3
LEAP. *See* Liberal Education and America's
Promise (LEAP) framework
learning and development (L&D) departments, and cross-company collaboration
in employee education, 71–72
learning engineering. *See* liberal arts education reforms to produce high-order
competencies
Lewis, Earl, 109, 110–11
liberal arts education: benefits beyond
employability, 119; core curriculum as
key element of, 132; declining number of
students, 112; as education in "robot-
proof" skills, 77, 107–8; and employability,
112–14; and eradication of bias, 127–28;
and fragile workers, inclusion of, 108; of
future, formation of self-critical, ethically
aware global citizens as goal of, 124; of
future, goals and structures of, 109–11;
goals of, 131–32, 136; HEATS approach to,
110; and horizontal thinking, value of, 109;
importance of integrating with real-world
learning, 39–40, 41; and international
travel, 110; and LEAP framework, 108–9,
110; ongoing demand for skills taught
in, 77; openmindedness as goal of, 124;
as part of well-rounded education, 38;
relevance of, as growing issue, 2–3, 120–
21, 227–28; tech employers' recognition of